Life with an Impossible Person

Life with an Impossible Person

A Memoir of Love, Loss, and Transformation

Joan D. Heiman

Published by Leo Rising Press

www.joanheiman.com

Disclaimer: This book is memoir, a book of memories, and memory has its own story to tell. While all the stories in this book are true, some events have been compressed, and some dialogue has been re-created. Some names and identifying details have also been changed to protect the privacy of the people involved.

First Edition

ISBN-13: 978-0-692-16897-4

ISBN-10: 0-692-16897-4

For Philip—impossibly beloved.

"You were my home . . .
I had all that I needed . . .
I may search the world for Truth
But it's only another word for you . . .
You were my home. You are far not forgotten.
You were my home. I am found when I found you."

—Danielle Anderson, of Danielle Ate the Sandwich

Acknowledgments

Throughout the upheaval I faced while writing this book, so many beautifully supportive people moved tenderly and generously toward me. They deserve my thanks. There was the evolving love from my mother that deepened in reciprocal support and friendship. There was the sharing of pain and love with Misha and Tanya, who are my family. There was the love for my cousin, Susan, and an ever-deepening empathy for her life's pain and growth. There was the love received from and returned to a few ever-so-special relatives: Katya, Kathie, Phillipp, Phil, and Ben.

The evolving and loving appreciation for my brother and his family has been a gift. The sweet love and awe for having been given so much care, forbearance, and wisdom from friends—Pamela, Liam, Hania, Mary Kay, Margot, Beth, Teri and Joe, Phyllis, Enja, Michelle, and Amanda—makes me long for new words to express gratitude. And there were my two very special therapists, Bethany and Mia, to be inordinately thanked.

The support and feedback I received from those who read this book as it evolved was invaluable. Each of them gets my heartfelt gratitude:

My mother—who handed me my very first journal when I was ten and passed on her love of literature, who wanted to hear this story and believed in my ability to tell it in writing.

Pamela—who cheered, cajoled, and believed in me, who shared and supported, who understands grief from the inside out.

Liam—who listened caringly in initial conversations, gave me courage to begin and strength to carry on, who offered a remarkable understanding of what storytelling entails and encouraged me to "write it all down."

Mary Kay—who took the time to read through the manuscript twice with her skilled English instructor's eye, once for content and then again to catch my most absurd errors when, for instance, I wrote about Philip growing up on the "Great Planes."

Teri—my writing accountability pal, who helped me put in daily "chair time," listened patiently to all manner of bellyaching and growing pains, and offered countless resources and practical pieces of advice.

Debra—who scrupulously worked over my first chapter and in that one critique taught me countless lessons to be carried on through the book.

Regina and Jere–who read because they'd loved him.

Molly, of Inkbot Editing—my first professional editor, who handled me and the manuscript with care and realistic expectations during its development. And Molly, yet again, for bearing the weight of the detailed editing and organizing for self-publishing. This book would probably still be in manuscript form if not for her.

My writing group, Becky, Deb, and Molly—who read, considered, and identified changes with infinite compassion and perceptive skill, who coached, cajoled, and supported me all along the way.

Sue—who gave me "permission" and a sympathetic ear.

Amanda—who generously took the whole weight of designing a website off my shoulders and created something that reflects my humanity.

Danielle Anderson, of Danielle Ate the Sandwich—who kindly gave permission to include her lyrics in the book, and more importantly, whose music knocked at the door to my heart when it was numb, whose soul spoke to mine through her lyrics and voice.

And there are the many, many people—sometimes acquaintances, sometimes strangers—who have not known that or how their kindness has been deeply sustaining. My love and gratitude to each of you.

Finally, and foremost, of course, there is Philip . . . to thank, to cherish, and to love with all my heart . . . always.

Contents

Prologue

About eight hours into an exhausting twelve-hour trip from Costa Rica to San Diego, Philip takes my hand, eyes closed, face pinched and drawn with pain. His coloring has a jaundiced tinge that wasn't there this morning.

He whispers, "Can't do anymore. I'm . . . going . . . dying."

I press my forehead against his as we've done for thirty-seven years, push into the warmth of our overheated, plane-strained faces.

He opens his eyes, looks into mine. "Bye," he says, and closes his eyes again.

A jumble of fear, love, anger, and, yes, humor rolls through my chest. "You can't just say 'bye' if you're dying. You need to tell me you love me!"

He opens his eyes again and says, "I'm hungry."

A few hours after we land in San Diego, the rescue team says he's dying. The emergency-room doctors resurrect him.

I walk into his ICU room. Philip is awake, his beautiful body emaciated and collapsed against pillows, nose squashed beneath an oxygen mask, voice muffled and weak. Yet, he's alive, and . . . he's arguing. He, who has lived on nothing but fruits and greens for nine years; he, who has tried and failed to heal with eleven days of water-fasting in the mountains of Costa Rica; he, who has miraculously returned from death, is dueling with an exasperated nurse.

"Avocados," he insists, "are a good source of protein!"

PART I

Learning and Loving an Impossible Person

In a moment that now seems slipped outside of time, a charming, if slightly zany, figure stepped out of a hot tub into a starlit summer night, took me—a complete stranger—into his arms, and rearranged my life.

But the story doesn't begin there—in fact, it all starts with a dog. These two beautiful beings, dog and man, are forever connected as the greatest loves, and greatest losses, of my life.

1

A Curious Connection

Dogs weren't allowed in my childhood home. I did, however, grow up with a string of adopted stray cats—each one smuggled from the dairy farm up the road (a last holdout from a quieter era in an increasingly sprawling 1950s Long Island suburb). I would sneak these tiny, defenseless creatures into my mother's hermetically sealed and immaculately ordered house. In an attempt to end my juvenile wheedling, my parents reluctantly allowed me to keep three of these strays, though not all at once.

I have fond and hilarious memories of my otherwise sedate and serious father running breakneck through our quiet, neat-as-a-pin house. He's pulling an aluminum foil ball attached to a string while being pursued by a large black cat. Scrabbling wildly, feet flying out from under, Midnight slides across linoleum floors, gleefully tearing after my uncharacteristically rioting father. Each of those cats saved me, comforted me through childhood and teenage woes. Each initiated me into a deeper experience of nurturance than I'd known, returning my devotion and first maternal stirrings with animal warmth, affection, and friendship.

However, years later, after living with my big-city, pretending-to-be-a-tough-guy college boyfriend and his absurd but noble Boston terrier, I set out to find my own dog. After having a taste of the unique relationship between a dog and his person (so different from cats), and, at age twenty-two about to start out on my own without a male partner for the first time since my early teens, I went to a nearby dog shelter and found the puppy I was looking for in a litter of three. In between two blond female pups sat their brother, looking smart in black tuxedo with white shirt, tip of tail, and socks. He was my "dog come true." Since he was to be my closest companion, I dubbed him Buddy—not very original, but fitting.

Even though the people at the shelter told me Buddy's mother was a Great Dane and his father a Labrador retriever, the little seven-pound pup with admittedly large feet didn't look (to my inexperienced eye) as though he would really get all that big. Over the next three years, however, he definitely got big. When I sat on a kitchen chair, he sat beside me—eyes level with mine. When he jumped up to greet me, his paws were on my shoulders, tongue gleefully washing my face. He got big. In fact, he far surpassed me on the scale. At 120 pounds, he was not terribly intelligent, but unquestionably and endearingly goofy, loyal, and loving.

Buddy went to graduate school with me, attending the classes of my more tolerant professors and snoozing in the hall outside the doors of the stodgier ones. Invited to parties and weekend retreats, he often wreaked havoc, but rarely left behind a bad feeling.

"Hey, everyone, look at this!" yelled a member of my adopted grad school "family"—a communal household of five guys playing at being grown-ups. "Buddy's got the volleyball stuck in his mouth."

Gathered on the back porch, we all looked up from our books and papers. Buddy, galumphing around the yard, was being chased by one of the group. I joined in and, catching hold of him, saw that all four of his canine teeth had punctured the ball, and were stuck.

Now what? Was my dog going to be a permanent ball carrier? Would he die of literal lockjaw? At this point, a voice bellowed from the kitchen window.

"The hell with the volleyball," shouted our resident chef. "He's eaten half the chicken for tonight's dinner! Where is he! Wait 'til I get my hands on him . . ."

The ball extracted from his mouth, Buddy—panting but otherwise fine, which was more than I could say for the rapidly deflating ball—managed to slobber his affection on his favorite guys, trample papers, muddy books, and knock over a glass of iced tea with his rapidly rotating tail. Moving on, he raced into the kitchen to share his enthusiasm with the guy he loved best, our irate cook. Out on the patio, we all held our collective breath. If anyone could get angry at Buddy it was our chef, who'd been robbed of his chicken.

Silence. Then, "Aw, the hell with the chicken. Joan, this damned dog is just too lovable. It's pasta tonight, guys." We exhaled.

Buddy was even allowed into my parents' house, tail knocking against vases and his presence filling the small house with an energy it hadn't seen since my brother and I were little. He was barely scolded, even when he was left alone for a few hours and chose to nap first on the living room sofa (a sacred piece of furniture my brother and I were invited *never* to sit on) and then on my mother's bed. Even gnawing on the wooden legs of an end table got nothing more than a *tsk-tsk* from my mother.

"Poor guy," my mother crooned as she rubbed his ears. "We left you alone too long."

"I'll just run 'round to the Carvel store and get him a dish of vanilla ice cream," my father said on his way out the door. Buddy butted his head lovingly into my mother's lap while I stood there, dumbstruck.

When I started my first job in 1976 as a therapist at a university in Pennsylvania, Buddy accompanied me to work most days. In winter, he snoozed in the corner of my office and acted as the center's unofficial therapy dog. In warm weather, he liked to be outside, tied under the shady tree in front of my open windows. My very tolerant supervisor and colleagues welcomed Buddy to our staff meetings, where he would nap belly-up, as if humorously commenting on the interest level—or lack thereof—of our professional conversations.

Outside of work, we shared a small house next to a lake on state park land about eight miles from town. Buddy ran free much of the time, exploring the scents and wildlife in the surrounding pine forests and along the lakeshore. Much to my dismay, he'd often return from his escapades smelling acridly of skunk or bearing other "gifts" that turned my stomach and dismayed my vegetarian heart. On one occasion, I thought I'd lost my mind when, from a distance, I saw him galloping across the field behind the house looking as though he'd grown tusks. On closer, if somewhat horrified, inspection, I found he'd picked up a discarded set of antlers.

I deluded myself into thinking I was an independent and self-sufficient young woman who had nobly rescued and adopted a dog, but that clearly was not the whole story. Instead, all the love I'd historically shared with men was now being given to this big, black pony. And as every dog lover knows, I was receiving the unconditional love that dogs give their people, a love the likes of which I'd never before received or known how to give.

On a fateful day in March 1978, when Buddy was in his third year, my best friend and I were strolling through a quiet neighborhood in Elmira, New York. Sun bringing an unusual warmth for March, spring teasing an upstate New York town, we were walking, talking, and laughing our way through a late, lazy weekend morning. Buddy, leash-free and deliciously exploring and cavorting, was as elated as we were with this first hint of spring.

Suddenly and irrevocably, the day—and my universe—changed. A squirrel darted into the street. A car pulled away from a stop sign. A sickening thud rearranged everything.

In pursuit of the squirrel and unable to swerve out of the way quickly enough, Buddy and his 120 pounds hit the car head on. In the slow-motion way that time jags during crises, I ran as though through quicksand. I heard a car door slam and feet running toward me.

"Oh my god. Oh my god," a woman's voice cried. "I wasn't going fast. I was hardly moving. I couldn't do anything. He hit the car . . . I am so sorry."

I sank to my knees, gathered Buddy's head into my lap, and watched in stunned horror as a thin trickle of blood ran from his ear.

Gone. One minute exuberant, animal vitality filled with energy and life, and the next . . . gone.

In the following weeks and months, that godawful scene replayed itself over and over. I heard the thud and felt the weight of Buddy's head in my lap. I dreamt and awoke, heart pounding with horror. Just as his boundless loving had been like nothing I'd ever known, so now was this nightmare loss.

Then there was grief, an emotion totally unfamiliar to me, wretched, heavy, constant. I hated going to sleep because waking—either from the temporary relief of unconsciousness or worse, from dreams of his return—dropped me back with a thud into a day-world of gray despair.

I struggled to understand the depths of devastation I was experiencing, and finally realized how Buddy had opened up and fed that place of unconditional love unique to relationships with dogs. I loved people profoundly, and I grieved when I lost them, whether to death or a parting of ways. But the love Buddy introduced me to was more generous, openhearted, and uncomplicated than any love I'd known. And while I'd been aware of and grateful for the unqualified and unreserved love Buddy offered me, it wasn't until he died that I began to fathom the uniquely effortless and unqualified love I felt for him.

People eventually do *that something* that is intolerable, unacceptable, and *that something* diminishes, even destroys, love. I'd come to learn this in a series of relationships, as many of us do, and had subsequently learned to hold back just a little in self-protection. My love for Buddy, on the other hand, allowed for the flowering of a love that was unguarded and unreserved. His sudden death smacked right into that place and overwhelmed me.

Being in "our" house was impossible. I moved to a farmhouse in a slightly less isolated spot and then felt unprotected and vulnerable without Buddy there. I worked late, slept on friends' couches, sought comfort I didn't find in men's beds. Winter returned, as it so predictably does in a Northeastern spring. I trudged the barren countryside for hours, hoping to exhaust myself, tears freezing on my lashes and cheeks. The bleak, desolate Pennsylvania winter walked with me. I wept more than I ever had and felt stranded in a life that no longer felt warm or welcoming. Life without love was misery. I became restless. The job I had loved, the new professional life about which I'd been so enthused, living independently, my little lake house, people, solitude . . . nothing eased the pain. Not surprisingly, I sought escape. I applied to a doctoral program for which I wasn't qualified, nearly went to Jamaica with the Peace Corps, spent every weekend on the road, visited friends, stopped visiting friends, and felt more at ease in the impersonality of motel rooms than in my own home.

At work, a therapist colleague invited, listened, provided tissues, and sent me home early with "doctor's orders" to rest and treat myself kindly—"as though you have a psychological flu," he advised. The friend who'd been there when Buddy died was care and empathy personified. My mother lamented, "For the first time in your life, I feel helpless to console you." Another friend took me to her artist's cottage on the grounds of a large, dilapidated estate out in the Pennsylvania woods. She lit candles, banked the fireplace with sweet-smelling pinecones, baked and cooked, sang and massaged. Yet with all this loving support, I was alone with grief, alone with dreams of his return, alone waking to emptiness.

One day, a flyer for a year-long internship program showed up in my office mail. It offered five hundred hours of supervised training in human relations and group facilitation, and better yet, it was spaced throughout the country, starting in Denver and then moving down the West Coast from Vancouver, Washington to San Diego. Perfect! I'd found the opportunity for change I hungered for. I quit my job, gave away nearly everything I owned, packed what remained into my car, and headed out for a year of solo travel with the quasi-legitimate pretense of professional development serving as the cover for my escape.

It was June 1978, and I, twenty-six years old. My best friend drove from Pennsylvania to Denver with me; it was to be our last adventure together for at least a year. We'd been through graduate school, first jobs, and Buddy's death together, but now I wanted . . . needed . . . to leave everything behind. I bravely hugged him goodbye at the Denver airport and turned west toward the Rocky Mountains, and the future.

A few weeks later, at an evening social hour for the program, I met a man named Ben. This thirty-nine-year-old, charismatic, larger-than-life devotee of the Indian guru Rajneesh was dressed in shades of orange to identify his disciple status. I'd never met anyone whose spirit so vividly enlivened his body. Though not what I initially would have called handsome, he was one of the more attractive men I'd ever met. He radiated playfulness and a great deal of sexual energy. Being with him rekindled a joy and enthusiasm I hadn't felt since Buddy's death.

When we walked into Denver cafés together, heads turned. My five-one height next to his more than six feet of long-limbed, thin, and agile grace would have been contrast enough. But with Ben garbed in orange and booming in animated conversation and boisterous laughter, every outing became an event. He was bright and flirtatious without being offensive. He also had an uncanny knack for dissolving barriers of inhibition—I recall a night when he managed to get twenty-some strangers snake-dancing and cavorting gleefully through Zach's Café, an artsy watering hole popular with young singles.

He invited me to stay at his house for the summer, where I met many of his friends. These were a hilarious collection of New Age healers and spiritual seekers. By day, they were therapists, professors, holistic health practitioners, astrologers, martial artists, massage therapists, and community organizers. At night and on weekends, they drummed and danced and partied. They also talked, philosophized, and organized festivals and conferences.

Ben's dilapidated but comfortable 1890s Victorian house was a magnet for unique people. One night I came home to great wafts of nag champa and the sounds of soothing music incongruously drowned out by laughter. I found Ben on a massage table in the living room, stark naked and punctured from head to toe with acupuncture needles. A scantily dressed and very attractive practitioner and he were jubilantly laughing their way through stimulating his chakras. On another night, I walked into a fug of sweet-smelling smoke to find a room full of belly dancers in head-to-toe Middle Eastern dance garb, smoking from hookahs passed to them by dark-haired, sultry-eyed Arab men in velvet jackets and skin-tight jeans. Ben was happily at the center of the circle, surrounded by exotic women.

One late afternoon, I came in from jogging to meet yet another curious figure in Ben's caravanserai. A woman was standing in front of the mirror in the bathroom. She introduced herself to me as Tanya. She lived in Greeley, but on the weekends, she worked as a belly dancer at a Middle Eastern club in Denver. Ben had given her a key and invited her to use his house to dress and put on her makeup, since driving the sixty-five miles from Greeley to Denver in her belly dancer costume might have resulted in any number of awkward situations.

I sat on the edge of the tub in my running shorts and shoes, watching the transformation of an attractive, young American woman into a bewitching and exotic creature. Her costume included a pair of voluminous, silky-pink harem pants topped by a bare midriff, a tiny rose-colored top, and a flourish of diaphanous scarves ready to drape around her shoulders. Gold coins dangled and jangled from her low hip belt. Tiny bells tinkled on ankle bracelets. Her expressive hazel eyes grew larger with kohl and emerald-green shadow.

As Tanya became ever more colorfully foreign, she and I seemed to grow increasingly familiar. She felt like someone I'd known for a long time, a sister and a friend. She talked about the more mundane life she lived up in Greeley, running a vegetarian café and caring for her three-year-old, golden-haired son named Misha. At last, she bid me adieu, leaving me behind in a cloud of musky rose and sandalwood. *Did I just dream that?* I wondered. I hoped we'd have a chance to meet again.

A month later, Ben invited me to a small gathering of friends from Greeley who regularly drove down to Denver for evening meditations. Following their hour-long meditation, they would all relax in the hot tub under the summer night sky. Ben generously sacrificed his time in the hot tub to pick me up to meet the others for a late supper.

We pulled up in front of a typical, 1960s suburban house that adroitly disguised the unusual activities going on inside. As we walked up to the house, the front door opened and four very tall people—laughing, with arms draped around one another—tumbled out into the summer night like a pack of large, happy puppies.

One of them paused, auburn-gold hair haloed by the light behind him. He looked at me and broke into a radiant smile. As in a dream, he came toward me—a lithe, graceful cat in want of stroking and certain of getting it. I stood bemused, transfixed.

In a magical moment, my vision and intuition expanded, and I saw both a whimsical, beseeching child and a sexy, madcap man, an unlikely contrast of vulnerable longing and manly self-confidence. This leonine creature tapped playfully at barriers I hadn't known I'd constructed around my heart.

An unexpected yearning startled and disarmed me. He wrapped his arms around me and said, in a voice laughing and mellifluous like warm honey, "Ah . . . it's you."

That was Philip. And that was, if you'll forgive the cliché, the first night of the rest of my life.

2

The Goal on the Way

Philip and I only had a few weeks together before I had to leave for the West Coast to complete the next part of my internship. Those were wonderful, confusing, electric weeks, throughout which we both knew I would soon be leaving. On the morning of my departure, Philip helped me load my car, dutifully admiring the curtains I'd made in case I needed to sleep in it along the way, and pointed me in the direction of Wyoming.

His final words hummed in my ears and tugged at my heart as I watched him walk away. "Come back, sweet darlin'. I'll be waiting for you."

Driving north on I-25, I tried to make sense of my mixed feelings. *How can I feel so connected to this person after knowing him for less than a month? Will I find my way back to him? Will he still be here?*

My scheme was to drive all night under a starlit sky, arriving in Yellowstone National Park in time to see the sunrise. I drove north into Wyoming, passing through Cheyenne and Rawlins, two names that were familiar from the cowboy shows my brother and I watched as kids on our black-and-white TV set. I headed northwest toward Grand Teton National Park, which would then take me into Yellowstone.

Around midnight, I pulled into a solitary gas station at the edge of the foothills. It appeared to be the last outpost of civilization (and gas), and when I walked in to pay, the scene hit me like a stage set for one of those old cowboy shows I'd been remembering. A single, unshaded lightbulb hung from the ceiling, illuminating four cowboys sitting around a table, playing cards, chewing tobacco, and drinking beer. Empty Coors and Bud bottles filled a trash can.

These guys were probably just around my age, but they seemed so *other*, like inhabitants of another time and country, possibly a different planet. And, in many ways, they were. Cowboy hats worn indoors, mud-caked boots with toes so pointed I wondered what kind of feet this species had, T-shirt sleeves folded up to hold packs of unfiltered Camel cigarettes, tarnished belt buckles worn like trophies. Still quite new to the West, I was thrilled and admittedly a little scared to find myself alone at the edge of the world with four "real" cowboys.

As a young woman traveling alone and walking in at midnight, I must have appeared equally *other* to them. Wearing a long, flowered skirt and a jean jacket, my crazy, curly hair tumbling out from under a blue bandanna, I bravely (shaking in my sandals) greeted them.

"Hey. Do you think I can make it from here to Yellowstone in time to catch the sunrise?"

Expressionless faces looked back at me. Then, slowly, one guy turned to the next, and he to the next, and so on round the table. In the void of their silence, I began to babble nervously.

"Wouldn't it be great? I mean, this is my first time in the Rockies alone . . . and Yellowstone's such a beautiful place . . . and the moon's nearly full. I'm wide awake, and, well . . . you know."

One of the cowboys peered up at me from under the brim of his hat. "You know there's five feet of snow up there?" he said.

That stopped me . . . for a moment. "Is that snow on the ground? Or on the roads?" I queried, voice a bit less bold.

They repeated the eyes-round-the-table routine before the same guy—apparently the only one who could speak—spoke. "Well, probably just on the ground . . . most of the way."

Well, then what's the problem? I wondered. "I've got a blanket, food, and water, so I should be fine," I assured them . . . and myself.

I paid for the gas, bought a couple of chocolate bars, and, bidding them a good game and a good night, swaggered out with all the remaining bravado I could muster. Back in the car, I blew out a huge breath of relief. I wasn't sure whether I'd just escaped danger or not. I pulled out fast just in case.

Heading straight toward the shadowed hulks of the foothills, I quickly forgot about the cowboys, so awed was I by the dark outlines of the mountains rising against an indigo, moonlit sky.

The night was magic—no snow on the roads, but, yes, about four or five feet on the ground alongside it. *Those guys know their mountains.* The moon lit up the snow more brilliantly than my headlights; I turned them off and could see perfectly well. Zillions of stars blinked, flashed, and flickered, while super-bright planets looked down placidly on the unearthly landscape. A ghostly cow put my heart into my throat when it wandered out of mists that rolled off the mountains and fell onto the road in light, filmy blankets. When cow and mist disappeared, the trees and snow-bordered roads reappeared in ethereal clarity. I wound around and up, steadily climbing, ears popping, spirits soaring.

At some point, I wanted so badly just to *be* in this incredible wonder of night and light and shadow, with nothing between myself and my mystical surroundings. I pulled into a rest stop, turned off the engine, and stepped into startling stillness. An open expanse of snowy meadows lay below while huge peaks soared all around me, outlined against the midnight sky. Every sense came alive: the cold night air thrilled my skin, clean scents of pine and ozone filled my lungs, water rippling over boulders created the tingle of negative ions in the air. A handful of snow lifted to my lips tasted pure and icy. Every ounce of me felt attuned to that singular moment.

I laughed aloud, imagining myself a pioneer steering my wagon across the Great Plains and up into the Rockies. I certainly hadn't achieved anything more than driving my 1971 Ford Maverick in a westward direction, unlike my pioneer ancestors who had made this incredible journey on horseback, on foot, or in covered wagons. Nonetheless, as a suburban girl standing alone at midnight in this wild and pristine place, I was elated, feeling I'd accomplished some great feat. Falling stars streaked across a blue-black sky as my ears adjusted to the stillness that was not still at all. This was a high like none I'd ever known. I melodramatically imagined this as a possible culmination of my life, thinking, *If I die here and now, I can let go gracefully and without regret. This is enough.*

I made it to Yellowstone about two hours before sunrise. Feeling self-satisfied with accomplishing my first solo traveler's goal, I rigged up my curtains with Velcro and curled up in the back seat of my pioneer wagon to nap until the sun came up. No surprise, I woke up to find the sun high in the morning sky. Something of an anticlimax, but the world I awoke to was so pristinely beautiful, I hardly blinked at having missed the sunrise.

I stepped out into a dazzle of morning light. All was quiet, not a sign of human life anywhere. I'd slept under the protection of ancient evergreen trees. They stood all around me, nurtured and fed by the rippling river that wound its way beside the rest stop. Embraced by peace, I listened to the occasional calls of birds and the gurgle of water gently passing over boulders.

Who needs the sunrise? I thought. *I'm sure it was grand, but this . . . this is a quiet piece of heaven.*

Gathering all my New Age wisdom, I sat down on a boulder still cold from the night and contentedly scribbled in my journal:

> Sometimes, we know what our aspirations are and the way to reach them, but other times, if we remain watchful and open, we may unwittingly stumble upon something more amazing on the way to the goal.

3

At Home on the Moon

My immediate attraction to Philip surprised me. He wasn't my "type" (that type having been formed by the dark-haired, olive-skinned Jewish and Italian boys I'd chased throughout my teens and twenties). In contrast, Philip was fair, with summer sun–burnished skin and hair late-sixties long, the auburn color of autumn, glinting red and gold in the sun. A cleft chin, softly rounded yet decidedly determined, betokened a strong will—little did I know just how strong. His eyebrows tilted endearingly, sometimes suggesting a touch of worry, other times topping a wink of whimsy. He had a mobile face, with emotions continually rolling across it and very little hidden.

When I returned to Colorado in the spring of 1979 after nine months of traveling for my internship, I studied and learned Philip. His eyes were tawny green, gold-flecked like sun-touched pebbles that glimmer at the bottom of flowing rivers. Riverbed eyes, I called them. He was tall, lean, and lithe—a "yoga body," graceful and flexible, agile, playful, and enlivened by a great capacity for pleasure. Dancing, doing yoga, wrestling with his four-year-old son, Misha (it turned out that Tanya was his ex-wife), or stretched out in the grass with me, he was at home in his skin and at one with a body strong, lightly muscular, and vital.

Comfortable in this physical form he'd never worked out for, he was self-assured, and, consequently, sexy—mostly without knowing it. A young saleswoman who was once helping him with pants couldn't resist lingering as she placed a hand on his bottom to smooth the fit. When his laughter bubbled out in tickled surprise, she jumped back, startled by her own audacity. When she turned toward me, red-faced and baffled by her own impulsiveness, I laughed indulgently and reassured her. "Don't worry. You've just made his day."

He was proud of his shapely, refined hands with long, graceful fingers that loved to improvise on any borrowed piano he could find and played guitar fairly well with minimal instruction or practice. Those hands, light and tender in loving, were incredibly powerful in massage, reassuring as he reached for me.

Emotionally, he was vibrant, vulnerable, and very in touch with his inner life. Attracted to these qualities, I was both enchanted and disarmed. I felt as though I was being seen and valued in ways no one had acknowledged before. It was like coming home to myself. One part of me felt like folding myself into his arms and never stepping out.

"He gives the best hugs in the world," a friend once said. There was no fear in his hug, no holding back from pleasure or pain. A natural inclination to inhabit his life fully made being in his presence both exhilarating and scary. When I finally surrendered my defenses and sank into his embrace, I felt enfolded in safety and connected to the authentic warmth of another human being.

A more cautious part of me, however, pulled back, no doubt owing to cowardice in the face of the vulnerability and longing that threatened to bring down my well-constructed boundaries. I'd had a late start finding independence, my high school and college years having been taken up with two successive five-year relationships. When I met Philip, I was finally on a heart-healing, soul-searching journey.

"I can't commit to anything," I told him one night. "I don't even know who I am. I need a year of solitude—maybe ten—to make up for all I've given away."

"I hold this to be the highest task of a bond between two people," he immediately recited. "That each should stand guard over the solitude of the other." This was one of many lines of the poet Rainer Maria Rilke he knew by heart. I was won over, wooed.

Philip wanted very little from the conventional world of ambitions, consumption, or conforming to the status quo. He owned a guitar, a journal, a backpack full of books, a bicycle, and two milk crates filled with classical, folk, and sixties-rock albums (with no stereo system on which to play them). He had a few colorful T-shirts, three pairs of drawstring pants, a pair of boots, and the flip-flops on his feet.

He was living at the center of a large alternative community in Greeley, fondly dubbed the "Greeley Group." Two close friends had taken him into their home, believing his presence was an inspiration to both their creative work and their marriage. They generously wished to support a poet, and he was content to shuttle himself and his few possessions between their home and Tanya's apartment when she was down in Denver (sharing care for Misha).

He was asked to write songs, sing, and play guitar at the weddings of friends. He wrote poetry, limericks, and short stories. He pondered, explored, and invited others to join him through astrology, past life regressions, creative writing, and guided imagery. He was invited to give poetry readings at public and alternative schools, and was even offered (and predictably and infuriatingly turned down) a poet-in-residence position at a high school in Columbus, Ohio. He danced and drummed gleefully at the center of gatherings and parties.

Being shy and much more introverted and inhibited than he, finding him at the center of this large group of friends was unnerving for me. I was intrigued but hesitant. When I retreated, he would hold out an inviting hand or pull me close to him. If I resisted, he'd kiss me gently before leaving my side to wade into a circle of dancers and drummers. Watching from the sidelines and knowing he'd return gave me a sense of certainty, acceptance, and freedom to be myself.

Not everyone was sure that we were the right match. From early on, I was confronted by friends and family members who pointed out—without hesitation or tact—what they perceived as my weakness and foolishness in staying in what they saw as an imbalanced relationship. Focusing on how he didn't meet their expectations, and possibly finding their own constructs of relationships threatened, the sting of criticism for choosing to stay was sometimes hard to stomach.

"Why doesn't he get a regular job?" friends would ask repeatedly.

"I have a regular job that supports both of us," I'd reply. "And money from his astrological readings contributes, too."

Even as I answered these challenges, I wondered at the tactless willingness on the part of others to intrude, to march into the privacy of my decisions and our life together.

"But it's not fair," I'd hear. "You're shouldering the weight of responsibility."

"If I were on my own, I'd have this same responsibility to support myself. If Philip and I choose to live frugally on my salary, and I'm okay with our situation, why is this a problem for you?"

"I don't want him taking advantage of you," they'd say.

"I don't feel taken advantage of," I'd answer. "If I were the man in this relationship, I wonder if we'd be having this conversation at all."

No matter how I explained that I felt I was receiving more than I was "sacrificing" by supporting us financially, I was judged as less than the strong, independent, assertive woman I had been and was expected to be.

Once my friends got to know Philip, however, their protests and protectiveness would almost always melt away. If he sensed acceptance, if he felt loved, he would open like a flower. His dreaminess, his imaginative way of seeing the world, and his unique way of expressing himself—along with his kindness toward the frailties of others—made him irresistible.

He inspired and reminded others of who they could be. His quest to find his own authentic voice often gave others permission to seek theirs. He was strong-willed, stubborn, and lived with the courage of his convictions, qualities that were both irritating and admirable. If he was uncompromising, and he was, it was first and foremost his soul he was fighting for. I loved him for that.

I, too, was fierce in the face of any attempts to rein in my independent spirit. Within our first month together, with my hand on the door, a question stopped me short.

"How many times, how many men are you going to run from?" he asked.

"But doesn't this feel as impossible to you as it does to me?"

"Being committed to a relationship," he answered, "is one of the best ways to learn who we are in reality—not in fantasy. It's the place where we unfold as psychological and potentially loving beings. This is where spiritual lessons—mirrored and embodied most clearly in the person of another—can be learned, where spiritual evolution unfolds."

"Maybe," I said. "But at what price? When we fall into these deep spiderwebs of contention, I can't see how we'll find resolution or mutually satisfying compromise."

"I know. It's hard work. But when you and I have touched each other's hearts as deeply as we have, don't you think it's our responsibility, to our souls and to each other, to stay and work for this beautiful possibility?"

This was possibly the most salient challenge anyone had ever posed to me in my brief twenty-seven years.

As we continued to be together, I felt my life opening out . . . and in. Much that had come before dropped away: ideas, values, people. Even my body began to change, weight melting in a way that years of dieting had never accomplished. The world felt more vivid, colorful, and enriched, but also surprisingly familiar. I seemed to be discovering, or recovering, a sense of home in myself.

Right beside the sense of safety and wonder he evoked in me, however, lay a complexity that made Philip a very unsettling partner. His uncommon sense and perspective challenged me to go further in my understanding of who I thought I was, and of how two people might be together. His longing for a depth of communion both attracted and dismayed me throughout our years together. He was always searching for "something more." This was at times deeply alluring; at other times, it left me feeling inadequate.

"Why does it have to be so complicated?" I'd ask him. "Why am I . . . why are we never quite good enough?"

"There's just so much more that can happen between two people," he'd reply. "I want that with you."

Sometimes, we'd be lying together in what I experienced as a loving communion, and he'd suddenly say, "I'm lonely." This hurt and bewildered me, especially when I felt so at home and complete with him. I struggled to understand, and, at times, feared I never would.

"Lovers ultimately need to transcend the divisions of ego and gender," he'd say. "I want to meet you beyond duality."

Never having faced this kind of deep yearning, I felt as though I'd landed on the moon. I was simultaneously baffled and charmed.

4

A Literary Love

Literature created vivid and vibrant worlds for Philip; he'd climb so fully into whatever he was reading that it would pervade both his consciousness and our home. When a character he loved was in trouble, Philip was in trouble. When a character made one more bad decision in a growing succession of disastrous choices, when Thomas Hardy or John Cowper Powys sent fate to disrupt yet another meeting of lovers, a book would fly furiously across the room or out the window.

There were books I could barely endure, and I waited impatiently for their endings as he read aloud to me. He identified so strongly with characters and their struggles that living through some of them became nearly as difficult as when he was dealing with his own inner trials and tribulations. Virginia Woolf's agonizing conflicts with Leonard Woolf—combined with Philip's conviction that Leonard was largely responsible for Virginia's bouts with depression, mental breakdown, and finally, her suicide—created a tension in our home that was hard to bear. At the same time, the sensitivity and courage that Woolf brought to each of her novels gave us delicate glimpses into another way of receiving and perceiving life. D. H. Lawrence filled the apartment with sensuality and quirky socialist ideologies. Dostoevsky's mad, textured, and intensely Russian atmospheres of obsession and passion engulfed us for days on end.

He consumed books and was ever on the lookout for the next one by a favored writer or a new author. But he was also very selective about what he'd read, almost exclusively choosing novels written and set in eighteenth, nineteenth, and early twentieth-century England or Europe, since those were the places and time periods where he most wanted to be. He had little taste for modern American authors, reflecting his relentless desire to live in an idealized, gentler, and more cultured Europe.

Our first Christmas together, in 1979, was in our first apartment—a romantic, well-lit studio in a 1920s building in Denver. We were scraping by on very little money.

"Let's agree to spend a maximum of twenty dollars on gifts for each other," he said one afternoon.

"Twenty dollars won't go very far," I said, thinking about the Irish cable-knit sweater I'd had my eye on.

"It's enough," he answered. I let go of the sweater.

In the week before the holiday, we parted each day for a few hours of secret shopping and returned with our carefully chosen loot hidden in our backpacks. We each chose a separate shelf in the closet for hiding gifts. A childlike spirit of the holiday permeated our little apartment.

On Christmas morning, when we woke to a huge blizzard that stopped the city, we were enchanted. With pleasure and relief, we snuggled in to watch the world outside our windows grow ever whiter and more quietly muffled as inch after inch of heavy snow blanketed the city. Cars became humps of snow, the building right across the street disappeared as wind blew snow horizontally.

We were left magically cocooned, delighted that all obligations to spend the day with others were completely undone.

"Ah, isn't this beautiful?" I said as we stood leaning against each other at the window, warming our hands on steamy cups of tea.

"Yes! We don't have to go anywhere . . . just stay here at home together." He squeezed me closer.

"Merry Christmas, my love. If I were a cat, I'd purr," I said.

We shared a candlelit, Mozart-accompanied breakfast of toast loaded with vegan cheese, veggies, and seasonings. In that first year together, we lived almost exclusively on creative vegetarian sandwiches, yogurt, soups, and salads. We playfully dreamed of starting a café, which we'd cleverly named Strange Breadfellows, but never wanted to do any more than offer what we thought was a great name and a growing list of unique sandwich recipes to some more ambitious entrepreneur.

When it was time to open gifts, we both brought out our collected hordes. Without having discussed it, we'd both spent our entire twenty dollars on books. Unwrapping one treasure at a time, first me, then him, then back to me, and so on, we were amazed at our combined collection of seventeen new books without one repeat. I'd rummaged through used bookstores to find books by D. H. Lawrence, Storm Jameson, Elizabeth Bowen, Rosamond Lehmann, and Wilkie Collins—authors Philip had introduced me to, but books by each he hadn't yet read. Our lifelong habit of reading aloud to each other began on that long, wintery and wonderful afternoon, in which we felt perfectly cut off and warmly protected from the outside world.

There was a wonderful claw-foot tub in that apartment. We painted the outside of it rose and turquoise, to highlight the colors in the print of John Waterhouse's "The Lady of Shalott" that we'd hung above it. I learned the art of taking baths from Philip. I'd lounge in the tub with sun pouring in through the large bathroom window, making rainbows on a blanket of scented bubbles. Philip would sit cross-legged on pillows in the doorway and read to me. He also discovered that he could make that bathroom into a second living room by filling the dry tub with cushions.

"Now we have a bit more space," he said when I came home to find him for the first time ensconced and reading in the new couch. I squealed with laughter, tickled by his creative eccentricities. I couldn't imagine my parents dreaming up a bathtub-couch!

Philip's Christmas books for me included an introduction to three new genres. Having grown up in a literary home and having been "fed" good books by both my parents until I left home, I was awed by the hitherto unexplored doors Philip opened for me. First, there were books written largely by women who took classic fairy tales, fables, or myths and translated them into contemporary or fantasy realms. Patricia McKillip, Marion Zimmer Bradley, Ursula K. Le Guin, Robin McKinley, and Madeleine L'Engle were my adult introductions to folktale and fantasy. I was entranced.

Next, there was young-adult fiction that I'd somehow missed reading as a young adult. Susan Cooper made Celtic mythology rise off the pages with modern-day English children exploring the basic tenets of light and dark, good and evil. Alan Garner created suspenseful worlds based on traditional English folktales. We were ensorcelled by T. H. White and his retelling of the Arthurian tales, and C. S. Lewis's *The Chronicles of Narnia* captured our imaginations.

And then there was mystery and mannerly crime, almost exclusively from the golden age of British mysteries of the late nineteenth to mid-twentieth centuries. We started with Agatha Christie; I think we read all sixty-six of her novels! Dorothy Sayers and her inimitable sleuth Lord Peter Wimsey had us on the edge of our seats night after night until we'd read all his adventures. The romance between Lord Wimsey and Harriet Vane became a mirror through which we saw our own romance reflected and enhanced. The keen intellects of authors like Margery Allingham, Michael Innes, Patricia Wentworth, Edmund Crispin, and so many others surrounded us in the atmosphere of old English country houses and created a more poetic and romantic ambiance around us than Denver might otherwise have afforded.

And then there was poetry. Like so many young Americans who'd had poetry ruined for them in high school, I was intimidated by it, its meaning seeming to be locked behind impenetrable walls. But with Philip as my guide, I saw, for the first time, how poetry could distill emotion and thought succinctly into words as clear and precise as jewels. The poetry of Robert Bly, Mary Oliver, David Whyte, Rilke, Neruda, Kabir, Hafiz, and Rumi was woven into the new and enriched tapestry of life unfolding with Philip, who would also recite his own poems to match a moment or express a feeling or a thought.

One of his early poems captured the sense of communion he so longed for us to share:

Should I pretend
to be just a man

with a man's body
with a man's hands
and with those hands
reach out to you
with a man's understanding
of what a woman can do—
that arm's length between us
would always be there
man to woman
and little to share
of the person inside you
of the body
unaware

I was so in love with Philip at that time. We spent hours curled up together or toe-to-toe on a couch reading separately or aloud. Books wove a spell of magic and romance around us, coloring our days and nights and creating something more intimate and transformative than the reading I'd done on my own.

5

Impossibly Beloved

A year or two into our relationship, we were browsing through an old used bookstore when the title on a small, weathered volume jumped out at me: *Impossible People.* Lingering in the musty atmosphere that permeates used bookstores—even in Colorado where moisture in the air is minimal and book mold less of an issue—we gently fingered the delicately worn and yellowing pages of that small, leather-bound book, published near the end of the nineteenth century.

"This could be the title of a book about you," I said. We both laughed, and from that day on, I thought of him as my impossible person.

And he was impossible, in so many ways. He was a charming and stimulating (if often maddening) conglomeration of contradictions: goofy, dramatic, serious, playful, provocative, and childlike. Depending on mood, circumstances, and audience, he shifted from an extroverted flirt to an introspective philosopher, poet, and spiritual seeker. He moved effortlessly from wacky, uninhibited, and madcap to wise, thoughtful, and at times, brilliant.

A quixotic and romantic longing and sensitivity combined with a deep-seated fear of abandonment and judgment compelled and haunted Philip throughout his life. There was something in his nature and experience that left him raw and open to a fathomless well of dissatisfaction, depression, and fear. The default mode, the feeling most familiar to him, the background music to his life, was that of pain and disappointment. Many of his poems reflected this inner life.

walking
back and forth
back and forth
I miss the opening
the opening beneath my feet.
pain makes such
solid ground.

This often undefined but ever-present uneasiness could leave him self-absorbed, insecure, and emotionally insatiable. He'd become dark, broody, unable to see his way back into the light. Panic attacks—unnamed as yet by either of us—would grab hold of him, especially at dusk when the sun couldn't light his way. If I were late getting home, I might return to find him caught in an emotional spider's web.

One night, I came home a few minutes late to find him waiting at the door.

"Where were you?" he cried. "I thought you were never coming home. What if the earth had just swallowed you up or you'd just evaporated?"

"I'm only twenty minutes late," I said, baffled by his overreaction.

"People do just disappear," he spluttered through tears.

"I'm not going to disappear, you goose."

In our first years together, I didn't understand. His illogicality angered me, and I resented what felt like an attempt to rein me. He had no words for what he was experiencing, and although I'd been through a graduate-level education and was working as a psychotherapist at the time, I had barely even heard of anxiety attacks, much less dealt with them.

Held up in conversation by my rather long-winded and self-centered supervisor late one afternoon, I turned at the look of surprise on his face to see Philip walking right into the office.

"I've been outside waiting for you since 4:30," he said. It was 4:40. His eyes had a wild look and the hand that took hold of my arm was shaking.

"Hello, Philip. I'm sorry to have held Joan up," said my boss. "I needed a few words with her." Obviously taken aback, he was not sure how to respond to this distraught intruder who was breaking the rules of office and employee etiquette.

"I'll be right out, Philip," I said, hoping to regain some semblance of normality. "Five minutes."

When I met Philip outside, I asked through angry tears, "What do you think you're doing? You can't just barge into my boss's office."

"Sorry," he said. His eyes filled with tears.

Being female in a culture that teaches women to blame themselves, I quickly regretted hurting him and sank into utter bewilderment at how to resolve this painful dilemma. Those were difficult, fractured moments between us.

This dark-tending aspect to his nature contrasted endearingly with a hugely leonine love of life and warmth for people. Once, following a period of feeling unable to connect with or like anyone, he suddenly decided to cook dinner for the couple who'd just moved into the apartment below ours. I came home that evening to find them happily engaged in conversation.

Later that night, when I remarked on how he'd managed to open up again and enjoy their company, he acknowledged his contradictions, even delighted in them. With the lift of an eyebrow and a puckish glint in his eye, he trotted out Walt Whitman's "I contradict myself" statement, and the next thing I knew, my frustration and anger had melted away, replaced with laughter and a sense of awe for this man who never ceased to surprise me.

Living beside this unpredictable personality was an enormous, if paradoxical, gift. Drive me crazy as he did, in surviving and thriving alongside him, I learned to acknowledge my own contradictions, to confront my limited sense of who I was, and to embrace more of who I might become.

As our relationship grew, Philip shared more and more of his early life with me. Intellectually, if not emotionally, advanced beyond his years, he was often in trouble in school and later in college for asserting what he believed.

First, there was the "famous" argument with his fourth-grade teacher. "Henry Ford didn't invent the first car," Philip interrupted during class one day. "Francois Isaac de Rivaz did. He designed the internal combustion engine." Nine-year-old Philip had done his research.

Then there was the classic book, *The Red Badge of Courage*, for which Philip expressed his dislike. His eighth-grade teacher, initially angry at this precocious kid who didn't appreciate "good literature," was eventually awed by the thirteen-year-old's reasoned explanation for his contrary opinion.

In college, in the late sixties to early seventies, he convinced professors not to grade his work, insisting he could and would only produce his best when there was no judgment. "I promise to do my very best in this class. I'm here because I love literature and want to learn from you. But I can only do my best if I don't feel judged. Will you trust me to be an excellent student as I trust you to be an excellent professor?" They often did.

He persuaded instructors to accept a poem when a paper was due and petitioned for changes in course syllabi and grading policies. A less flexible philosophy professor burst into tears during class one day, after Philip interrupted her lecture yet again.

"Please, if you allow time for more class discussion," he said, "I'm sure we'd all learn more from an authentic exchange of ideas."

After class, she asked him to wait. "Please drop this class," she said, still teary and upset. "I can't keep my train of thought in the face of your constant questions and comments."

Philip described this scene years later with a touch of humor, but admitted to being perplexed at the time. He couldn't imagine why she wouldn't want him there when his contributions and thoughts seemed—to him—so relevant and illuminating.

Philip listened in a disconcerting fashion, often with an ear tuned to challenge or question rather than being receptive to a new idea. This was not solely out of orneriness, though he clearly had a mule's worth of obstinacy and a predisposition to oppose any norm. Nor was he primarily motivated by an unreasoned or conscious desire to cause trouble. Rather, his contrariness arose from genuinely seeing the world in a different way . . . and enjoying the difference.

In the early seventies, before I met him, he was invited to sit on the Denver Holistic Health Network's philosophy committee, to listen for and challenge any set or unquestioned beliefs from the doctors and therapists who made up the committee. He was essentially assigned the role of a modern-day renegade, trickster, or court jester. You can imagine how this appointment brought glee to his contrarian nature.

Philip's thinking was grounded in and colored by emotions and intuition, as well as a sharp, if quirky, intellect. Initial and instinctive feelings guided his responses to people, places, concepts, politics, art, literature . . . everything. His thought processes followed a very different course than the expected or encouraged. He sought connections, bringing unlikely points together into surprisingly coherent intersections—if people would only hear him out. For many, he was disconcerting and threatening, for others stimulating and challenging.

Early IQ scores ranking him at genius level probably contributed to his overall inability to fit in with the norms of schools, family, or the world around him. A blessing and a curse, his thinking leapt from one idea to another via metaphor and imagery, rather than moving along lines of linear logic. While most of what we do in school and university—and in day-to-day communication—encourages sequential thinking that moves predictably from A to B, Philip's mind sprang maddeningly from A to D, not stopping to fill in the gaps verbally. When following his own train of thought, he had little patience for those who couldn't or wouldn't travel with him.

In our first years, I felt as though I was learning a new way to think, stretching my mind and imagination. While he generally gave up quickly on others, he assumed I could and would follow him easily. I often felt like he expected me to read his mind, and I protested. Other times, he'd apologize for something I wasn't complaining about while leaving the transgression about which I was miffed in the dust.

When confronted with this, he'd tilt his head like a puzzled puppy at my seemingly petty concern. "The mistake I'm apologizing for is much worse than your complaint, but if you want, I'll apologize for that, too."

"I don't know whether your apology makes me feel better or even more infuriated," I'd reply, my head in a spin.

While I learned to expect Philip to disagree with an idea or opinion, I could rarely guess from which direction the disagreement would come. He was perfectly imperfect, predictably unpredictable. When I'd bring home a quandary or uncertainty about something that had happened at work, I could count on a response that no one else had articulated. If there was a question about someone's behavior, or if a colleague had a struggle with an administrator, I could bank on Philip siding with the underdog—but for reasons other than those I or anyone else had considered. On the other hand, if it was me who needed support or an empathetic response, there was no one to whom I'd rather turn. Finely tuned to my pain or insecurity and bringing a nurturing disposition, a protective love, and a solid belief in me to any conversation, if I were hurting, he was more on my side than I was.

The contradictions in his personality and the effect he regularly had on me made my head whirl. I was shocked when, in our fourth month of living together, he proposed marriage. Not with an engagement ring or by kneeling, but with a rational—to him—argument. I couldn't grasp his thinking at first (I was too shocked), and I couldn't believe I was hearing such a conventional idea coming from a man about whose radical thinking I was so in awe.

"To stand together in the eyes of the world as married gives a certain energetic validity to a relationship. It doesn't happen outside of marriage," he said.

"But we're fine as we are," I insisted. "Why should it matter how people or society see us?"

"It's not that," he said. "It's a kind of magic that comes with the symbolic energy of the tradition," he explained. "Marriage is an archetypal commitment that ties people into something greater than just the two of them living together."

"Maybe, but I'm not ready."

"Okay. Let's have breakfast."

I toasted bagels, trying to get my head around what I now sensed was far from a conventional desire to conform to a societal rule. Through mouthfuls of fruit and yogurt, he continued to explain the astrological and archetypal influence of the planet Saturn, and its laws ruling traditions and conventions.

"Hmm . . ." I mumbled with interest but little conviction.

He let it drop.

Often sparked by the conflicts engendered by our differing constructs of reality, he could be unbending and infuriating. When talk became so convoluted and irrationality prevailed, I would storm out of the house to walk furiously through torrents of frustration I'd never experienced to that extent before. I didn't know if my head or my body was going to explode first. I'd walk blindly through town for hours, finally falling in the grass of a nearby park, mentally preparing what I would say when I broke up with him, or picturing myself getting into my car and driving away without a word.

By the time I'd thundered across town and back, however, the intensity of my anger would burn off. I'd return ready to try again, even while secretly—*Just in case*, I'd think—holding onto my escape plan for "next time." My resentments would fall away quickly, perhaps because I'd return to a person who had also calmed down and regained perspective, or because I was attracted to so much about him, or possibly because I was falling ever more in love with him and who I was with him. I often couldn't even reconstruct our arguments. He was fire to my water, intensity to my calm. And in his vulnerability, there was too much honesty, too much gentle, childlike, healing humor to want to turn and walk away. I'd never met anyone remotely like him.

I am reminded that the word courage comes from cor, the Latin word for heart. Philip lived, thought, and responded from his heart. His personality was fiery to the point of combustion, teaching me to scent danger and walk gingerly through potential minefields. I learned to intuit when negotiation with him was possible . . . and when not.

One of Philip's favorite stories of "living from the heart" happened before he and I met. In 1967, pulling out his suitcase and seriously looking toward Canada when faced with fighting in Vietnam, a war he could not believe in, he was summoned to the army recruitment office in Denver. A pacifist both by nature and philosophy, he walked up the steps and through the imposing, intimidating doors of the military establishment with fear and loathing.

A few hours later, rejoicing to learn that he'd failed the physical exam due to terrible myopia, he literally whooped with joy as he made his way to the exit doors. Nearly flying, elated with relief, he danced his way out past the uniformed officials who he despised as regimented, dehumanized, and dehumanizing.

"You should be ashamed to be so happy!" an officer shouted at his back. But Philip gleefully flew out the door to freedom. Tanya, to whom he was soon to be married, was anxiously awaiting him and the news. She knew instantly that all was well when he lifted and swung her wildly in his arms.

"Never thought I'd love my lousy eyes as much as I do today!" he said, laughing.

Whether it was anger, indignation, or fear, once he fell into the grip of intense emotion, there was little room for reasonable discussion until he'd cooled down. Being confident in what he knew to be true for himself, rarely doubting or questioning his perceptions or intuition, he could argue with an arrogance that would bulldoze others' opinions or ideas. In the heat of controversy and impassioned by what he called "objective truth," he could be provocative and even insulting.

"How can you be so certain that what you say is the one and only way to see this?" I'd ask, red-faced and fuming. "Why can't I disagree? Can't we each have valid, if differing, opinions?"

"But this isn't my opinion," he'd counter. "I'm expressing a universal truth." Then, he'd insist I listen to his argument again. "You only disagree because you haven't fully understood. When you understand, you'll agree."

What could be more infuriating? At times, he could be maddeningly obstinate, rigid, and inflexible—even bordering on fanatical.

"I can easily picture him in an evangelical priest's collar, vehemently pontificating from a pulpit," my mother once said, expressing her utter frustration. "He's an extremist. He doesn't understand the 'everything in moderation' approach to life."

He surely didn't. But as suddenly as the fiery defense of an argument was ignited, he could turn, bow (figuratively and metaphorically), and become disarmingly contrite, realizing he'd been overly forceful. His eyes would suddenly fill with tears as he'd ask my forgiveness for being so insistent and persistent.

"In the end," he would whisper into my neck, "our loving is much more important than my being right or getting my way. Please, don't ever let me forget what really matters."

This was one of the guiding principles of our relationship—it made compromise possible and healed many of our conflicts with a wider perspective. The first time we were able to put it into words was during a bike ride we took early in our relationship.

We were pedaling at an easy pace along a quiet, tree-lined country road in a South Carolina beach town. It was a pleasant spring morning, and saltwater breezes were blowing in from the ocean, keeping us cool. We talked and laughed as Philip continually sped up, leaving me behind, only to turn recklessly and pedal back to circle wildly round me—acting as though he were on a horse rather than a bicycle.

His laughter bubbled up at my half-protest as he grabbed hold of my handlebars and pulled me along so I could coast with no effort. The day was perfect, and all was well with the world.

Until we reached a fork in the road.

"Which way?" he asked lightly.

"To the left," I replied. We paused, straddling our bikes as Philip peered as far as possible in both directions.

"Nope, to the right."

And there we stood. Who would decide? Who would win? Our eyes locked—mischief in his, sparks of challenge in mine. He twirled a lock of my curly hair and pulled me closer, nearly toppling both bikes. Our kisses warmed and momentarily diverted the conflict.

Yet the divergence hovered, a disturbing presence inserting itself between us, threatening to darken the day. We dismounted and sat down in the grass under the shade of an old live oak tree draped with Spanish moss.

"If we go your way, then I'll feel resentful," he said. "But if we go my way, I'll feel like a bully, and you'll feel bullied."

I remained quiet, chewing on a blade of grass, lying back and dreamily watching two squirrels racing and chasing each other high up in the branches above.

"We'll just stay here!" he declared, falling back beside me in the warm grass. Our hands entwined. We breathed together. But the disagreement was there too, trying to wiggle between us. We instinctively rolled to face each other—nose to nose, heart to heart, dark-brown eyes searching golden-green. He tickled me, and I wriggled and laughed.

Still, the dilemma waited . . . insisted. We grew quiet, rolling apart and staring up into the blue sky.

"Here's the thing," he said at last. "To fight over this . . . to make winning, being right, or getting my way more important than loving you is to get everything all wrong. Only this"—he kissed me—". . . only love matters. Do you see that, little darlin'?"

I smiled, feeling lazy, languid, but also deeply certain of this man and this love.

"Let's go back the way we came!" he said, delighting in his idea.

And that's what we did.

"The bicycle ride and the fork in the road" became one of our signs to return to what mattered: the love that was more important than being right or getting one's way.

6

Torn Between the Two

Philip was disturbingly iconoclastic and anarchistic when faced with the typical expectations of society or family. He would rebelliously trounce upon the most commonly accepted conventions, scoff at ideas like the need to earn a paycheck in a secure, nine-to-five job, and disregard long-held family norms without seeming to sense the toes on which he was treading. My close tie to my parents was often confusing or threatening to him because he saw us as having chosen an essentially different path from their middle-class, security-oriented life. This set up a painful, and in my mind unnecessary, dichotomy between my love for my parents and my love for him. It was one of the largely unreconcilable struggles that pained us throughout the years.

Even in little things, he was baffled when confronted with one of those "but this is the way we do it in my family" statements. Early on, we were visiting my parents and waiting for them to return home. We were out in the yard, Philip shirtless and enjoying the first warm sun of early summer. When I heard my parents' car pull into the garage, I instinctively threw his shirt to him.

"Here. Quick. Get dressed!"

"Why?" he asked.

The bewildered look on his face made me realize how automatic and ingrained my adherence to my family's sense of decorum was.

"They'll be embarrassed."

He laughed, then grabbed me and was swinging me round and round against his sun-warmed chest when my parents appeared. They were predictably mortified. He was impishly delighted. I—caught between.

He could provoke defensiveness, frustration, and exasperated incredulity in those who were unaccustomed to, and hence threatened by, his vehement challenges to their world view. Early in our relationship, my parents were repeatedly thrown off by both Philip's unexpected, not-to-be-pigeonholed opinions, as well as the intensity with which he presented them. In fact, he regularly drove my usually mild-mannered father more than a little crazy by challenging even the liberal beliefs my parents assumed that any friend of mine, no less my partner, would share.

In a fully packed diner in the tiny provincial town in Vermont where I was working at a college in the mid-eighties, Philip and I were having a weekend breakfast with my visiting parents. This little one-horse town had a main street that included a bank, a tiny library, a pizza place, the diner, and a post office combined with a general store. The old-fashioned diner was one of the few places in which town and gown peaceably rubbed elbows. On that morning, however, there was little peace while Philip and my father argued vociferously over stacks of blueberry pancakes. The topic? Sex education.

In the era of the AIDS crisis, Philip's objection to sex education was shocking to my liberal parents, and probably to a number of people trying to have a pleasant Saturday brunch.

"It's demeaning to expose young people to the beauty and wonder of sexual intimacy in school, not to mention their being taught by dried-up, so-called sex educators who know nothing of the joy of orgasm and sexual communion," Philip said.

My parents swallowed hard, but hung in there. "But too many parents neglect to teach their children even basic information about prevention and safety," my mom said.

"Sex education is an anomaly," Philip said, his voice rising. "I say take it out of the classroom and leave it in the bedroom or field, where it belongs."

A moment of silence followed, both at our table and in the diner as a whole.

My dad, a guidance counselor at an all-boys high school in inner-city New York, pushed aside his mostly uneaten blueberry pancakes and took a long gulp of coffee. "You're being idealistic and unrealistic," he said. "The schools are trying to regain some control in the thick of your generation's sexual revolution and the resulting AIDS epidemic."

"Realism will never lead to the respect and affection found and needed in healthy sexual relations," Philip said. "The sexual revolution tried to free us to be authentic and loving. What's more practical than that?"

This controversy was never going to become a conversation. My father and Philip were shouting at each other from distant planets.

"It's necessary in a time of increased promiscuity to teach teenagers to be responsible, and that includes handing out condoms in school health centers," my father said.

Philip's fist came down on the table, sending the water glasses and plates jittering. The diner collectively inhaled as everyone waited for Philip's response.

"Young people are better off learning about sex and love from parents, siblings, friends, literature, even farm animals, and their own firsthand experiences in loving relationships," Philip said. "To have this sacred act diminished by practical, hands-on classroom instruction is a travesty. Do you demonstrate how to put those condoms on?"

Another hush descended upon the diner.

He continued, "To reduce the complexity and enchantment of love and sexuality to definitions, regulations, and safe-sex instruction manuals is anathema!"

Philip couldn't stomach the idea of what he saw as a private, personal, and romantic experience being brought into the impersonal and sterile milieu of the classroom. Talking and teaching about sex in an objective, academic manner was, to him, tantamount to killing spontaneity and passion.

Listening to them debate, I realized I'd never considered my unquestioned liberal stance on the topic. Of course I thought sex education was a good thing. I had vague memories of tittering girls and snorting boys in my tenth-grade sex-ed class, in which, sure that we knew more than the teacher, we'd set out gleefully to embarrass him. My teenage initiation into sex had been tinged with guilt that was neither addressed nor alleviated by that class, so I doubt the curriculum included an exploration of values. Most of what I'd learned about the mechanics of sex had come by word of mouth from more experienced friends, and, more directly, from my high school boyfriend. So, I didn't think the class either helped (my parents' position) or hindered (Philip's position) my sexual development.

At that breakfast table, I found myself wondering how I'd made my way to my less-than-conscious opinion. Listening to this vehement debate between my partner and my father (who was much too modest to ever say a word about sex to me), I wondered what other thoughts and opinions I was carrying without having questioned or explored them for myself. Now, Philip—coming from his own planet—was yet again causing me to doubt something I hadn't even known I'd adopted: my parents' world view.

That discussion probably provided hilarious conversation material for any number of dinner tables around town later in the day. My red-faced parents decided to return to their motel room to "wash up" while I walked a still-irate Philip into the woods to calm him down. Once again, Philip's way of seeing things was unpredictably *other* and predictably troubling. And the disarming thing was his blindness to this. He couldn't see how others didn't see what he saw. The bewildered and pained expressions on my parents' faces as I walked away with Philip that morning tugged at my heart.

About a year later, at yet another disastrous meal out with my parents, I thought my dad would be pushed into apoplexy when Philip nonchalantly asserted that Franklin D. Roosevelt knew about the bombing of Pearl Harbor before it happened and was willing to let 2,400 American military personnel die so he could finally convince the reluctant American people to enter World War II.

"Roosevelt was fully aware that the only way to save the country from the Depression, and, consequently, his chances for re-election, was to enter the war. He was willing to sacrifice those men for his own gain and ambition," he said.

Philip was audaciously arguing this to a man who'd volunteered to serve in WWII and had held FDR as a hero for forty-some years. (A treasured photo of my father shaking hands with Eleanor Roosevelt hung like a religious icon on the wall of my parents' bedroom for sixty-six years.) During the war, my dad had been stationed at one of the airfields in the South Pacific that was poised to bomb Japan (and ultimately did). He'd faced the dangers of being a pilot-navigator in the Battle of Tinian, and wouldn't have wanted to be anywhere else.

Not surprisingly, he shot out of his seat in furious indignation at Philip's sacrilegious assertion. "That's outrageous!"

Philip, to be fair, was not yet aware of my father's allegiance to FDR. He had simply launched into one of his many tirades about false flag operations and the treachery of governments. Nonetheless, he was more than willing to engage in controversy, only fully recognizing how utterly he had trespassed on "holy ground" for my father after the dispute ignited.

This was yet another of many calamitous encounters between Philip and my father that left me helplessly caught in the middle; I loved them both, and was equally loved by both. Much as I'd argue with Philip, entreating him to be more peaceable with my father, he couldn't resist articulating his widely different views. He was always up for a good verbal fight—neither exclusively liberal nor conservative, but always unconventional—and always opposed to what he saw as unexamined, party-line thinking on either side of the divide. He could be impatient and intolerant with people or ideas he found limited and limiting; his tilt on the world came in at a different angle. I simultaneously admired and inched away from this part of him, flinching as it threatened to divide me from the people I loved most in the world.

Though my parents tried their best, he was far too *other* for them to fully fathom. He didn't set out to cause trouble or be divisive; he just couldn't compromise or keep quiet, especially with people he wanted to love and be loved by. The more he cared about someone, the more insistent he'd become about "helping" them see what he believed to be right and true. This was frustrating, infuriating, and threatening for all of us. I struggled with him repeatedly, begging him to back off and let my parents comfortably be who they chose to be.

"What good is comfort?" he'd ask me in exasperation. "Isn't it better, and more loving, to open their eyes and show them how limiting their thinking is?"

"They're satisfied with who and where they are. It isn't your responsibility to change or improve them," I'd reply. Then I'd ask, in equal amounts of exasperation and desperation, "What about loving people unconditionally?"

"We owe it to the people we love to show them where they're blind. I always want you to do that with me."

"Yes, but you and I have agreed to this. My parents have not."

Deadlock.

In addition to all their radical divergences of opinion, my dad (a security-oriented man who'd struggled to survive the Depression) more generally was not convinced that Philip was a suitable husband for his only daughter. In fact, both my parents must have been deeply dismayed to find Philip utterly without worldly ambition—he was about as nonmaterialistic, impractical, and unworldly as it gets. Emblematic of his improbable idealism was his dropping out of college in the final quarter of his senior year. Upon hearing this, my mother was incredulous. My father, white-faced and speechless.

"What made you do that?" my mother asked.

"It just lost meaning for me," he said. "I looked around at all my literature professors and saw cynical, disillusioned alcoholics. I didn't want to participate in that world, so I quit."

"In the final quarter of your senior year?" my mom persisted in amazed disbelief. He just shrugged. I sat there inwardly torn between admiring his idealistic and principled stance versus sharing my parents' disbelief at what seemed foolhardy and incredibly short-sighted.

Later that year, Philip and I were invited to my cousin's posh summer wedding in New York City. At the time, we were living in a communal house in Asheville, North Carolina. Philip borrowed a pair of "nicer" sandals and a sports jacket from one of the other men living in the house. Amid hoots of laughter, we all agreed he looked quite dapper as he modeled his dress-up outfit for us. However, up in New York, the "nice" sandals were unappreciated.

"Who wears sandals to a wedding at the St. Regis?" someone behind us whispered.

My mom, also overhearing the comment, looked at me with a quizzical eye, to which I shrugged. My father rolled his eyes and blew out his cheeks.

"Why would anyone care about my feet?" Philip wondered aloud.

Stifling my giggles and poking him in the ribs, I had an uneasy premonition as I glimpsed just how *other* he was from the world in which I'd grown up. He had zero interest in that world, was mystified by it, and never ceased to wonder how I'd emerged from it. I, on the other hand, felt as though I'd pulled a butterfly into Times Square. My impulse was to protect him and get him away as quickly as possible. At the same time, however, I was becoming uncomfortably aware of the different level of "leaving home" I was facing—something I'd never imagined or planned on.

7

Not a Human Doing

"What do you do?" I asked Philip when we first met.

"I'm not a human *doing*, I'm a human *being*. Ask me who I am, not what I do." He said this with the mischievous grin I would come to know so well. The response initially startled, then dumbfounded me, and finally won my heart. But even in this realm of non-doing, what *did* he do? Or, in his terms, how was his *being* reflected in his *doing*?

He wrote, never thinking to publish. I'd find poems, limericks, and little stories on scraps of paper he'd walked away from. He'd choose an illustration and write a fanciful story about it for me or Misha, pen flying across the page, rarely hesitating. He'd leave these gifts lying about or stuffed in books, often forgetting about them as soon as the pen dropped from his hand.

Before I met him he'd taught creative writing at a free university, but I doubt he ever got paid. He encouraged me to write, suggesting ways to use writing to explore, articulate, and share feelings and create images of beauty and wonder. He encouraged me to "exercise my imagination." He'd write a few sentences and then pass the page to me to continue. Back and forth the piece would go, each of us adding to the original, ultimately producing something neither of us could have created on our own. I'd sit near him or know he was in the next room or out on the porch while each of us wrote in journals. At age twenty-eight, I'd found a partner who shared and supported my creativity, who recognized my love of words, and who wanted me to explore an unexplored potential. I began to find my writer's voice.

In addition, he filled my life with song. Throughout high school, he'd sung in choirs and a cappella groups, and later in a local rock band and a folk duet. He had a memory that held a seemingly endless collection of lyrics and melodies from the sixties and seventies. He played acoustic guitar, serenading me with a melodious voice that kept perfect pitch and moved from baritone to tenor with ease. He filled our days with songs—even his talk was often punctuated with a song that fit the conversation. As we walked, as he cooked or cleaned or tended the small urban gardens he'd plant, Philip sang continuously. He even got me shyly singing along when he realized that, despite terrible self-consciousness, I could hear and carry a tune.

Our first major purchase together was a stereo system. Those crates of albums came to life, and Philip introduced me to adagio movements of classical music and the equilibrium of baroque pieces when I objected to the bombast of full symphonies. We explored New Age music that evoked great calm and sometimes moved our hearts with sweetness. He'd sing us back into the sixties, one song leading to another as we sang and danced around the many apartments we lived in during those first years. The peace, pleasure, and beauty of his music collection was a gift.

He was also incredibly well-read, and equally well-informed on much related to literature, art, music, and history. (He'd dipped into at least that many majors in college.) Being with him was like walking into a box of brilliant and multicolored jewels. He read aloud to me before bed in a honey-toned voice that soothed me sweetly into sleep. I cherished ending my days lying next to him, his hand running through my hair while his voice and a story lulled me into dreams.

Professionally, and even as a way to contribute financially, Philip practiced what he called soul astrology. Characteristically unambitious, he never promoted or advertised, preferring to rely on word-of-mouth referrals as they came his way. These readings would, at times, have him contentedly preparing for and meeting clients a few times per week; at other times, months would go by with not a reading in sight. While he seemed satisfied either way, I was ever on the lookout for an open-minded client, colleague, or friend I might steer his way. The insight of his intuitive gift combined with the symbolic tools of astrology seemed wasted when he would let it go for long periods.

"You're so good at this and seem to love doing it," I said one day. "Don't you want to build and develop a serious practice?" I was trying hard not to let my frustration come through.

"It all happens as it's meant to," he replied. "You can't force it."

I bit my tongue and continued quietly looking for clients, temporarily shelving my proposal of business cards and flyers.

I'd propose astrological readings to my counseling clients when they were feeling stuck after talking for months with little evidence of change. Whenever I had the opportunity to sit in on a reading, I was amazed at what transpired. Astrology's capacity to identify inclinations, patterns of behavior, major losses, creative longings, or specific relationship struggles can disarm people, opening them up in a way that more traditional talk therapies do not. Whenever Philip quickly pinpointed a relationship issue or a creative struggle, something that psychotherapy failed to elicit in its tendency to let the client lead, the "magic" of astrological insight acted much like a key turned in a locked door. People, myself included, were startled into a new level of honesty by this intriguing system of symbolism.

"The predominance of the element of water in your chart makes you inclined to experience your life through your emotions," he'd begin.

"Yes, that's true."

"This can be very threatening to your father."

"Yes, I seem to drive him crazy whenever I do anything with feeling—cry, get angry, even show joy."

"Well, your father's predominant element is air, so, he's more inclined to think and analyze his way through any situation. He would be quite uncomfortable with your watery emotions. I imagine you feel as though he wants to shut you down as quickly as he can."

"Yes, and that only makes me angrier."

After an hour-long conversation with Philip, my clients were generally more willing to explore issues in greater depth with me. It was a fascinating and illuminating collaboration that added to my respect and awe for his psychological interpretations of the planets and signs and the intuition and sensitivity he brought to each person.

And then there was the deeper understanding that this ancient art brought to our relationship. It helped us through many tangles. Rather than attaching to identities, being bound by who we thought we were and had to be, Philip could step back and explain a controversy using astrological insight. Somehow, the more objective language and the archetypal planetary symbols and their signs provided a new way to explain and respect divergences and disagreements. It allowed for a clarity and detachment that afforded us a wider, more inclusive perspective by connecting us to something more universal.

"I feel like you're judging me," I'd say.

"I'm sorry. My masculine Aquarian moon can be hard on your feminine Scorpio moon."

"So . . .?" I'd ask, arms tightly crossed, still feeling defensive and annoyed.

"So, I need to be more careful not to crush your sensitive, feminine nature with my more masculine tendency to assert my sense of right and objective truth."

"I like that," I'd say, beginning to thaw.

"On the other hand, we'll be better off if you can remember that your Saturn conjuncts my Moon, and can leave me feeling stiff or inhibited."

"Hmm . . . really? So, what am I supposed to do with that? I never think of you as inhibited by much of anything."

"Yeah, my six planets in fire signs make it look like I'm all confident and brave. But this other thing is also going on, and it makes me feel self-conscious just when you're feeling free and easy."

"Yikes . . . this sounds hard for us."

"Well, yes, it is. But if we're aware, then we can be gentle and forgiving with each other."

This kind of conversation usually allowed the emotional tone between us to shift from contention to reconciliation. Just as we'd be about to topple into fault-finding or attempts to change each other, an astrological insight would save the day. Astrology gave us a way to respect and include more of who we were individually, and to celebrate the unique alchemy we created as a couple. This complex system, along with Philip's way of combining it with intuition, poetry, compassion, and whimsy, made it a whole lot easier for two fixed and implacable people to go forward in an ongoing and loving exploration.

Added to his serious and philosophical traits, Philip had a tremendous capacity for joy often expressed in a rather wacky sense of humor. There was something in his smile, his laugh, and his eccentric sense of humor that transported and transformed my days and nights. In our first months together, we played an inane and oddly addictive naming game that often kept us up laughing through half the night. The game was inspired by Mr. Gotobed, a character in an Anthony Trollope novel called *The American Senator*. Trollope often gave his characters descriptive names, and Mr. Gotobed (go-to-bed) had a penchant for spending a good deal of his time sleeping when he was supposed to be attending to matters of state.

We started with Philip-laughs-a-lot and Joan-giggles-and-jiggles. Then we named the people we knew. There was Myra-wiggles-wow, Sue-smacks-her-lips, Noah-knows-it-all, Greg-goofs-around, Peter-puffs-his-chest, Rose-rushes-in, and so on. Something about being cozily wrapped around each other, whispering, giggling, and alliterating these ridiculous names into the small hours of the night while the rest of the world slept, added a goofy and warmly comforting intimacy to our unfolding relationship.

At other times, with oversized pants pulled up to his armpits, Philip would perform a slapstick act for Misha, Tanya, and me. Falling, stumbling, tripping, and dancing around the room, he'd have us rolling around, clutching our sides and begging him to stop. At other times, we'd see, hear, or read something that tickled one or both of us, and suddenly laughter would become an intense, thigh-slapping, face-crumpling, bellyaching hilarity that quickly grew way out of proportion to whatever it was that had started us off. One person's laughter sparked the other's until we'd collapse in satisfied exhaustion that was better than a good meal, as good as good sex.

Sometimes, we'd be in separate rooms and I'd hear a chuckle, then a snort, then a chortle. Finally, unable to resist seeing what was going on, I'd wander in to find him totally cracked up, tears streaming down his face as he pounded on an open book, helplessly convulsed with laughter. Without the slightest idea of what he was laughing about, I'd soon be pulled into bellyaching hysterics too. The pure joy of seeing and hearing him laugh was a profound gladness. I'd rarely laughed so freely and spontaneously—or at least, not since childhood.

Like everything else about him, there was something idiosyncratic and eccentric about his sense of humor. This quirky poem shows his peculiar knack for juxtaposing the unexpected:

Is delicious a word
we should use very much
between the two of us
about the way we touch?

If I were eating
chocolate cake
then I think
that it would be no mistake
to use it
but if I am biting
into you
each time I feel alone
and calling you delicious
it won't be too long
before you're all gone
and I'll have to wash the dishes

Children were especially drawn to Philip, probably because he was childlike himself. Early in our relationship, my young nephew and niece were spending a day with me, Philip, and my parents. Philip was sitting on the living room floor, something not typically done in my parents' well-ordered, well-mannered house. He was playing guitar and singing for my six-year-old nephew. My niece—no more than two or three and still shy of strangers—clung to my mother in the kitchen. Attracted by the music and his voice, however, she ventured to the door and peered out, quickly returning to the safety of her grandma. Slowly, however, she edged ever closer, until finally, letting out a gleeful laugh, she ran into the living room and jumped into his lap—joining the guitar with giggles of glee.

Philip's way of parenting Misha was, to me, remarkable. (Misha's name, by the way, was inspired by a rash of Dostoevsky reading during Tanya's pregnancy.) Having myself grown up with routines and kind-but-definite boundaries and discipline, Philip's approach to being a parent was much more egalitarian.

I remember a time when four adults waited ten minutes to leave because Misha wasn't finished playing at whatever he was playing. In my upbringing, a four-year-old would have been gently but firmly picked up, carried to the car, and plonked into his seat; adults in my world did not generally wait for children.

"Why couldn't you have hurried Misha?" I asked later.

"He's got just as much right to do what he's doing as I do. What's the big deal if we wait ten minutes for him to be ready? He'll be a happier guy when he comes of his own will." And it was true—he was one of the most easygoing and secure little boys I'd ever known.

When Misha came the first time to stay with us for a summer, Philip entranced him (and me) with daily and nightly readings from Tolkien's *The Hobbit*. After only a few chapters, neither Misha nor I wanted to do anything other than be read to. This was fine with Philip, who always worried that Misha might want to do more "sporty" activities for which Philip had no great liking.

We spent happy hours every day lying around on the carpets and couch, drifting through the afternoons with dappled light and shadows marking time across the room and words weaving their spell around us. We were transported into Tolkien's mythical landscapes. We trekked out of the Shire with Bilbo Baggins and Gandalf, through the dark caves under the Misty Mountains, into the black forest of Mirkwood, all the way to Mount Doom.

At night, Misha resisted bedtime until we'd had a final reading. He was enchanted by Bilbo's adventures, often extending the tale and creating adventures for us during the day. The grocery store, the park, or the library became places where we might run into Gollum; giant spiders, wargs, elves, or orcs awaited us around every corner. Philip's reading bewitched and accompanied us throughout that entire summer—the summer of *The Hobbit*.

8

The White Glove Tests

Any number of times in our early years together, I was sure that Philip would get a good punch in the nose or a plate cracked over his head from one of the irate parents he confronted. Eating dinner in a café, voices from the next table would reach us with parental admonitions or threats to some little person. I would feel Philip stiffen and go silent. Next thing I knew, he'd be on his feet and headed for that table.

"Hey there, I just want you to know that not all grown-ups are as mean as your parents," he'd say, kneeling at eye level with the berated and now startled child.

I'm pretty sure the only thing that saved him from getting a black eye or a broken nose was the daring sort of lionheartedness that filled him with rage at any unkindness to children. He seemed to grow in size as he would glower down at the flabbergasted parents, fiercely suggesting they rethink their bullying approach to parenting. In these situations, I was torn between wanting to evaporate and wanting to shout, "Bravo!"

Philip's fierce protectiveness over children, his belief that they should be allowed to develop without heavy-handed attempts to change their nature, and his own tender, loving parenting style with Misha were all firmly rooted in a lifetime of struggles with his own domineering father.

For years, I heard Philip criticized, cajoled, and questioned by family, friends, and therapists about his stuck position regarding his father, Gale. They'd say things like, "I rose above dysfunction, why can't you?" "You have to move on. That time is over . . . done . . . gone." "Why let him ruin your life?"

I would watch Philip's eyes when some frustrated soul would tread on this marshy ground. Ultimately, a look that bespoke his felt helplessness would travel across his face. Like it or not, want it or not, choose it or not, he was stuck. Taking his hand in mine and squeezing encouragement was all I could do in those difficult moments.

Endless hours of stories told and therapy paid for circled round and round the obsessive disappointment and heartbreak Philip felt toward his father. In fact, I've often thought there could easily be a book entitled *Life and Struggles with Gale.*

Physically, Gale was a slightly stockier and earthier version of Philip. He was one or two inches shorter, a bit heavier, and more muscular. In moments of arrogance, his chest became prominently provocative, "like a puffed-out Pouter pigeon," Philip would say in disgust. The contrast between Gale's and Philip's hands always struck me. Gale's were big and heavy, reminding me of the term "ham-fisted." Philip's hands, in contrast, were slender, strong, and graceful, with long fingers made for stretching tenderly over the keys of a piano, the strings of his guitar, or my cheek.

Philip's early years were deeply affected by his father's ambitious pursuit of upward mobility in the banking world. As Gale moved from smaller to increasingly larger banks, the family moved from tiny to increasingly larger towns on Colorado's eastern plains: from Grover to Hereford to Sterling to Denver. He strove relentlessly, advancing from bank manager to vice-president to president. In fact, he was named the youngest bank president in the country at one point.

By the time Philip was in high school, his father was president of a large bank in Fort Collins. By 1960s standards, the family had become prominent in the community and possessed most of the trappings of affluence. There was the Frank Lloyd Wright–designed house by the country club, the Lincoln Continental family car, and Philip's baby-blue Fiat, complete with unlimited use of a credit card for gas. Gale sat on local boards and charities and belonged to every service organization and club a bank president should belong to: Rotary, Lions, Elks, and so on. The family was even nominated for and competed in the "Colorado Family of the Year" contest.

"Ironically," Philip once explained, "the contest was discredited and shut down when it was discovered that the competing 'ideal' family had stuffed the ballot boxes. What a bust!"

"Really?" I said. "The ideal family cheated?"

"Yes! And after endless freezing and humiliating winter weekends of standing outside supermarkets and handing out Heiman-family flyers, the whole thing was cancelled, all the amazing prizes—a mansion in Denver, another house in the mountains, all kinds of gadgets and gizmos—forfeited."

Because a bank president and his family were considered public figures in small-town America during that time, it also became necessary to belong to a church. The family obtained a front-row pew in the United Methodist Church, and all four children were in Sunday school each week without fail.

"I had badges for seven years of perfect Sunday school attendance. Even on family holidays, we'd have to find a Methodist church, and the pastor would stamp our attendance passports," Philip told me with a mix of amusement and disdain.

Gale's worldly ambition for material wealth and status became anathema to seventeen-year-old Philip, who was coming of age in the late sixties. Much to his father's chagrin, Philip kicked off his shoes, threw off his Young Republicans tie, grew his hair long, and took his guitar to hang out in Boulder to the tunes of Bob Dylan and Judy Collins.

"What caused such strife between you and your father?" I asked early on.

"Read this," he said, digging out a poem written in his late teens.

where are you
in all that you've learned
what have you lost
in all that you've earned
have you gone so far
in the direction you've chosen
that the stream of life
within you

is still now
and frozen

As Philip joined the sixties' generational swell of changing consciousness and values, the music and world view he embraced expressed a growing aversion for the materialistic values of his father's generation. Added to having grown up under the heavy hand of old-world, paternal dominance, Philip moved into full-fledged teenage rebellion.

It was during drives to church that he began openly voicing his contempt for what he saw as Gale's hypocritical striving after income and possessions. When Philip began singing Porter Wagoner's "Satisfied Mind" from the back seat of the car on Sunday mornings, he and his siblings had to duck from Gale's heavy hand as it came swinging wildly over the seat in search of a target.

Philip painted such a detailed figure of Gale that I felt as though I knew him—or Philip's version of him—long before I met him. In fact, it was months into our relationship before I met either of Philip's parents, or learned that we were all living in the same town.

"I'm an orphan," he told me when we first met.

"Really?"

"Well, we're estranged. I only visit my Granny Annie when I'm sure my parents won't be around."

When I finally met Gale, it was impossible to approach him without bias. In Philip's eyes, his father held all the wrong values and priorities, was dominating, controlling, power-hungry. Needless to say, I headed into our first encounter with trepidation. I expected a monster, and was thrown off-balance when I met a charming man who graciously welcomed me into his home.

Philip's ogreish descriptions of his father certainly weren't all there was to the man, but they weren't inaccurate either. As I came to know Gale, he was indeed a formidable personality with an arrogance that sometimes frightened, often overwhelmed me. He was not an exaggerated figment of Philip's imagination.

Gale's ambition eventually led him into reckless risk-taking, resulting in professional ruination for his embezzlement of a trust fund.

"Of course," he said, "I always meant to pay it back."

The prosecutor was unimpressed with Gale's defense, and disregarded with disdain the many character references from the community.

"So he's a *nice* guy," the prosecutor drawled sarcastically.

Gale narrowly escaped imprisonment, but he lost his job and was charged a weighty fine. The hasty sale of the country-club house and the move to the basement of Philip's maternal grandparents' house in Greeley was a comedown (literally and psychologically) causing deep shame and suicidal depression. Headlines and local news coverage during the weeks of the trial were devastating.

Even from this disaster, however, Gale bounced back. With his banking career gone up in smoke, he made a career change, but not before struggling through months of rejected applications, his smeared reputation preceding him wherever he went—even as far as Nairobi. Not a little ironically, he eventually assumed a post as professor of business law at a community college in Greeley. Who better to teach the law than one who had broken it?

Unlike his early-eighties colleagues who showed up for classes in jeans and T-shirts, Gale managed to emerge from the chaos of a depressing basement apartment in immaculate business suits and silk ties. He'd stop before an upstairs mirror for a final adjustment to his tie and a last smoothing of his wavy, silvering hair. Then he'd dash from the house for class, always at the last minute.

"Why does he like to rush like that?" I once asked.

"He thrives on racing against time," Philip said. "He's an adrenaline junkie. It makes him feel important."

Gale was so different from my mild-mannered father, who was careful, quiet, cultured, security-oriented. Indefatigable and determined, Gale was also vain, arrogant, and pugnacious.

"You'd think this disaster would have humbled him," Philip said. "But no. As you can see, Humpty Dumpty just put himself back together again and carried on in the same proud and pompous manner."

A determined jogger and marathon runner, Gale was ever on the move until collapsing late at night in front of the television. On average, he slept less than six hours a night.

"I have to keep going until I fall into a stupor—otherwise, I lie awake tormented by a bad conscience," he once said.

This occasional and surprising rise to self-honesty was one of his more admirable traits. His demanding and critical approach to his wife and children, his extramarital affairs, and his financial shenanigans all weighed heavily on his conscience, but sadly, not heavily enough to compel change. He was always running, racing, speeding against the clock and his conscience.

Philip's mom once showed me a proudly preserved front page from Sterling's newspaper, *The Journal Advocate.* A full-page black-and-white photo showed Gale Heiman running down the main street of town, briefcase in hand, tie flapping in the breeze. The accompanying headline humorously (and possibly presentiently) read, "Why is this man running?"

"He figured out a route to the college that avoided all the traffic lights so he'd never have to stop," Philip told me. He collected speeding tickets, burst into the house late and breathless for dinner, and forever picked himself up, both literally and figuratively, from falls and troubles. I watched once, helpless and transfixed with horror, as he fell ten feet from the top of a tree (from which he was attempting to rescue his granddaughter's kitten). He landed unharmed on the roof of a parked car, and then proceeded to climb yet again to retrieve "that danged kitten."

"I'm convinced he's not fully human under the skin," I told Philip after that incident.

"You're starting to see what I mean about him," Philip said, laughing.

Sitting down to a Sunday dinner at the Heiman family dining table was like stepping into a Joyce Carol Oates novel. There was so much drama, so much larger-than-life feeling.

At times, undercurrents of tension forked across the room in bolts of lightning. At other times, shouting matches exploded, thundering with an intensity I'd not witnessed in the childhood scenes of my polite and temperate family. But there were also many hours filled with boisterous laughter and great storytelling that included the near-mythologizing of a frontier-like birth out behind a rock near Colorado Springs, isolated prairie houses with frog ponds for basements, and mountain homes invaded by cows.

As time went by, Philip added other stories and examples of his multifaceted family. Gale was a larger-than-life figure whose influence on Philip (and most likely his other three children) was profound. As the father of young children, Gale appeared to be training his progeny, particularly his two sons, for a tough and competitive world.

"We were expected to clean our rooms every Saturday to pass Gale's white glove tests," Philip told me. "Any dust found on or under the furniture meant 'doing gigs.'"

"Gigs?" I asked.

"Yeah, marching up and down the hall until we were permitted to stop. As kids, my brother and I initially thought that playing soldiers, with Gale as the sergeant, was fun. But week after week, it got old."

Integral to Gale's world view was an unexamined assumption that his family would do as he bid—unquestioned and unchallenged. Sitting at the head of the table, an unabashedly old-world Germanic patriarch, it never occurred to him to set a table, pick up a plate after a meal, or wash a dish. He had no idea how to shop for food or run the washing machine, had never run a vacuum (except in detailing his cars), never washed a dish or wiped down a kitchen counter. In his world, wife and daughters should serve; sons should obey.

"One of his favorite things to say was, 'As long as your feet are under my table, you'll do as I say,'" Philip told me.

"And your response?" I asked.

"My brother and I set up a separate card table in the dining room and sat there. We took our feet out from under his table."

"What did he do?"

"He snorted and ordered us back to the table. But everyone else got a good laugh."

"I can just see the scene."

"Yeah, pretty ineffectual in the end. But living with Gale was like being a sniper in guerrilla warfare. Just to survive, we had to keep resisting. Even if it didn't work."

Gale's white glove inspections and commander-like control of the family home were undoubtedly inspired by his military experience. Although he was never called to active duty during WWII, he had spent the war years on air force bases in Colorado Springs and California, teaching pilots. When he contrasted his wartime experience with that of his brother's, I heard his chagrin tempered with hero worship for this older brother who had been called to active duty.

"When my brother returned from service in the Far East with stories of jungle skirmishes, malaria, and an Asian girlfriend left behind, I saw him as a returning hero," Gale said one evening after dinner. "He and his squadron were abandoned on a small South Sea island where they hid from the enemy in the jungle for weeks before rescue finally appeared. In contrast, what was I doing?"

"I know it must have sounded thrilling to you at the time," Philip responded with unusual compassion, "but it must have been terrifying enough to create a lifetime of trauma for your brother and his men."

"Maybe, but I wanted to serve my country. And what was I doing but sitting safe?" Gale replied. His voice held the disgust and anger of a twenty-year-old.

"But your intelligence was apparently more valued than your soldiering," Philip said. "You were serving the country in a really important way."

But Gale blew out his cheeks in disgust. This was no consolation to him even forty-five years later.

Philip described the contrast between Gale and himself with incredulity.

"How could we have been more different? I was leisurely while Gale was on fast-forward. I was learning to cook brown rice and beans while Gale grabbed his hamburger on the run. I strolled or rode a bike while Gale was pressuring my brother and me into go-karts and teaching us to drive hot rods on back roads by the time we were thirteen. I hid up in the attic of the house with my older sister reading novels and writing poetry while Gale read *The*

Wall Street Journal, rooted vociferously for the Broncos, and liked nothing better than tinkering with cars. I was dreamy and impractical—Gale was eminently pragmatic. I was reflective, he was an action movie. I loved using words and the power of my voice to beguile, persuade, or seduce. Gale boomed. I was interested in literature, history, and art, Gale in business, law, and cars. Is it any wonder we were at odds from the very start?"

"As far back as I can remember," Philip continued, "he was an insensitive bully who could not accept me. When I was five, he swooped me up off a beach blanket where I was sorting the shells I'd found that morning under the shade of my mom's umbrella. Gale hoisted me up, tucked me under his arm like a football, and ran down to the water laughing and tickling. He plunged both of us into the sea, and then lifted me—the live football who didn't know how to swim—and chucked me into the waves. Apparently he thought this was the best way to overcome my fear of the water. It was terrifying."

When I met Philip, he could still barely swim—a dog paddle in shallow water was about it. Most of the time, loving water as he did, he chose to walk along shores, dabble his toes, and watch me swim.

"Another time," Philip said, "he lugged me up the steps of a high playground slide and at the top, he plonked me on my bottom and, without pause, pushed me down what seemed like a mile-high slide. I couldn't do a thing to slow or stop myself as I slid wildly to the ground."

In his early teens, Philip once tried to stop Gale from beating his younger brother, who doggedly refused to admit to a lie he hadn't told. Gale flung Philip off with the flick of his arm. Philip said he felt like a fly being swatted away, making him realize how powerless he still was against him.

"It's ironic that Gale was so vehement, and, if he deemed necessary, violent about disciplining us regarding honesty, of all things," Philip said. "It was only a few short years later when it came out that he was having an affair with his secretary and embezzling money from clients at the bank. How honest is that?" Philip spat this out with anger and disgust as though it had happened yesterday.

Even family road trips were Gale-dominated.

"Gale's idea of a vacation was to drive as many miles as possible in as short a time as possible," Philip once explained when we were on one of our many drives from Colorado to the East Coast.

"That sounds horribly tedious," I said.

"There's the famous story of the trip to Baja California," Philip said. "After days of nearly nonstop driving, we all climbed stiffly out of the car to view the Pacific Ocean. After a few minutes for a stretch, Gale announced, 'Well, that's the Pacific side, now let's see how fast we can get to the Gulf.' The family chorus of groans only seemed to make him all the more gleefully determined. Sometimes I really think he was demonic."

"Gale's preferred way to travel was literally nonstop," Philip went on. "When he was beginning to nod at the wheel, I would slide under as he slid over—the challenge being never to take a hand off the wheel or a foot off the gas, never to slow down, and, certainly, never to stop."

After I heard this story, I understood why, on our trips, I had to beg for bathroom stops or insist that we eat at least one meal sitting still in a café or a rest stop. It was during these early cross-country trips, on uninterrupted stretches of interstate highways, that I listened in amazement as Philip unfolded his history. These stories revealed how Philip had inadvertently learned this style of travel from his eccentric father. Again, in contrast to my own family travels, where regular stops for treats were part of the fun, this was bizarre and unacceptable to me.

"If we drive another mile, I'll go mad!" I shouted during one of our trips as he zipped past one service exit after another. "I hope you know you're acting just like your father."

This was probably the most incendiary thing I could say to a man who wanted to be nothing like his father. Following a blowup and a subsequent sulk, he pulled over and ungraciously invited me to lunch at the first unappealing greasy spoon in sight. It took a few of these lengthy trips and my continued protests before he finally recognized the absurdity of his behavior . . . and worse yet, where he'd gotten it.

Philip's family, complete with its dramas, traumas, and deeply felt loyalty, was intriguing—certainly never dull. I came to love them, and I felt increasingly grateful for having been allowed into what I came to understand as a fiercely protected, and protective, family circle.

In the six months prior to Gale's painful death from pancreatic cancer, we discovered a radically different man; one who had never been able to fully disregard or dispel a bad conscience fueled by deep regrets for his faults and failings. After so many years of hubristic pride, when confronted with a fatal diagnosis, his façade crumbled instantly. He apologized, asked openly for forgiveness, and put the gratitude and love he felt for his family into words never before spoken.

I'll never forget the surprised tears filling Philip's eyes when, just a few weeks before he died, Gale said to Philip, "I always admired and respected you. I wish I could have been more like you."

Too little, too late, and yet Philip and I both grabbed onto this remarkable moment.

"What do you wish you'd done in your life that you haven't?" Philip asked Gale.

"I always loved singing in choirs and wish I'd done that more," he answered without pause, causing my jaw to drop in amazement. "I also would've loved to be a musician."

Knowing him as a practical businessman whose main recreations were watching sports on television and tinkering with cars, we were shocked by this unknown, artistic longing to sing or play an instrument.

"He had a really good baritone voice," Philip remembered from the days of churchgoing. "You could always hear his voice during the singing. It was resonant and well-timbred."

In those final months, his whole demeanor shifted. His face became gentler, more childlike and vulnerable; he was softer; his sense of humor blossomed. He looked increasingly baffled, unable to fathom the demise that was happening, and happening so quickly. After years of watching this face that rarely expressed doubt or uncertainty, that huffed and puffed at any of our hesitations, this change was both unnerving and heartbreaking. Watching him walk, bent over and holding himself up with the help of the chairs and tables, broke my heart.

Humbled in a way I couldn't have imagined, he cried openly, asking for help in ways never dreamed of. Following chemotherapy sessions, I held the pan for him to vomit into with one hand while wiping sweat from his face with the other. I smoothed and combed his once proudly thick hair, and felt a love and sorrow I didn't know I had for him. Philip massaged his aching shoulders, feet, and hands when we visited him each weekend. This was more physical contact and shared tenderness than had passed between the two since Philip was a baby. It may also have been more gentle, loving care than Gale had received in many, many years.

"If you lie down flat, I can give you a better back massage," Philip said one day. Getting him back up when he'd lost all muscle strength was surprisingly harder than anticipated. When Philip had finally pushed and prodded him back to sitting on the edge of the bed, he was fully exhausted. I could only keep him upright by leaning him against me.

"Sorry I'm not softer, Gale," I said as his head rested on my less than voluptuous chest.

He chuckled and replied, "You're fine. Good. Soft."

It was both heartbreaking and heart-healing to be with him through those final months. The transformation was inspiring, what one might call a good dying. With bittersweet pain, we embraced this much more lovable man and were grateful to have the opportunity to see who he might have been. Sad to say for Philip, this side of Gale emerged far too late. Perhaps this was equally so for Gale himself.

9

A Place on the Planet

Being surrounded by beauty was as essential to Philip as food and shelter. In addition to seeking it wherever we went, he sought it in people, looked for it in art, music, literature, and nature. He searched selectively for it in clothing and jewelry for me ("little bits of beauty are much preferred to quantities of mediocrity," he'd say). He created atmospheres of aesthetic enchantment in each of our many homes, hanging filmy material from the ceilings to divide studio apartments into more than one room and taking down light fixtures to replace them with Japanese paper umbrellas turned upside down. Middle Eastern colored-glass lanterns, Buddha statues, fairy lights, and Pre-Raphaelite prints surrounded us wherever we went.

We never had much money or many possessions and we repeatedly left everything behind when we moved, but Philip loved and adopted the idea planted by a neighbor in Denver. As we toured his very eccentric studio apartment, he told us, "One should buy or find one thing of beauty to bring into one's home at least every few weeks." Canvases that could find no more wall space lined the floor three and four deep. Artifacts—antique and 1950s retro—sat side by side, creating an atmosphere of whimsy and wonder. This pleased Philip no end. We began wandering antique stores and dropping into estate sales in the Cheesman Park and Capitol Hill neighborhoods of Denver to see what beauty we could find.

Having grown up in the post-war pragmatism of 1950s suburbia, my eyes were not trained to seek beauty outside of museums, theaters, and concert halls as his were. My perspective expanded under his tutelage, and I learned to look at Victorian-era architecture with new appreciation. Moving into apartments carved out of mid-1800s Gold Rush mansions created a sense of intrigue and romance, resonating with parts of me I had yet to explore.

Our attic apartment was two blocks from Cheesman Park, in an 1886 Victorian house. Given a free hand by an easygoing and trusting landlady, we repainted that apartment more than once. Philip inclined toward primary, jewel-toned colors—especially deep blues and reds. In my childhood home, off-white and beige predominated, and the Scandinavian furniture was simple and clean. With Philip, I drank in rich colors with a thirst I hadn't known I had. He once painted the walls of the living room a deep red topped by a ceiling of powder blue.

"It's our womb room," he announced with delight as we surveyed the completed work.

We would sit together as the afternoon light streamed in through the windows, our heads bent over travel books for England, France, and Germany. Philip talked about the places he'd been during his travels and told of adventures had. His enthusiasm for art, culture, architecture, history, and natural beauty was contagious. My travels up to that time had been solely in the U.S. and Canada, and being introduced to England, France, Germany, Austria, and Switzerland through his stories ignited longings to wander farther than I'd ever been.

Those books took us from mad King Ludwig's castles in Bavaria to the fairy-tale fountains of Salzburg; from Thomas Hardy's thatched cottage in Dorset to the open spaces and wild ponies of Dartmoor National Park in Devon. My hunger to travel grew. The wider world invited and enticed. And the idea of exploring it at Philip's side made it seem more possible and attractive.

I'm not exactly sure why it felt as though Philip was opening the lock to a new and more cultured world. I had, after all, grown up with parents who went to college, read constantly, and used New York City to immerse themselves—and me—in art, music, and theater. At home, classical music filled the house whenever my father was there. Weekends included trips to museums and theaters. I loved Leonard Bernstein's children's concerts, where artists spontaneously painted on huge screens and dancers improvised to the orchestra's music. I sang along to most Rodgers and Hammerstein and Gilbert and Sullivan operettas from a very early age. My parents returned from travels to Europe, England, Israel, and Russia with exotic gifts and exciting tales of their adventures.

So why did being with Philip feel so different, so much more enriching? Perhaps it was being in love. But it also had to do with the way he experienced everything. From my parents, I received a wondrous appreciation and respect for the long lineage of historical greatness we call Western culture. Philip, on the other hand, seemed to discover each painting, cathedral, book, poem, and piece of music as though it and he were new to the world. I found myself passionately participating rather than observing and standing back with my parents' respectful regard.

Even at a literal level, in the spirit of the poet Denise Levertov, Philip wanted to "taste and see" life and art up close. Much to my dismay and his chagrin, he would regularly set off alarms in museums when he'd get too close to a painting. Guards would come running, and Philip would stand back, dramatically holding his hands over his head in surrender.

"Forgive me," he'd say, "I only meant to look more closely. Have you noticed the remarkable delicacy of the brush strokes in this painting? The artist must have used two hairs of his brush to do it."

More than once, a guard, so taken by Philip's enthusiasm, would also lean in too close to marvel at brush strokes, depth and subtlety of color, and other minute details. When the alarm would sound again, the guard would either laugh or sheepishly send us on our way.

Philip didn't want to stand back, observe, or critique art, life, or places. He longed to get as close as possible, to taste, feel, and experience everything from the inside out. In this way, my life with him—in all aspects—became more vivid, personal, colored, and intimate. His love for travel also expanded my world view in ways I had never dreamed possible.

Before I met him in 1978, Philip had spent four consecutive summers exploring Western Europe with Tanya and his brother. He fell ever more in love with castles and cathedrals, countryside and Alps, cities and villages, rivers and lakes, and, of course, bread, wine, and beer. More than the sights and experiences of being in different cultures, however, he talked about meeting different aspects of himself in new places.

"In Germany, when I woke to the clanging of cow bells, the scents of flowers and sun-warmed hay, and German being spoken by the farmer and his wife in whose house we were staying, I felt different. Different from how I feel when waking up here."

"Was it the foreignness? The otherness?" I asked.

"Maybe. Walking into the nearest village to buy bread, yogurt, and chocolate, I'd look down at my feet on those ancient, cobbled streets and feel grounded in a way I don't feel in Colorado. It was a . . . familiar otherness."

"Familiar otherness?"

"Yeah, it was like a door I'd forgotten was there, and now it was open and inviting me in, inviting me back to a place in my soul I'd nearly, but not completely, lost touch with."

"And what was behind that door?" I asked.

"Poetry! And my self! I wrote more in those weeks than I have in years. And . . . I know this sounds corny, but I felt poetic. I felt like a poet."

"And you think this was at least partly because of where you were? It wouldn't have happened here?"

"Well, it hasn't, has it?"

I reflected on this as I recalled feeling nearly electrified with a sense of awe when I was exploring the West Coast during my internship. Standing on a cliff to get my first view of the Pacific Ocean in Oregon, wandering through Carmel-by-the-Sea, sitting in candlelit hot springs in Esalen overlooking the coast of Big Sur, and driving along Route 1 down the coast of California, I had to keep pulling over to write in my journal.

"I felt older and younger, more open and inwardly expanded," Philip continued. "It's as though I was discovering more inward space, and the outward spaces were reflecting forgotten places in my psyche. I also had moments of recognition, feeling as though I'd been there before and had known myself differently there."

"A possible glimpse or sense of a past life?" I asked.

"Maybe. It's hard to put into words. But I know I felt more alive, more like the person I want to be. If we're not living on ground that resonates with our souls, we'll never fully grow into the people we were put here to be. We are interdependent with place. We need the support of place to find our true voice and authentic self."

"Surely not just one place per person," I said.

"Oh, my little silly. Of course there's more than one place for each of us, but it certainly isn't any place or every place."

"Somewhat akin to finding a soul mate, yes?" I asked, wrapping my arms around him.

"Yes, we're soul mates in search of our soul place," he said. "There are specific places where each person's soul coheres most fully and is most at ease and at home."

"It's an energetic thing?" I asked.

"Yes, primarily. And then, on the surface, we feel attuned and harmonious with the people, language, food, clothing, climate, custom, architecture, music, and art. A place to live," he insisted, "needs to reflect one's values and aesthetics."

Philip had always been searching for his "right" place. He was unwavering in his need to find this kindred place on the planet, and found support for this idea from the branch of astrology known as astrocartography.

He sought communities where we'd be more likely to find like-minded people, natural food choices, and alternative, holistic health care. He looked for organic farmers markets, health food stores, and vegetarian cafés. Equally important were book, music, clothing, and home design stores where we could find nurturance and beauty for mind, body, and home.

This kinship, he was convinced, was also sensed in our being drawn to the natural beauty of a place.

"I'm drawn to the green of the Alps in Germany, Switzerland, and France, but I feel distinctly uncomfortable in the craggier, browner Rocky Mountains," he said.

"But you've lived in Colorado most of your life," I said.

"I know . . . that's the problem! Even in England, I love Sussex, Devon, the Cotswolds, and Cornwall, but the Lake District is too rugged and not nearly green enough for me."

A Scorpio and lover of water, he felt nurtured by lakes, rivers, and oceans while feeling parched and desiccated in land-locked, arid Colorado.

I'd never been conscious of this sense of a kindred place on the planet before. Or, at least, I'd never articulated it. But once explained, I recalled the keen sense of relief I felt when I left Long Island at eighteen to move upstate for undergraduate and graduate school. I immediately felt more at ease, more aware and appreciative of my environment, when I moved to the small college town of Oneonta. Earlier, I'd loved childhood summers on Schroon Lake in the Adirondack Mountains, and in later years, I'd felt eased by two separate homes on lakes—one in rural New York and the other in northern Pennsylvania. So I resonated with Philip's longing for a place that felt like home, but hadn't ever considered deliberately going in search of this place. Up until that time, I'd gone wherever school or a job took me.

This quest, initially intriguing and attractive, eventually created a growing sense of disquiet in me as Philip and I spent a lot of time driving through towns and cities across the U.S., with Philip rejecting each one faster than I could catch my breath, no less get the "feel" of the place.

He hungered for green, verdant places, so I suggested a visit to Massachusetts, where I'd once spent a summer. But when we got there, he kept moving, passing through the towns of Amherst and Northampton—both filled with the book and music stores, food co-ops, vegetarian cafés, and counter-culture atmosphere I thought he'd love.

"New England is claustrophobic," he said. "There's no open space, no big sky."

I'd lived in the same house until I left home for college at eighteen. I was accustomed to a sense of stability that Philip, whose family had moved repeatedly, did not seem to know or value. His rejection of one place after another had my head spinning and my whole sense of belonging in upheaval. I felt dizzily ungrounded, and began to feel caught in a sped-up whirlwind from which we'd never land. Images of Dorothy's tornado-lifted home floated through my head as we spun crazily back and forth across the country in our searches.

"I understand this idea of a place on the planet," I said, "but making it happen seems like a different story."

"Well, it's not easy," he conceded.

"What if your place and mine aren't the same? Is that grounds for breaking up?" I said, only partially in jest. I was weary and disoriented.

In the end, it was the need for a steady income that pulled us down to earth. Sitting on the curb outside a laundromat in Brattleboro, Vermont during our first summer together, we had one of our first pragmatic conversations.

"Your career in counseling will more easily guarantee a steady income and a home than my astrology practice," he said. "So should we focus on your career? I can do astrology wherever we land."

Relieved to have a plan, and one that even sounded feasible, I readily agreed.

Our strategy involved my going back to school again. Philip discovered Antioch University's London campus and its student-designed independent master's program in archetypal psychology. A friend had unwittingly introduced us to this growing field when we'd asked for a book to take on a trip to the beach earlier that year. "Here's just the thing," she'd said with a mischievous twinkle, handing us a book called *Suicide and the Soul* by James Hillman. That book sparked my interest in the field, and I wanted to pursue it further.

"We could combine your studying for another degree with a year of living in London," he said.

I was thrilled with the prospect; Philip's wish to wander had sparked a new thirst in me. We started to plan our trip to England. Sitting there dreaming, however, I had no idea how far he'd take me.

10

In This Together

"But why do we need to get married just because we're going to England for a year?" I asked. Three years into our relationship, I was still quite content with living together.

"When Tanya and I were in England just a few years ago," Philip said, "we came across provincial attitudes that were still intolerant of 'cohabitation,' as they so politely called it. I'm afraid we'll have trouble finding a place to live if we're not married."

"Isn't that a crazy—not to mention terribly unromantic—reason to get married?" I asked.

"We've been together for three years," he said, pulling me close. "I'm here to stay. Are you?"

I smiled my assent. It wasn't a typical marriage proposal, but then nothing with Philip was.

"As well as people can know these things, we feel we're in this together," I explained to my friends. I realized that at age twenty-eight, I was, after all, ready to take that next big step, and Philip was the person I felt sure I wanted to take it with.

The first justice of the peace we approached to marry us was around seventy-five years old, complete with an alcoholic's veiny, bulbous nose, unnaturally flushed cheeks, soup stains on his tie, and a sickening cologne that couldn't cover the alcohol oozing from every pore.

"Lucky guy," he said as he looked me up and down and then nudged Philip.

I ignored his ogling and stuck close to Philip.

When the judge began pulling out forms, I thought it was time to make my wishes clear. "I don't know if there's something special that needs to be done or signed, but I plan to keep my maiden name," I said.

Suddenly, everything changed. "Get out. Get the hell out of here!" he shouted. In an instant, he'd metamorphosed from ogler to ogre.

"You do know this is 1982 and there's been a women's liberation movement?" I spluttered.

Stunned and bewildered, I quickly discovered an anger uncommon to me. Hot-faced and eyes flashing, I turned to Philip for support only to catch a glimpse of his back as he hightailed it out the door and down the corridor.

When I turned around again, the judge's sneering face compelled me to put in one last barb before I also stalked out. "You're a doddering, drunken old fool who should retire if you can't keep up with the times! Not to mention stay sober enough to be civil."

I caught up with Philip, who hadn't exactly been my knight in shining armor, on the courthouse steps. I was ready to transfer my anger onto this deserting not-yet spouse.

"Why'd you leave me there with that creep?" I demanded. But one look at him and my rage dissipated. He was laughing so hard that he was holding his sides, tears running down his face.

"There are times to fight and times to walk away, little darlin'," he said. "I don't want him within a hundred miles of my marriage to you."

We headed off, arms wrapped around each other, sharing our indignation and hilarity at the strange scene in which we'd just participated. A few days later, a lovely young judge married us with genuine pleasure. We celebrated with a simple gathering of Philip's immediate family over a picnic lunch in our favorite park.

Philip's parents, his Granny Annie (still spry and witty at ninety-one years old), seven-year-old Misha, and Philip's three siblings and their children gathered with us. He and I each read a favorite poem, toasted and were toasted, and broke bread. The adults politely partook of the tofu burgers and brown-rice salad I'd prepared. Much to the relief of all the kids, Philip's parents arrived (predictably late and expecting our "boring and weird" healthy food) bearing buckets of Kentucky Fried Chicken and gallons of Baskin-Robbins.

We asked my parents, much to their dismay, to wait to celebrate with us until we came to New York en route to London. Perhaps it was the failure of Philip's first marriage—one complete with minister, white gown, bridesmaids, tuxedos, and best man, as well as large, not overly congenial extended families on both sides—that made him leery of another big ceremony. Or perhaps it was our sense that this was more a formality; an homage paid to Saturn. For me, the emotional commitment had grown steadily in the three years we'd been living together.

"Would you mind if we just keep it simple?" he'd asked as we were making plans.

"Not at all," I replied. "After living together for three years, I would feel absurd putting on virginal white. Besides, I've always watched those walking-down-the-aisle scenes sure that I'd either trip or burst out in a fit of hysterical and inappropriate laughter. Just the idea of everyone's eyes on me makes me feel like breaking out in hives." Philip laughed and squeezed me.

Philip also had the very eccentric idea that we'd be better off keeping our families apart. By this time (he was thirty-five to my thirty), I think his family was so accustomed to his quirky thinking that they didn't question it.

"They'll gang up on us," Philip said, only half in jest.

"Well," I said, "I can see that the chasm between my New York, Jewish-atheist parents and your western, small-town-Methodist family is a wide gap to bridge."

My parents were understandably baffled and wounded at the idea of not participating in my wedding day, however.

"So, listen, Dad," I said. Without taking a breath, I told him of the decision to get married, move to London for a year, and begin another master's program. "We've decided to do this in a somewhat unusual way."

"Oh? How's that?" he asked, sounding wary.

"We're going to get married here next week with a justice of the peace. Just the two of us. Then we'll have a little party with Philip's immediate family, just a picnic lunch."

"But . . ."

"Hang on," I interrupted. I knew I had to keep going, and was relieved it had been my father who'd picked up the phone. I could always get around him more easily than my mother. "Then, when we're on our way to London in October, we'll stop in New York for a few days and have the same kind of simple party at your house with our family."

"Oh? That is unusual," he said. "Uh . . . don't you think your mother would like to be there for your wedding? I mean, you're our only daughter."

"Yes, I know, Dad. But this is the way we want to do it. There's really no sense in you two flying all the way out here for a picnic, is there? And we can do something nice, but simple, with you. I know Mom doesn't like cooking or preparing, so either I can make a few salads, or we can order a few platters from a deli."

I managed to get that all out and end the conversation while he was still too flabbergasted to object. Of course, within a half hour, my mother called back. We went through the whole thing again, this time with a lot more questions and requests for details, but in the end, she conceded.

A few days later, she called again to tell me they'd begun planning "their" celebration. "I don't want to have people at the house," she said. "It's too small. So, we've rented a private room in a nice restaurant. Your father has hired a pianist and your uncle Marty will take photos."

"But—" I tried to get a word in edgewise.

"I want to talk about the seating arrangements," she interrupted.

"Seating arrangements?" I asked. "I didn't know we were sitting."

"Yes, first there will be a cocktail hour with hors d'oeuvres, and then a sit-down dinner."

"A sit-down dinner? Really? Won't that be expensive? And who's coming?"

"Well, we're up to around seventy-five people now."

"Seventy-five? I don't know seventy-five people!"

"Of course you do. There's our family, Dad's friends from work, my friends from work . . ."

"But Mom . . ."

"Never mind," she rolled on. My mother could be just as hardheaded and determined as me. (In fact, where did I think I'd gotten it from?)

So, in October, two days before our departure for a year, maybe two, in England, this second, larger, and somewhat more conventional celebration took place on Long Island.

It was a lovely evening, and Philip—once he'd gotten used to the idea and had a few glasses of wine—was surprisingly easygoing and accepting of this "slight" amendment to his simplicity plan. He was also greatly surprised, as was I, when we got back to my parents' house and opened all the plain white envelopes we'd been handed throughout the night. We had suddenly acquired an unanticipated booty that would cover our expenses for our first six months.

My parents looked on with satisfied, Cheshire-cat grins, undoubtedly working hard at not saying, "See? See what we did for you?"

11

England and East Berlin

"Let's take a day off and go to the Victoria and Albert Museum, my honey," Philip said on our fourth morning in London.

"Are you kidding? How can you think of doing anything other than searching for a place to live? All our money is dribbling out on this awful hotel," I huffed. "And why do we need a day off? We've only been here for four days!"

"We need a break," he replied. "You haven't seen any of the reasons why I want to be here yet." He cuddled up next to me.

I wanted to laugh and cry . . . and did both. As we continued to struggle to find a flat in the unwieldy and expensive city of London, the stress of not knowing how best to proceed, combined with watching our wedding-gift money slipping away on hotel bills and restaurant meals, was making us edgy.

Our temporary lodgings weren't helping either. In an attempt to save money, we were staying in a seedy old hotel in an area of London referred to in novels as "the mean streets of Pimlico" behind Victoria Station. The hotel, perhaps once charming but now dilapidated, as were most in that area, was run by Indians who had different standards of cleanliness and "quiet hours" than those to which we were accustomed. A good bit of beer-drinking and Hindi singing happened in the halls most nights. We'd answer a knock on our door after 10 P.M. to find the tipsy, turbaned, and grinning face of one of our hosts standing there, hand extended.

"Have beer, madam? . . . Sir?"

These invitations were initially unsettling. As our month-long stay progressed, however, we accepted the goodwill behind the offers, alternating between resignation and fits of laughter. We accepted the bottles of beer along with the sagging mattress, greasy English breakfasts, and the occasional cockroach.

More out of desperation than satisfaction, we finally settled on a place to live when we gave up on London and hired an agent who drew a circumference of no more than an hour's train ride in all directions from the city. Philip bemoaned the semidetached, 1970s East Sussex flat's lack of old-English character.

"I didn't come all the way to England to live in suburbia," he lamented.

"But it really isn't suburbia," I said. "At least, not American style. We're on the edge of a quaint little village and can walk out into green, rolling countryside in minutes."

"But look at this place," he said as we dropped our suitcases and stood in the little kitchen on the first day. "Built when? Five minutes ago? No character. No soul."

"Yes, but we can stop paying the exorbitant prices at the Jewel of India. We can unpack our suitcases and settle in, which will make both of us feel better. It's light, simple, and clean. Not perfect, I know, but it's our own place. Let's just give it a try."

However, the month of homeless stress and strain had taken its toll. We both felt battered and bruised by our many senseless arguments; it hadn't helped that we'd gotten out at the wrong train station to get to the flat. Our fight about whether or not to spend the money on a cab when we learned we were a mile and a half away from home had left both of us feeling testy. Had we gotten out at the right station, it would have been a five-minute walk.

Philip had won the argument, and we'd walked with the overly heavy suitcases my mother had so adroitly packed to maximum capacity. This was before the days of rolling luggage, so each time the heavier suitcase smacked into Philip's shin or heel, his anger with my mother, me, and life in general got hotter.

When he furiously hurled a handful of almonds at me as we put our suitcases down and surveyed our new home, I was appalled. What had I signed on for?

In the three years that Philip and I had lived together, whenever we bumped into each other's ego, I'd absent myself for a few hours and temporarily retreat into fantasies of leaving. These escape daydreams gave me a renewed sense of freedom whenever I suspected that Philip and I were just not right together.

The fantasies, when allowed their full, imaginative scope—what I'd say, how I'd pack my car, where I'd go, and the huge relief I'd feel as I got back on the open road—carried me over the hurdle of each new controversy. Then, having let off steam, my angst would evaporate, leaving me willing to try yet again. I'd return, having made my way back to the affection I felt for this impossible person. I'd often open the door to the scent of a good dinner. The table would be set with flowers ("just a few taken from the neighbor's yard—surely he'd want to share"), and I'd be greeted with a hug and a sheepish grin.

That worked as a living-together strategy, but now that we were married, I felt trapped and panicked.

"Marriage means no escape, no exit," I explained to my newly found British therapist a few weeks later. "And our arguments feel so much more threatening in a foreign country where we have no friends or support."

There was also a good deal of money and importance weighing on the need to stick this out. I had gotten a $10,000 student loan to pay tuition to Antioch, and my family had given us a lot of money in wedding gifts. I was sure they were just waiting to see whether or not we'd finally show some real-world maturity and perseverance.

My grandmotherly therapist's insight finally allayed my marital jitters. "Well, dearie," she said, "'divorce' fantasies are as much an option now as 'leaving' fantasies were prior to your marriage."

It sounded like a simple solution, but one I hesitated to consider. "But what if I carry through?" I asked. "With all this bad feeling between us, I'm afraid to allow the fantasies."

"A fantasy is not an action," she said. And, after a few practice runs with her, my sense of humor returned. I turned my attention to my studies, and the excitement of being in England.

Almost as soon as I set foot on English ground—dark, wet, and soggy as it was in mid-October—I felt I'd come home.

I knew almost instantly that England was speaking to parts of me that had long gone undernourished. Every day in London, on every street, in every park, public garden, and open-air market, with free lunchtime classical music pouring out of open-doored cathedrals and more museums, galleries, and theaters than I could imagine, I drank in London's centuries-old history, architecture, and culture.

Next to all the history, I also loved finding myself in a hub of pop culture. I saw my first mohawk, on my first real-live punk, while waiting in line at the post office. The young man—more outlandish in leather, tattoos, spikes, and studs than any of the long-haired hippies I was accustomed to—attracted no more attention than the little white-haired lady standing next to me in her practical brown shoes and sweater set.

"The English are so tolerant," I said to her in lowered tones.

"Or we're masters at ignoring that which we wish not to see," she suggested with a twinkle of China-blue eyes.

Much as I loved Colorado's semi-arid climate, I was beguiled by the way the wetter, softer English air carried scents of earth, leaf, and flower mixed with an ever-present tang of sea salt. I loved the constant shifts from sea-blue to pearl-gray skies, and the ever-changing cloud castles that rolled in off the sea.

Each regional accent—from Yorkshire to Cornwall, Scotland to Wales—charmed me. Philip and I marveled at how our neighbors from Scotland were speaking our language, yet we hardly understood them. We giggled with pleasure when waitresses and shopkeepers called us "dearies," "loveys," and "ducks."

Philip and I became friends with certain museums, especially the Tate Gallery, where we found the Pre-Raphaelite paintings we'd admired so much in books.

"Meet me at 3:30 in front of 'The Lady of Shalott,'" I'd say on the days when Philip was coming into London. I loved sitting with the original of the print we'd hung over our bathtub in Denver.

We learned how to get cheap tickets to the theaters, and found a wealth of free cathedral concerts. London—a city more like a sequence of interconnected small villages, each with its own color and character—provided endless exploratory walks and unplanned adventures. Philip eventually found ways to walk for miles through central London's interconnected parks, barely using trafficked streets.

Local street markets, cafés, music from around the world, and people in all manner of eccentric styles of dress turned each outing into an unpredictable adventure. London spoke to my hunger for depth, centuries-old culture, diversity, and eccentricity. Everything English captivated me. I filled letters to family and friends describing my enchantment.

"Right here and now," I said to Philip, "I understand what you mean by finding my place on the planet."

But there was also that "something more" that Philip had tried to articulate. Something immaterial—an energy or atmosphere, a soulful connection. Not only was I exploring a new city in a new country, but I also felt new or hidden aspects of myself being revealed, reflected, and awakened. I experienced a sense of enhanced aliveness in the self I watched gradually unfolding.

Philip, on the other hand, had surprisingly not found his kindred place in England, the place to which he'd so longed to return. Being far from the support of his friends and spending long hours alone while I was often in London unnerved him, leaving him nearly undone with panic at times. In November in England, the first shadows of evening roll in as early as 3:30 P.M. It was a lot of time in the dark for a Colorado boy accustomed to wide blue skies and daily sunshine.

We learned that our cul-de-sac had recently sprung up on the edge of an overgrown, long-abandoned quarry that was now home to owls, rabbits, foxes, and other critters. The footpath that went through this area was wild and heavily wooded. In the growing shadows of coming darkness, the calls of animals and birds spooked both of us. The first time we heard the screamy, high-pitched screech of a fox, we stopped dead in our tracks, hearts racing, afraid to move but braced to flee from we knew not what.

"It sounds like a spook," I whispered, only half joking.

"I have no idea what it is or even where it's coming from," he replied.

"Should we turn back?"

"Take my hand and let's run for home. Make a lot of noise. It's probably some animal or bird we don't know." We ran, hollering all the way. If it hadn't been so scary, it would have been hilarious.

While I loved London's excitement and the contrasting stillness of our little village, Philip didn't have the balance that days in the city gave me. When he was alone in the long, gray hours of the gloaming, he became fearfully panic-stricken, his thinking irrational, fantastical, and superstitious. I'd return home to a frightened and needy person I'd not met before.

"I heard weird sounds outside the house. I was scared stiff," he said once when I got home. He was pale, hands cold and shaky.

What's more, the contrast between my excitement with my studies and days in London versus his isolation was difficult to reconcile. I had never been so engaged in study. My self-designed program in archetypal psychology had evolved into an intriguing and intellectually enriching experience. The tutors I worked with, the research and writing I was doing, and the growing desire to spend hours reading and writing when I was at home put me in a very different state of mind than Philip. He had more free time and solitude than he knew what to do with. I was afraid that this was going to be his undoing, but I couldn't think what to do.

"Do you think I'm going mad?" he asked one evening, tears springing to his eyes. "It's so lonely and dark, and I'm afraid you'll never come home."

"I'll always come home to you, my darling," I said, wondering how he was going to survive this year in the country he'd dreamed of for so long.

Even in the midst of his anxiousness, however, Philip rarely wavered or swerved, consequences be damned. His courage and a tricky situation collided one night when we were walking down a street in Cambridge. Rounding a corner, we came upon a circle of toughs complete with motorcycles, black leather jackets, and chains. Voices were raised, and the ugly energy of mob psychology was thickening palpably under the sickly light of a streetlamp.

I saw the glint of a chain as it swung wildly, heard someone shout in pain, and before I knew what was happening, Philip, no longer at my side, was in the middle of a roaring circle of subhuman hostility and aggression.

"Stop being idiots!" he hollered as he grabbed the guy with the chain.

His voice, so sweetly tender in loving, was resonant and commanding, projecting over all the others. Within minutes, the shocked crowd had dispersed, and the chain dropped in a clatter from Philip's hands.

"Who's the idiot?" I spluttered, running up to him. "Why in the world would you risk your life for a bunch of hoodlums?" I hugged him to me in relief, pride, and exasperation.

"I don't know," he replied, looking dazed. "I didn't know I was going to do that. But violence like that is just stupid and wrong. I had to stop it."

Attractive and intriguing to my hippie soul, his reckless rebellions also scared me. I witnessed this part of him again and again with a mix of pride tempered by more timid fears of reprisal. *Is he courageous or foolish? Or both?* Many would have no trouble answering my questions and qualms about Philip, but they didn't love him.

When my parents came to visit us a few months into our time there, the tension got so fraught that I thought we'd all finally crack. My parents' usual veneer of polite tolerance wore thin, Philip was like a powder keg, and I was tempted to walk away from all of them.

During an after-dinner stroll through an idyllic Cotswold village one evening, we walked past a thatched-roof cottage perched on a canal. We were able to peek through open curtains into a book-lined study where an archetypal Englishman sat reading, pipe in hand, fire on the grate, cat on the arm of his chair, retriever at his feet.

"Why does he get to live here in this perfect life?" I asked.

"He works!" snapped my father.

I quickly grabbed Philip by the arm and crossed over the canal before he or I could snap back.

When my parents finally left after their three-week stay, I slept for sixteen hours and emerged feeling battered and bruised. I was therefore deeply surprised to receive this letter from my mother a week later.

"Despite your father's struggle to understand and accept Philip," she wrote, "he said he couldn't help seeing the joy in the love that flows between you. 'It's a true romance, a love story,' he said."

This was a remarkable acknowledgment from a pragmatic and down-to-earth man, not to mention a father who was naturally protective of his only daughter and not at all sure he understood or liked the strange world she'd apparently stepped into . . . or the stranger who'd taken her there.

When December rolled around, we flew to Berlin to spend Christmas with Philip's older sister, Kathie. Although Kathie and her young family lived in West Berlin, one of Kathie's good friends lived on the other side of the Berlin Wall, and Kathie made regular trips through Checkpoint Charlie to visit her.

When Kathie's friend invited us all to spend the holiday in East Berlin, I was a bit daunted. A frisson of fear shot through me as we drove up to the infamous wall with its barbed wire, spotlights, and heavily guarded gates.

"Okay, guys," my brother-in-law said to all of us kids in the back seat, grouping Philip and me along with his four children. "No talking and no horsing around."

"This is something to write home about," I whispered as I slipped my hand into Philip's and welcomed the warmth.

"Yeah," he said through closed lips. "Eerie."

We all drew in our collective breath as my brother-in-law rolled down his window to pass his papers to the guard for clearance. Teaching for the U.S. Department of Defense gave him permission to cross the border.

The whole scene—complete with uniformed guards, guns, and even a pair of German shepherds—was so intimidating that one part of me wished I were back in merry old England for a safer version of Christmas, while another part was fascinated to be exactly where I was. Philip and I were gripping each other's hand so tightly that an hour later, I found the mark of my ring where it had pressed into my flesh.

It was already dark when we arrived, and the blinding glare of the guard's flashlight scanning my face was unnerving and surreal. He surveyed each of us and did a quick check of the trunk. Once through the gate and breathing again, we drove through quiet, dimly lit streets, everything grim and dismal under the stark white glow of the streetlights.

Inside the small apartment, however, we were greeted with warmth and laughter. Candles lit the small rooms, creating an amber glow of intimacy. The table was beautifully set, and handmade paper and wood decorations adorned every available space. With the winter night air still clinging to our coats and cheeks, all eight of us tumbled gratefully into the tiny apartment. The five East Berliners awaiting our arrival greeted us warmly, took our coats, and led us to a beautiful old ceramic stove to warm up.

"Herzlich willkommen," they said, welcoming us into their home. "Fröhliche Weihnachten!" (Merry Christmas!)

There was a hearty shaking of hands and hugs all around. I'd rarely felt so generously taken in by strangers whose language I didn't speak, but whose heartfelt welcome was unmistakable.

Kathie had packed baskets and boxes brimming with delicacies, items not to be gotten on that side of the wall. The East Berliners' oohing and aahing over fresh fruits, vegetables, chocolates, and cakes made our privilege and their deprivation painfully apparent. Small, artfully wrapped gifts were placed under a tree simply decorated with handmade wooden angels and elves.

When the gifts were unwrapped, exclamations of joy and gratitude—"vielen Dank!"—rang throughout the apartment for simple things like pens, paper, candles, and a book or two. Philip received a small book of Novalis's poetry, and I unwrapped a midnight-blue shawl of the softest spun wool and draped it gratefully around my shoulders. The festive evening was filled with laughter and toasts being made throughout the meal.

We repeatedly lifted glasses brimming with red wine that looked like liquid garnets in the candlelight. "Prost!" (Cheers!) and "Zum Wohl!" (To your health!)

"This seems like one of the lessons our parents and grandparents would always talk about, come to life," Philip said quietly in my ear. "About the good old days, when people had less and appreciated more."

"Yes, it feels like a real Christmas, possibly my first," I said, taking in the candlelit tableau of smiling faces before me.

After dinner, we were invited out for a walk and a trolley ride. With a nearly full moon sailing in a clear sky, the wintery air bit into my face and fingers. The streetlights—a stark white—made us look ghastly. The boys pointed out bullet holes in the buildings, as well as bombed-out sites that still, nearly forty years after the end of the war, had not been cleared.

The trolley itself was from a bygone age. "I feel like we're back in the 1930s," I said as we rode along.

When we got out to walk for a while, the streets were empty, with only an occasional person quickly passing by, head lowered, hat pulled down to cover their eyes. "Fröhliche Weihnachten," Philip offered, but no one responded. No one looked at anyone. Even on Christmas! It was unsettling, unlike anything I'd experienced.

Around midnight, when the party was breaking up, my brother-in-law offered a lift to a guest who lived on the other side of town. There was a good deal of vehement discussion about this, since it was illegal for an East Berliner to be in our car.

"He shouldn't," said one of Kathie's friends. "He can be arrested for being in your car."

"It's so cold," her husband said. "No one will be out tonight. The Polizei will be warming their toes and sipping black-market whiskey inside."

"You don't know that."

"It's risky," said Kathie.

My brother-in-law, always up for a dare and a chance to defy authority, insisted it would be all right. In the end, it was agreed that our fugitive passenger would sit on the floor in the back seat.

"We'll put a blanket near him just in case," said one of Kathie's young sons, excited by this cloak-and-dagger adventure. But this was not play, and I was edgy. And then, the "just in case" happened. We were stopped for *eine routinemäige Kontrolle*, a routine check, by the Polizei.

With the young man crouched and covered and Philip and our three nephews sitting with their feet stretched out on top of him, my brother-in-law's talent for smooth-talk got us through an unbearably tense moment. The meaning of having one's heart in one's throat had never been so clear to me. When the headlights of two armored tanks blinded me as they drove toward us on the otherwise dark and empty street a few blocks later, I felt again as though we were in a black-and-white war film.

After what seemed like hours, we finally dropped off our new East Berliner friend and headed west.

"Checkpoint Charlie looks beautiful," I said as the lights of West Berlin appeared beyond the wall.

A sense of surreal detachment followed us throughout that visit. East Berlin was a hushed and colorless world, turning us into ghosts in a ghostly city. Driving back into West Berlin, it was as though someone had flipped on sound and color . . . and freedom.

A few weeks after we returned from Berlin, we met a woman at a meditation class in East Sussex. At first, we both liked her and hoped for a real friendship. But as time went on, she became more and more convinced, and even found a psychic who confirmed, that she and Philip were meant to be together and that I would also soon meet my true match—a happy ending for everyone. The fact that she had a husband and children seemed not to worry her in the least.

Philip reported all this to me with horror. What had started as a friendly and flattering flirtation appeared to be going haywire.

"She says you're finished with me!" he said. "Says you're sick of my melodrama. What's happening to us?" We both stared wide-eyed and open-mouthed at what felt like a bomb exploding in our living room. He sank down beside me, putting his head in my lap. He began to cry. "Did you say that? Did you mean it?" he asked.

"No, I didn't say that! I may have complained, but no, I didn't mean anything like that. But you are spending a lot of time with another woman. Would you rather be with her?" I asked, wanting some reassurance too.

"I have no desire to run off with another woman! For crying out loud, I love you more than I ever thought it was possible to love." That said, we came to our senses. In fact, we ended up laughing and crying together as we talked about it.

"A psychic, huh?" I spluttered, smiling through tears. "A new man for me? Hmm . . . I wonder what he's like." I hugged Philip tight.

That year in England was a strenuous test for our relationship—one neither of us was fully convinced we were going to pass. But in that one year, we imbibed, explored, and ultimately grew closer through struggle, adventure, and a shared love of England. Even at the time, I was infinitely grateful for Philip's determination, which had instigated an experience I wouldn't have had the initiative or courage to set in motion myself. It was one of the most stimulating and self-affirming years of my life. When we left, I wept much of the way back to the U.S.

12

A Still Life

Philip was often perceived as uncompromising and headstrong; he often was. He was probably most harshly judged for not shouldering the conventional financial responsibilities expected of an adult man. I, however, was far less troubled by whether he held an understandable job or made a respectable income, and more concerned for him at another level.

In Louise Penny's novel, *Still Life*, a person living a "still life" is one who waits for life to happen to them, a person who feels inexplicably and unalterably victimized, unable to act, initiate, or steer the course of their life. Strong-minded and intractable as Philip was regarding his beliefs and codes for living, in underlying, more unconscious ways (and in total contradiction to the determined and unyielding aspects of his personality), Philip's will was largely broken, his confidence undone.

Doomed by his own debilitating beliefs, Philip—this person with such creative vitality and potential—was unable to take an active part in his own life, and often passively and fatalistically waited for life to happen to him.

The odd thing is that much *did* happen to him. A first, short-lived but life-enhancing marriage to a beautiful soul brought into his life and this world an equally beautiful child. Friends sought his playful spirit and old-soul wisdom, returning love and affection. He had three exceptional nephews and an extraordinary niece who loved him dearly and saw in him a guide and inspiration. I happened to him, and with that came years of seeking, sharing, and loving companionship.

We traveled, lived in many places in the U.S. and overseas, met intriguing people, read widely and deeply, talked and dreamed and explored.

Love happened to him! And yet, there was this stuck place that trapped him in an inner turmoil he could neither resolve nor release.

Ultimately, and most distressing to me, was the threat this posed to his rich and deeply colored potential—the creative energy and profound perceptiveness that coursed through him and gave an intensity and fiery force to all he said and did. The conflicting streak of defeated passivity in his nature was—and continued to be throughout our years together—baffling, and sometimes heartbreaking.

Despite years of self-inquiry with the help of philosophy, astrology, literature, and psychology, as well as extensive dives into all kinds of individual and group therapies, he was caught by the belief that he'd been psychologically derailed by his parents, particularly his father, and could not get himself back on track. Any belief that he could be, do, or have what he deeply longed for had been undermined long before I met him.

This inner struggle too often had him pushing and pulling against himself. Bottled-up, unexpressed energy would cause his opposing strength to erupt with unexpected force. Torn between the internalized voice of his father's diminishment and distrust versus his own genius and originality, his thoughts and emotions were alternately expressed in beautiful or unruly ways. He could neither honor nor take his gifts seriously—even while, in most of the wrong ways, taking himself too seriously.

He once joked about a prior girlfriend who was forever saying, "Lighten up, Phil."

"Really," I sighed.

The intensity of inner dissonance in which Philip lived was also, perhaps, partly what contributed to the beginning breakdown of his physical stamina and health.

In the mid-1980s, after we'd returned from England, we were living through the gray, wet frosts and thumper snowfalls of a brutal upstate New York winter. We were rarely without layers of clothes in the light of day. It wasn't until spring, when we stripped off the thermal underwear and layers of sweaters, that we saw—with alarm—what had happened to him. Not yet forty years old at that time, we were shocked at his weight having dropped by twenty-plus pounds over a seven-month period, falling from 140 to 120 pounds hanging off his five-eleven frame. Along with his weight, his energy had mysteriously drained out of a body that had up until that time been vital, strong, and fit.

A psyche at war with itself had begun to manifest physically.

13

Wanderlust

Throughout our next seven years back in the U.S., Philip and I lived in small college towns where I worked as a psychotherapist at universities. Poor Philip continued to feel displaced in towns and cities from upstate New York to Vermont to Tennessee, where we'd most recently landed. None of these places met the external criteria he sought, nor did any of these temporary homes resonate even remotely with that more elusive and intangible sense of his right place on the planet.

It was now 1990, and I was burned out, diagnosed with adrenal fatigue. The weight of listening to people's anger, depression, and confusion eight hours a day, every hour on the hour, was bleeding me dry, wearing me out. Living on hourly cups of caffeine and chocolate bars to stay alert, I knew I was wrecking my health.

Philip was increasingly concerned and said it was time for a change. Although we'd enjoyed a few shorter excursions across the U.S. and Europe, our time living in England made us hungry to live abroad again.

"I have an idea," he said when I dragged in from work one evening.

"Uh-oh," I said, knowing how "dangerous" Philip's ideas could be. They typically led to a major upheaval of one kind or another—an expensive move, a job change, an investment in more education. I plopped down into his lap, leaned against his shoulder, and said, "Okay. Tell me."

"What would you think of teaching English as a second language?" he asked. "I had a friend who did it, and she loved traveling, living in new places, and getting paid to have adventures. It would be more neutral, less emotionally demanding work than therapy, don't you think?"

"Teaching English as a second language?" I repeated.

"It's a way to live in other countries indefinitely," he said with that enthusiasm I'd grown to love . . . and fear. "We could experience different cultures. Every couple of years, we could try someplace new."

But I was weary to the bone, and thoughts of returning to our early, unsettled years of wandering left me feeling even more exhausted. "I'm not sure I can live with that ambiguity and financial insecurity again," I said.

"But this would be different. You'd have a job . . . with a salary. We could stay in each place for as long as it felt good. Then, when we wanted a change, we could move on. Think of it . . . Spain, Portugal, eastern Europe, maybe even places like Thailand or Japan."

"Hmm. Well, maybe. Let's think about it." I was too tired to think of anything other than bed.

My sleep was interrupted, however, with yet another urgent call from a student thinking of taking their own life. The call had my adrenaline pumping and my thoughts racing. As I threw on my clothes and dashed out of the house into the dark for the fourth time in two weeks, I wondered, *Could ambiguity and insecurity really be any worse than this*?

I returned at dawn, exhausted after yet another night of talking yet another young person who hated their life into living for another day. "I'm beginning to think the entire world is depressed, struggling with eating disorders, abusing drugs, or suicidal," I said.

Philip put his arms around me and handed me a cup of steaming tea. "You shouldn't go on like this. It's weighing you down, ruining your health and your life."

I nodded, sipping my tea.

"Teaching adults English overseas would be interesting," he said. "You'd have motivated students and you'd meet teachers who share our love of adventure. And you'd be working with healthy people . . . much more hopeful work, don't you think?"

"But will you get lonely or end up feeling panicky, like in England?"

"Well, I might or I might not," he answered with characteristic impossibility. "If we go to places that are warm, in latitudes that don't get dark at 3:00 in the afternoon, and where it doesn't rain every day, I should do better, eh?"

"Yeah, maybe . . . I hope." That was all I could come up with for this man who I'd come to know as having little long-term memory. His here-and-now way of living was optimistic when he was dreaming us into a better situation. Past defeats and disasters were left in the past.

This dream would mean my going back to school yet again, paying for it, relocating again, and, if successful, moving to places farther afield than ever before. But I was so tired of my current life. Despite my fears, I was finding the idea of living abroad again increasingly hard to resist.

Watching my face and catching a glimmer of hope, Philip's eyes brightened. He began scanning the room looking for what to eliminate, what to sell, what to pack. I was torn between excitement and hesitation, between hope and fear, feelings I'd become quite familiar with in my life with Philip.

Philip's lack of desire for worldly or career success didn't mean he lacked dreams or goals. It was just that his dreams were personal, not professional. So, as the breadwinner, I was the one to make many of those dreams happen. The good news about this was that I didn't have to negotiate changes with a spouse who wanted to stay put or whose career might move us in a different direction.

From that long-ago moment when we'd sat on a curb in Vermont waiting for our laundry to dry and deciding that following my career would provide more financial stability, we'd adopted a mutually satisfying agreement—a gender role–reversal that suited both of us. Philip readily assumed care for household tasks while I went to work. He did astrological readings to supplement our income, spent hours in university libraries finding old, out-of-print books for us to read, and wrote poetry.

"I can do astrology wherever we are," he said.

"In Japanese?" I asked.

"There are English-speaking expats all over the world nowadays," he was quick to answer.

We embraced the plan. That summer, after resigning from my counseling position, we moved back to Colorado where I began taking classes at Colorado State University in Fort Collins. I was going to add two more years of graduate study and a third master's degree to my résumé, this time in English. I stepped happily into another academic field, perpetual student that I was delighted to be. Philip and I found a 1920s apartment in Old Town and settled into our latest new life.

"How many times do you think we've moved in our eleven years together?" I asked.

"I've lost count," he said, laughing.

Once again, I was off to classes, meeting new people, exploring a new subject, and enjoying a more liberal college-town atmosphere than the one we'd gleefully driven away from in Tennessee. Philip embraced his house-husband duties and felt comfortable, if not overly enthusiastic, about resuming residence in the town where he'd spent his teens.

"How'd I end up back here again?" he complained.

"It's only temporary," I said.

"Yeah, you're right."

"Remember the goal, old boy."

"Right," he said.

14

Corfu

After graduating from Colorado State University in 1992, I received a job offer for a teaching position on the Greek island of Corfu. On the day I received the letter, I was alone in the house waiting for Philip to return from the library. Unable to contain my excitement any longer, I ran out of the house in the direction I knew he'd be walking home. When I saw him strolling down a quiet street with his characteristic dreamy and graceful gait, I waved my arms in the air, jumping and shouting with crazy happiness.

"Corfu! Corfu!" I yelled. He ran toward me laughing, and, reaching me, lifted and twirled us round and round in the middle of the street until the gentle honk of a horn brought us back to earth.

We read about and looked at pictures of Corfu, soaking up everything we could find about it. Its ancient history dated back to the start of Greek mythology and evolved through Venetian, British, and French rule, the influences of which were woven into its culture and architecture. Winding medieval lanes, Byzantine churches, esplanades and French arcades adorned its capital, Corfu Town. We pored over photos of its hidden coves, white beaches, and pristine blue waters.

We also read Gerald Durrell's funny, heartwarming *The Corfu Trilogy*, which describes life on the island just before World War II. The book is told from the simple and easily enchanted eyes of a young boy free to roam and explore silvery-green olive groves and sun-drenched beaches, and Philip and I predictably set off in search of *that* Corfu—still quiet, pristine, and reachable only by those adventuresome enough to come by boat.

Durrell's 1930s Corfu was not the same island we flew into that year.

We arrived nearly three months before my first day of work, having learned from our England experience how hard finding housing can be. We stayed at a small hotel in Corfu Town the first night. Philip had found a place that didn't cost too much, and, predictably, we got what we paid for.

The bathroom was the "jewel" of the experience. Communal and located down the hall, there was no shower curtain between the shower and the rest of the room. The floor was swimming with soap slime (at least I hoped that's what it was) from the people who'd used it before us. The toilet paper roll was a soggy, messy mass—impossible to use. And when we learned that one does not flush toilet paper on Corfu (something to do with island plumbing) but drops it into a provided pail, Philip was horrified.

There was one remarkable moment, however, when, from our bed early the next morning, I pushed open the wooden shutters. I can still feel the softness of the air and see the clarity of the light as it filled the room with our first Greek island morning. We looked over slate rooftops and chimney pots, a higgledy-piggledy confusion of old stone houses and winding steps and streets, geraniums in abundance, and city cats basking in the morning sun.

With the sound of gulls crying and the sea tang tickling our noses, we both leaned out into the new day and our new life with relish and anticipation.

"One night in this hotel with its grotty, slimy, probably disease-infested bathroom is enough," Philip said when he returned from his attempt at freshening up for the day. "I feel less clean than I did before I took a shower."

"I'll call the school and ask about the apartment the director offered for new teachers to use temporarily," I replied.

The director of the school, still out of the country on vacation, asked her assistant to pick us up and take us to the prearranged housing. The assistant roared up to the hotel that evening in her little red sports car, stuffed our bags and Philip into the tiny back seat, and—barely even waiting for me to close the passenger door—sped through the city at breakneck speed, windows down, wind and traffic making it necessary to shout our conversation.

Forty hair-raising minutes later, we pulled up to a villa just beyond the main street of the dark and sleeping village of Kato Korakiana. She pried the bags out of the back seat and carried everything herself into the apartment. She whirled us through a tour of the place, flashed a brilliant smile and a long, lean leg emerging from her red minidress, handed over the keys, and sped off into the night.

We awoke the next morning feeling a bit weary after a hot, mosquito-plagued night and a 4:20 A.M. neighboring rooster call. Philip was slightly queasy, but still raring to explore. We walked a mile down the hill to the nearest beach to find sunburnt British and German tourists sprawled like beached whales on the sand. We'd arrived at the height of the tourist season.

"There's hardly a space between beach towels," Philip said over his shoulder as we wound our way single file over a sea of bodies. Nonetheless, we took our first gleeful steps into the Ionian Sea. Philip dog paddled and I did the backstroke in bathtub-warm water. Not exactly cooling, but exhilarating just because we were in Greece and swimming in the sea that had birthed ancient mythology.

We eventually found other beaches that came closer to the ideals we'd packed into our suitcases. The next day, we made our way to one set in a beautiful cove below a cliff-top monastery. We climbed down from the road through tall grasses, and when we got onto the sand, we realized we were on a nude beach.

"Some of the monks up there must be having a great time with binoculars," Philip said.

And there we were. I in a demure, black one-piece suit and Philip—who refused official bathing trunks for some Philip-esque objection I no longer recall—sporting a pair of baggy shorts that went down to his knees. We were the prudes of the beach! Surrounded by statuesque naked bodies and breasts bouncing on tanned torsos playing water volleyball, we felt absurd. We scuttled in the direction from which we'd come and managed to find people in some semblances of bathing suits at the other end of the beach.

Despite the incessant heat, tourists, and mosquitos, we were still searching for Gerald Durrell's paradisal island. We were soon forced to the conclusion that it no longer existed. Government corruption and economic mismanagement had bankrupted Greece yet again. Extremes of poverty had caused despair so profound that there had been multiple suicides in our small village and more all over the island.

We learned about this firsthand from our neighbor, a lovely woman in her thirties who came to welcome us one day. Philip was still feeling queasy, and she ran out and quickly returned with a plunger for the backed-up toilet as well as herbal remedies for his stomach. She also brought home-cured olives, homegrown tomatoes, and feta cheese made from her goat's milk. We sat on our balcony under the shade of lemon and almond trees.

"My husband was laid off months ago," she told us.

"That's horrible," I said, feeling my response to be lame and inadequate.

"Yes. We are worried about how long we can manage without his income. Worrying about money for food, health care, and clothing for an infant, a three-year-old, and my aging mother . . . life grows more frightening by the day."

"What's happening here?" Philip asked. "I read in the English newspaper that the whole country is affected."

"Yes, all of Greece is in political upheaval and economic depression. Attempts to strike back at the government are only hurting the people, not those in power."

We soon saw what she meant as national strikes sporadically shut down electricity throughout each day. In the beastly August heat, food spoiled in the refrigerators of people who couldn't afford the food they bought, no less to throw it out. The post offices were closed indefinitely, so that we were cut off from our worrying families back in the States. I was horrified by the dead and dying rats I found on our doorstep, and the heat and humidity were so oppressive at night that we took to spraying water on our sheets and each other throughout the night. I slept fitfully, wet sheet pulled up to my chin and straw hat covering my face to keep the ravenous vampires—the biggest mosquitos I'd ever seen—from eating me alive.

Although the owner of the language school had generously provided this lovely apartment, it was too far from the school to live there. We set out to find an apartment in Corfu Town, which was indeed a challenge. Getting around in a place where even the alphabet was indecipherable made everything—from reading street signs to real estate listings—impossible.

Worst of all, Philip got increasingly ill, and even after two desperate trips to a local doctor in wild and crazy taxi rides, the anti-nausea injections didn't help for more than a few hours. Not only was he not recovering, he was getting weaker by the day. I began to wonder if we'd have to give up on Corfu. He had struggled with ceaseless vomiting and diarrhea ever since we'd arrived on the island.

"I can't understand why you've gotten this sick when you're eating the same food and drinking the same water as I am," I said as I held a cold compress on his hot forehead.

"Me neither," he groaned.

"God . . . what a mess," I said.

What if you aren't cut out for a life of travel? I wanted to say, but thought better of voicing my fears. In his misery, all Philip could do was roll his eyes in perplexity before dashing back to the bathroom. His consciousness was, understandably, sunk in misery and survival.

I, on the other hand, had a good deal of time to silently fear that we had made a huge mistake, not just with Corfu but with this whole idea of teaching and living overseas.

I sat one afternoon with our lovely neighbor, laughing as her curly-haired three-year-old chased chickens around her yard. Each day, Philip and I laughed to hear the grandmother calling this beautiful child to order with her screechy, "*An-ge-la!*"

My mood turned back to the growing desperation I was feeling when our neighbor kindly asked how Philip was doing.

"I don't know if he can deal with change or bacteria as a world traveler," I replied, shaking my head. "Should I quit my job and insist on going home before he gets any worse?" Tears of fear and frustration sprang to my eyes.

She took my hand. "You must take care of Philip," she replied. "His life and health are the most important thing—for him and for you." She handed me a handkerchief to dry my tears.

An-ge-la looked up at me through dark curls and out of olive-black eyes that expressed the kindness of a much older person. She gently patted my hand.

Later, I thought, *How selfish of me to burden her with my first-world problems.* Philip and I had the option to go back home and try something else. She, on the other hand, was stuck in a life that felt dismally dead-ended. Thankfully, she was providing food for her family from the almond, olive, and lemon trees in her yard, the yogurt and cheese she made from their goat's milk, the vegetables her mother grew, and the eggs gathered from the chickens. But with a husband increasingly depressed over not being able to support his young family, our neighbor carried not only the weight of providing for her family, but also the very real fear that her husband, like other men in the village, might take his own life. Suicide can be contagious.

I returned to find Philip hanging limply over the toilet and listened yet again to his horrible retching. What were we to do? What was I to do? Philip was in no position or frame of mind to make big decisions.

Our financial plight was also about to get worse. I had taken out another student loan to pay for this latest degree. My first monthly payment was due next month, and here I was thinking of quitting my job before it even began. Had Philip not gotten ill, we would have dealt with the heat, mosquitos, and rats, if only for a year. I would have gained overseas teaching experience for my résumé. But what was going to happen now?

With our neighbor's words echoing in my mind and the sounds of Philip's distress coming through the bathroom door, I decided. I settled Philip back on the couch and walked thirty minutes to catch a bus that took another forty minutes to get to Corfu Town. Three days before the start of the school year, I walked into the director's office and handed in my resignation. My news was understandably far from kindly received, but I walked away feeling vastly relieved.

At dawn a few days later, we pushed and pulled our luggage to the single-runway airport, making use of a derelict shopping cart found on the side of the street behind our motel. Philip leaned on the cart to support his poor, weakened body while I pulled all our worldly possessions over a rough gravel road. During this dream-defeated trudge to the airstrip, we stopped a few times for Philip to catch his breath while I watched the sunrise—"the time between the wolf and the dog," a new colorful expression I'd learned for the in-between, border times of dusk and dawn. I marveled at the ghostly gray sky growing lighter and the softest streaks of pink painting the clouds as the sun rose up over the sea.

"I'm both ashamed by and grateful for my relative affluence that I've taken for granted all my life," I said, standing in the early morning stillness of that quiet road and tasting the last of the sea air on my tongue.

"We might have re-created ourselves and our lives on this island if not for me," said Philip. "Now I've ruined our chances," he groaned. I reached for his hand, but we both felt something wished-for slipping inexplicably from our grasp.

Once onboard the airplane, however, we sat back in our seats breathing huge sighs of relief.

"I'm grateful to be getting out of this alive," Philip said as he clasped my hand for takeoff. As the weeks of intestinal distress, weight loss, and subsequent weakness had gone on and on, I realized we'd both secretly feared he might not live to leave.

Difficult as our Corfu experience was, the dichotomies it presented—the desolate village where we'd stayed and the gold chain–bedecked, wealthy tourists strolling through the ancient city; the poverty up the hill and the opulent resorts on the beaches; the rats that scrabbled in the dumpsters behind beach hotels, eating wasted buffet tourist lunches—made me more grateful for what I had.

The cultural richness we'd lived with on that tiny, economically ravaged but stunningly beautiful island was not to be regretted either, no matter that our stay was largely miserable for Philip and my first teaching job lost before it started.

The days we spent in Corfu Town, and the trips we'd been able to make around the island on Philip's better days, the tiny coves and quiet white beaches with crystal-clear, turquoise water all added to a lifetime's memories, images, and experiences.

Feeling philosophical and relieved as our plane took off and the island swam out of sight, I wondered what our future would hold, and how we would survive our upcoming time between the wolf and the dog.

15

Lisbon

A few years later, in 1997, I was offered a contract to teach at a private English-language institute in Lisbon. We went determined to stay for the entire year of my contract, even hoping to extend beyond the year and find "home ground" in Portugal.

It was a hard time to arrive, however. First, preparations for the 1998 Lisbon World Exposition were underway. The resulting construction and renovation meant noise, dust, and confusion everywhere.

Competing with us for limited housing, moreover, was a huge influx of *returnos*: thousands of people from former Portuguese colonies (Macau, East Timor, Senegal, and Brazil) returning to the fatherland. The cost of housing had skyrocketed.

It seemed to me that as soon as we walked into a real estate agency as *americanos*, the rents shot up even more. We would read an ad, show up at the agency the same morning, and be given a higher quote. It was infuriating.

"Mas isso nao e o mesmo" (But this is not the same), I learned to say, pointing to the classified page with the ad circled and the price highlighted.

"Nao, desculpe, madame. Falo sobre um apartment diferente. Este ja esta alugado." (No, I'm sorry, madam. I'm talking about a different apartment. This one is already rented.)

Again and again, we heard the same story. I'd walk out frustrated and fuming. Philip would take my arm, stroke my flushed cheek. "Don't worry, little darlin'. We'll find the right thing when the time is right."

Depending on my mood, his fatalism would either soothe or further infuriate me. Either way, the situation conspired to leave us with frustratingly few places to choose from. My teaching position had also already started, giving me less time to look.

In the meantime, we were staying in a small, well-preserved hotel that looked and felt much as it must have back in the 1920s when it was built. It was just a few doors down from the language institute and would have been a perfect location to live. I loved it. I also loved being called *querida menina* (dear girl) by maids with eyes dark as sloe berries. After our first week, they took my face in their hands daily to tenderly kiss each cheek. I felt so cherished.

Each morning, following a breakfast of crusty bread, tomatoes, and cheese in the hotel dining room, Philip and I would set out to search for an apartment and explore the city, though not always in that order. When I would leave to teach my classes each afternoon, Philip would continue to pound the pavement. It was all to no avail.

At our farewell dinner back in the States a month earlier, my eminently practical businessman brother had asked, "Is the salary commensurate with the cost of living in Lisbon?"

"Of course," Philip had answered impatiently. "Why would they offer the job to someone from overseas if the salary wasn't enough to live on?"

Sadly, that's exactly what they did do. Characteristically and impractically, we'd jumped at the offer of a job in Lisbon without figuring the finer points. We discovered once we were there that the salary I was earning was not enough to match the newly inflated costs of housing. One more typical Philip-and-Joan blunder, according to my family.

Nonetheless, this challenging situation turned into a rare opportunity. The Portuguese people we met were gentle, warmhearted, and sweetly shy. They were also appreciative and forgiving of our limited and bungling attempts at their language.

One day, when he got a little bit lost in the fairy-tale city of Sintra, Philip went into a library hoping to get directions. "Com licença. Olá. Pode me ajudar, por favor?" (Excuse me. Hello. Can you help me, please?)

"Um momento, por favor" (One moment, please), said the male librarian, peering over wire-rimmed glasses and breaking into a warm smile.

He rushed from the room only to reappear minutes later with two young women and another man. He gestured toward Philip, smiled again, and asked Philip to repeat. "Pode repetir, por favor, senhor."

Philip repeated his well-rehearsed lines for a kind and amused audience. One of the women clapped with delight at his recitation. "Muito bom." (Very good.) "Você fala português?" (Do you speak Portuguese?)

"Sinto muito. Não falo bem português. Falo dez palavras em português!" (I'm sorry. I don't speak Portuguese well. I speak ten words in Portuguese!) Philip answered. He was so happy to use this humorous phrase we'd practiced assiduously. The librarians burst into an uproar of laughter, applause, and goodwill and then broke into perfect English, happily marking Philip's map with the route he needed. (He was trying to find the house where Hans Christian Andersen had stayed in 1866—a typically Philip-esque adventure.)

On our mornings and weekends together, we explored one beguiling Lisbon neighborhood after another. The Alfama district, up on the hill, was a romantic medieval maze; I tugged Philip eagerly from one bendy alleyway into the next. We wound our way up to St. George's castle at the top of the hill, learning that parts of the castle dated back to the sixth century. Other than a cable dish, an antenna, and a pair of running shoes airing on a balcony, there were next to no signs of modernity in the Alfama. We were, predictably, charmed.

We found small, dimly lit clubs where local *fado* singers put so much ardent longing—*saudade*—into each song that our hearts ached. If we timed our excursions carefully, we would catch the sunset from a panoramic vantage point that looked out over the city and the Tagus River. We got deliciously lost, winding our way through streets so narrow I could stand in the middle with my hands touching opposing walls. Laundry fluttered on lines above our heads, pots filled with geraniums sat on tiny wrought-iron balconies, and yellow and blue canaries sang from cages swinging from window frames.

We kept one eye out for *para alugar* (for rent) signs, but were often so enchanted by each distinctive neighborhood that our more pragmatic mission would be forgotten for hours at a time. The Bairro Alto, a bohemian haunt of writers and artists with architecture dating back to the sixteenth century and colorfully painted buildings, lit my imagination.

"Look," I said as we were exploring this neighborhood one day. I pointed up to a third-story window with white lace curtains fluttering in the breeze. "We should live there."

"That will be us," said Philip, nodding toward a couple sitting at a sidewalk café with coffee mugs set before them, heads bent over open notebooks, ankles entwined. "We'll wear black berets and scribble poetry furiously into the night," he said. Giggling, I wrapped my arms around a happier version of Philip than I'd known in years. We wanted to live in this city that felt literary, intellectual, poetic, and largely unspoiled by tourism.

"We have to find a place to live here!" I said.

"We will," he replied. He was more relaxed, more even-keeled, in Lisbon than he'd been since our earliest days together, when he was at the center of the Greeley Group.

We found our way to Lisbon's alternative culture. There were two excellent macrobiotic cafés, each with community bulletin boards announcing everything from parties to workshops to every type of craft and service. Emboldened by our desire to make a place for ourselves in this magical city, we overcame our usual reticence and talked with others over delicious, unhurried vegetarian meals. We got tips on which parts of town to try for housing and laughed a good deal with strangers who felt like friends by the end of a shared meal. In fact, after a few visits to two favorite cafés, when we'd arrive, our new friends would greet us warmly and wave us over to their tables.

"Olá, Philip e Joana!"

One day, we shared a table with a man who spoke fluent English. Again, we lamented our housing problem. He sent us off to meet a real estate agent he called "the Captain." The Captain, speaking with a distinctly British accent and sporting the manners and trappings of a genteel, neck-scarf-wearing Englishman from an earlier century, graciously showed us two charming apartments in 1920s buildings. Sadly, they were both too large and too expensive, though lovely with their high ceilings, French doors opening onto balconies, frescoed walls, and beautifully tended hardwood floors.

"Well, there is another place, but I don't think . . ." the Captain reluctantly began.

"Please, Captain, let's just take a look," Philip said.

So, the Captain took us to an apartment in an utterly dreamlike setting. We climbed rickety wooden stairs on the outside of the building and came up on an open-air walkway leading to a series of five small wooden doors, each one painted a different color—red, blue, yellow, orange, and green.

"I expect hobbits to emerge from these doors," I whispered to Philip.

"This was once a whorehouse, and in the case of one or two of the residents, might still be," said the Captain, harrumphing sheepishly. Philip met my eye with a glint and a question in his raised eyebrow.

The building had been constructed in the late 1800s as a warehouse (not whorehouse). The apartments, more like caves than apartments, had likely been used as storage rooms. The only natural light came from the open door. Inside, I could barely see what I was seeing, even when the Captain flipped on a lamp whose dim, golden glow barely pervaded the darkness.

"This feels like another time, another world," I said as I reached for Philip's hand but couldn't find it.

"What the hell . . ." he muttered when he stumbled over a shadowy cat that leapt to a high shelf with a yowl of indignation.

Philip grabbed my hand as though fearing a witch or goblin might emerge out of the strange gloom. Without a single open space, we moved single file through paths that traversed old wooden furniture, rolled-up carpets, oversized pillows, and every other kind of unidentifiable whatnot. A bed was piled high with blankets and pillows. Suddenly, something moved.

"Senhora Silva?" the Captain called loudly. "She doesn't hear well," he said to us. There was another shifting under the blankets, and then . . . stillness. Philip squeezed my hand harder while I strained my eyes to see. I couldn't make out anything more than a lumpy hump in the bed.

"Senhora Silva," the Captain said again. "Just showing the apartment, madame. No need to get up." Stillness.

As my eyes finally adjusted to the dim light, I could make out tables and chairs laden with books, piles of fabrics and newspapers, peacock feathers, candelabras, and dusty, dried flowers. The cat yowled again.

"Uh . . . I don't think this will do, Captain," Philip said in a hushed and incredulous voice. And that was before we realized that there was no kitchen, no running water, and no bathroom in the apartment! Back on the street, looking shamefaced, the Captain quickly tipped his cap, apologized, and bade us a hasty farewell.

We laughed all the way down the street and back to our safe and sane little hotel. "Why can't we just live here?" I asked, only half joking.

Once we understood the difficulty of finding housing in Lisbon, we extended our search to include some of the nearby towns we'd already started exploring: Cascais, Estoril, and Sintra.

Sintra was an utterly romantic city dotted with palaces and castles and set in forests on Europe's westernmost point. Though an hour from Lisbon by train, we agreed that Sintra would be worth the commute.

"Imagine living in such beauty!" Philip exclaimed as we explored the town and its residential neighborhoods. "It's like a romantic nineteenth-century novel."

"I love it!" I said.

We spotted a three-by-five card in a greengrocer's window advertising a large, comfortable studio apartment five minutes from the town center. Jotting down the address and asking the greengrocer for directions, we purchased a pound of peaches and walked to the house, peach juice dripping from our chins. We stopped at a small stone fountain to rinse our sticky faces and fingers with water fancifully streaming from a lion's mouth.

A few minutes later, we arrived at a peaceful, vine-covered, early nineteenth-century stone house. The landlord answered the door on our first ring and greeted us in English. *Maybe our luck was finally turning.*

"May we see your apartment for rent?" Philip asked.

"I am so sorry," he said, "but the current tenant is out. I never enter my lodgers' apartment without their permission. Can you come back tomorrow, perhaps?"

We explained how we'd come from Lisbon to this sympathetic man with a gentle smile and dark, melancholy eyes.

"When is the apartment available?" I asked.

"You could move in the day after tomorrow if you want," he said. He walked us around the side of the house to a patio and pointed to French doors, the entryway to the apartment.

"How bad can it be?" Philip said to me as the landlord politely stepped aside to check his roses and give us a private moment.

"The house certainly is lovely. And the landlord seems kind and obviously respects the privacy of his tenants," I said hopefully.

"Still, it's risky to take an apartment without seeing anything more than the door," Philip said. "But we don't want to lose this opportunity."

Taking a deep breath, we nodded our agreement.

"Can we give you a deposit today and move in on Wednesday morning?" Philip asked the landlord.

Thus, in yet another Philip-and-Joan leap of faith, we rented the apartment sight unseen. Ignoring the risky element, we checked out of the hotel with all our belongings two days later. I hugged my favorite maid goodbye and felt absurdly teary when she kissed me and called me *querida menina* for the last time.

As we entered through the doors we'd viewed two days earlier, the landlord explained that the apartment was a converted wine cellar.

"Another cave apartment," Philip muttered.

"Well, at least the French doors let the light in," I offered, trying for optimism. Disappointed but resolute, we unpacked, putting our few belongings into the antique dressers and wardrobes.

"The furniture definitely gives the place a homey ambiance," I said. "And the stone walls give it a unique, old-world feeling, don't you think?"

"Hmm," Philip replied as he groped for a lamp.

Shortly after, I took the train back to Lisbon in time to teach my evening classes. Philip headed out to do some shopping and exploring.

On my train trip home at 8 P.M. that night, peering out through the window into that mystical time between the wolf and the dog, my anxious face was reflected back at me. I was sitting in an empty train car, feeling isolated and vulnerable. All kinds of "what if" scenarios attacked me as I imagined being accosted, kidnapped, murdered. When the conductor finally came for my ticket, I was so relieved that I nearly hugged him. I had to stop myself from begging him to stay with me.

When I wasn't worrying about gangs and muggers, I mulled over the critical comments I'd received from my supervisor that afternoon. "You should be observing my classes every morning to learn my methods," she'd said.

"I've been spending my mornings searching for a place to live. We've been paying for a hotel room for nearly three months now. No one at the school has been of any assistance," I'd retorted with annoyance.

"That's what Philip should be doing," she'd replied, equally tersely. "The school is not responsible for helping you with housing."

I gritted my teeth. I was furious. When Philip met me at the train station, I was in a state. Taking one look at my face, he pulled me close and searched my eyes. "What's up, my darlin'?"

My eyes filled with tears, and I hardly knew where to start.

That night, we lay in bed plagued by the persistent drip of water hitting the old-world stone walls. Apparently the humidity and rain that make Sintra and its surrounding forests so green was going to drip and plop through our nights.

"This is like Chinese water torture," Philip said after an hour of tossing and turning. As he pulled the pillow over his head, I wrapped myself around him for warmth. Added to the dripping and plopping, the sheets were impossibly clammy and cold, and try as we might to warm them and each other, we remained wretched and freezing.

Finally, giving up on sleep and taking turns rubbing each other's cold feet, we talked, admitting our latest disaster. In the morning, adding insult to injury, I had come down with a cold. To the tune of my nose-blowing, we repacked our suitcases and went to talk to the landlord.

"We're sorry, but the wine cellar apartment is impossible. It's damp and clammy, and water dripped incessantly throughout the night. My wife now has a cold that she didn't have yesterday. So, as you can see," Philip pointed to our suitcases, "we can't live here and hope you will return our deposit."

"Yes, yes. I understand. I have never slept there, as you might imagine," he replied. "But I think you may be right. In fact, the reason the former tenant has moved out is that he is now in hospital with pneumonia."

"Maybe you should return the apartment to its wine cellar origins," Philip suggested.

"The poor man," I spluttered through a sneeze as the door closed behind us and we walked away from the house.

"Which one? The guy dying of pneumonia or the landlord who can't rent his blasted wine cellar?" Philip asked as he shouldered his pack and steered us back to the train station.

So, after three long months of searching and not finding a place to live, after handing over almost all I'd earned to pay our hotel bill, after facing an unreasonably critical supervisor, and now, blowing, honking, and fearing pneumonia, we sadly admitted defeat. I handed in my resignation that evening.

It was hard to leave Portugal—it had been wonderful to find Philip feeling fully amenable with one place on the planet. Despite our failure to stay, we remained so enamored of the country that we kept it on our list of places to return to someday.

16

A Fig Tree and a Teenage Alligator

It seemed that Philip and I were destined to lead a nomadic lifestyle, and the years after we left Portugal were spent going wherever I could find a job teaching English. We lived in Denver again for eight years, then spent three years in the sweltering desert city of Abu Dhabi, in the United Arab Emirates.

During our time in Abu Dhabi, we traveled during the college's summer and winter breaks. In 2011, we stayed in a lovely Italian inn. Philip and I both loved the host, Roberto. He was warm, filled with humor, sensitivity, and intelligence. He was also (mostly) very patient with his often trying guests. Philip was in heaven at this small, quiet hotel perched on a hill overlooking the Mediterranean and the town of Santa Margherita.

In addition to the inn's charms—the quiet and comfortable rooms, porches overlooking the sea, and generous breakfasts—the property proffered the extra gift of many ancient fig trees. And we were there in fig season! Luscious, sweet, ripe figs dropped and plopped from the trees. Our mouths bulged with figs during our entire stay, and when either one of us bit into an unusually good one, we'd share the second bite.

"Oh, here . . . try this one!" Philip would say.

"Mmmm . . ." I'd murmur as he'd plant fig-sweetened lips on mine.

However, picking up treasures from the ground wasn't good enough for Philip. One afternoon, I stood beneath a hundred-year-old fig tree, anxiously peering up through the branches as Philip clambered his way to the top.

"The best fruits will be way up at the top, in the sun," he called down to me as, much to my consternation, he scrambled ever higher.

"This is probably not something Roberto would want you doing," I hissed up at him.

"Imagine the headline. 'Guest falls from hundred-year-old fig tree. But dies fully sated,'" he said, laughing. I stood helplessly below as he chuckled and rustled high above me.

How many other trees, walls, and high fences had I stood under all over the world while Philip had happily foraged for figs, cherries, apples, grapes, apricots, and even dates? After a few moments' thought, I conceded—what else was there to do—that being nervous about him falling (he never did), feeling anxious about facing an irate tree owner (which only happened once), and having ripe fruit splatter on my upturned face (fairly often) was just part of life with Philip. So, letting go of worry, I marveled at his boy-like agility at age sixty-four and laughed at his willingness to dare any heights for the sake of ripe, stolen fruit.

As fate would have it, within minutes, along came Roberto, proudly showing some new guests around the property. I'd just had time to shush Philip when they stopped to talk to me. Right then, of course, Philip's foot slipped, he rustled, and ripe figs rained down on all of us.

Looking up to see Philip peering down through the branches, Roberto shouted, "Hey, you crazy guy! Get the hell down from there!"

Moments later, my dearly beloved jumped down from the lowest branch, face and fingers fig-smeared, expression sheepish. Roberto scowled at Philip and, regaining his composure, quickly moved on with his guests, still shaking his head.

Later in the day, he arrived at our door with a bowl brimming with figs.

"Signor Heiman," he said, "*I* bring these to *you*, please."

Roberto was very gracious, but I'm sure he stored this memory of Philip away in his innkeeper's collection of tales about crazy guests.

When my contract in Abu Dhabi ended in January 2012, Philip and I moved to Tampa, Florida, where I'd been offered a teaching position at the University of South Florida.

After three years in Abu Dhabi, living eleven stories up and looking down onto eight lanes of honking, screeching, and incessant traffic, we were like parched nomads at an oasis. We drank in all the tropical Florida foliage and water in our new backyard. The quiet was heavenly.

True to our knack for wishful, idealistic thinking, however, when we'd contemplated our upcoming move, we had pictured Florida as it must have been one hundred years ago. We'd dreamed of orange groves (organic, of course), date-palm trees, nearby beaches with warm, balmy breezes blowing off the waters of Tampa Bay.

In retrospect, I think all of this was there, although finding organic food was a challenge in supermarkets called Piggly Wiggly and Winn-Dixie. With patience and persistence, one could probably peel back the skin of the highways, golf courses, and strip malls to find much of the state's natural beauty, but we were disheartened in our first days, as much as we savored the change from hectic, noisy Abu Dhabi.

With very little time between landing and beginning another new job, we quickly and grudgingly settled on an apartment in the least depressing complex we could find. In fact, we found, it wasn't half bad. From our living room windows and balcony, we looked out on nothing but a boggy wood and two ponds. The parked cars and the other hundred-plus cookie-cutter, two-story buildings were only visible from the bedroom.

The Florida weather in January was idyllic. For the first time in three years, we slept with windows open and relished the fresh air we'd been denied in Abu Dhabi's air-conditioned nightmare. When we awoke on our first morning, Philip grabbed a bowl of Florida oranges and headed out the door. "I'm going to break my fast outside, sitting on *real* ground by the ponds. Yahoo!"

"Bon appétit, mon chéri," I called after him. "I'll stick to the balcony."

My dislike of bugs combined with the signs warning residents to beware of snakes and alligators made the balcony more appealing, even though I thought the signs were more about remote possibilities than imminent danger.

Fresh from the shower, with my head still wrapped in a towel, I laughed with relief at the return of Philip's childlike ebullience. He was such a complicated soul who could be so simply pleased. Sunlight, oranges (which he called "liquid sunshine"), trees, and quiet were his idea of a perfect morning.

"No more concrete, urban madness!" he called up at me as I stepped out onto the balcony. This was the first time he'd been this happy in a very long time. My heart filled with love for him as I shook my wet hair free, feeling equally free of the Middle Eastern blowing sand, fierce sun, and oppressive heat . . . and the oppressive attitudes toward women.

I looked down at Philip, who sat cross-legged a few feet from the water's edge. It took a moment before I saw the teenage alligator parked in the water, facing him. After watching nature shows with slow and lazy alligators darting with sudden bursts of speed to capture unsuspecting prey, I froze in terror. The alligator was about five feet long, his back and tail just visible under the surface of the water.

Once I regained enough breath to speak, I hollered, "Get away from that!"

"He won't hurt me," Philip said. "He's just curious. How amazing is this? We're living in a nature preserve!"

Philip's nonchalant response did nothing to slow my racing heart. He had ironically (or infuriatingly) walked right past the sign that read "Beware of Alligators and Snakes." I began to long for the safety of eleven floors up in a Middle Eastern concrete jungle. Even the literally mouse-sized desert cockroaches that occasionally terrorized us in our Abu Dhabi apartment seemed relatively innocuous in contrast to the baby dinosaur who had joined Philip for breakfast.

That alligator, whom Philip fondly dubbed Clive, lived in our pond for the entire year we were there. Well-intended neighbors regularly warned and chided Philip (and me, since they couldn't make any headway with their impossibly foolhardy new neighbor) about the dangers of sitting head-to-head with an alligator.

Our downstairs neighbor, a college student who'd introduced himself as a lover of reptiles, agreed with Philip, promising that "an alligator never attacks anything larger than itself." His attempts to reassure me had little effect.

"You need to stand up every few minutes and show Clive how big you are!" I'd holler down to Philip. You can imagine the eye-rolling response I got.

Clive didn't just paddle or glide around the pond. Any number of times during that year, I looked out from our second-floor balcony with a mixture of awe and horror as Clive waddled down the sidewalk much as a cat might in a northern suburban neighborhood. Accustomed to growing up with squirrels, cats, and an occasional dog on the loose, watching an alligator meander along the same sidewalk I used was food for nightmares. In fact, alligators quickly became new and fantastical dream-figures that terrorized my nights.

Other much larger daddy and granddaddy alligators also appeared, though thankfully on the far shores of our ponds. We watched, borrowing binoculars from other fascinated neighbors, as these giant monsters basked in the sun, hardly moving for hours at a time.

"They've probably just lunched on someone's poodle," I surmised.

One day, we watched in horror as Clive took down a stork and dragged it across the water to enjoy as supper on the far shore. I hoped this might put a bit of fear into Philip, but no. Instead, to hide from the "hysterical and overreacting" neighbors and get even closer to nature, he found a favorite shaded spot on a small isthmus that straddled the two ponds and backed into the boggy wood.

"You have to turn around regularly to be sure nothing sneaks up on you from behind," I warned futilely.

From his place on the isthmus, Philip watched not only Clive, but storks, cranes, turtles, and even an otter. He called out to me regularly to come see the latest episode of our personal nature show.

One afternoon when we got home, I stepped onto the balcony and had to take a second look to see what I was seeing out on the isthmus. A turtle had managed to flip upside down while making her way up and over from one pond to the other. (We'd agreed that turtles were feminine.)

Fearless where I am fearful, Philip often sat within just a few feet of one of these slow neighbors, relishing his proximity to wildlife and throwing bits of lettuce or fruit to it as it scrabbled up and out of one pond, plodded past his toes in its steadfast manner, and then plopped down into the next.

"Philip, quick! Come see! You have to help," I called. He came running, and I pointed out the stranded critter.

"What can we do?" I asked. "Can you flip her back over?" These were large turtles, about the circumference of a Frisbee, so *I* was certainly not going to perform the rescue. Still, I could be a good cheerleader. Philip grabbed the dustpan and broom and headed down.

"Let's just hope she hasn't been out here too long," he called as he rushed onto the isthmus. With a few gentle pushes and prods, the turtle was right side up, returned to a more dignified position. Either stunned or frightened by this traumatic turn of events in her afternoon, she didn't move right away. I held my breath as we watched and waited. When she finally took up her slow transmigration and plopped back into the water, I let out my breath and cheered.

"You're a hero!" I clapped.

"Yeah." He grinned up at me.

By the time we moved away from Florida, Clive was at least a foot longer, which technically made him longer than Philip was high. Still undaunted, however, Philip continued to sit nose-to-nose with his reptilian pal. My heart stopped one morning when Clive decided to venture closer, clambering in slow motion out of the water.

"Move!" I shouted.

Philip stood, waved his arms, and said loudly, "Whoa, there, Clive, old man. Get back in the water." Which Clive cooperatively did, in a rather hilarious backward slither.

"You see," he said, "he's no danger." Now it was my turn to roll my eyes.

The one thing that finally did frighten Philip was a tree full of buzzards. Sitting out on his isthmus one morning, he heard a very strange and unfamiliar noise close by.

"It was like a cacophony of hoarsely barking dogs," was the way he described it to me when I got home that afternoon. "I stayed where I was because I was curious, but I was definitely ready to run. It was eerie, not like anything I'd ever heard before."

"Yeah?" I queried, anxiously thinking, *What now?*

"The noise kept getting louder," he continued, "and suddenly I realized it was coming from above me. I looked up into the tree and saw what must have been twenty to thirty enormous, ugly black buzzards perched in the tree, peering down at me. Did you know their heads are bald? They're horrible! I hightailed it out of there."

Oh no, here's more nightmare material for me, was all I could think when I saw them the next morning. Over the next four days, those buzzards showed up to sit and bark in that tree for hours before thankfully moving on. The monstrous creatures looked and sounded to me like menacing harbingers of foreboding.

"But I never saw a snake," Philip complained as we drove away on moving day.

My entire year in that tropical world was colored by uneasy fears. Fears *for* Philip and *from* the creatures and critters with which he was so happy to cohabitate. But this was living with Philip—always living between love and anxiety. With his honeyed laughter warming my heart and an alligator or illness threatening to snatch him away, I lived day after day, year after year between deep peace and frazzling uncertainty, between infinite love and threatening loss.

17

Madeira: Paradise Lost

After Florida, we returned to Fort Collins, where I had applied for and been offered a job teaching English as a second language for Colorado State University. The combination of my perfectionism, the less than ambitious students, and the demands of a new administration made it an increasingly taxing and disheartening experience. As the end of the academic year neared, I was worn to a frazzle.

"You're so tired and discouraged, little darlin'," Philip said as I moaned over yet another stack of ten-page research papers to be graded over yet another weekend. "You've been working fifty- to sixty-hour weeks ever since you started this job."

"I know . . . I know," I groaned.

"What's with this program? Who appreciates what you do? Your students keep making the same mistakes. Your supervisors are as caught up in the rat race as you are, and they can't see how the system is failing."

"I haven't ever felt this discouraged about work I once loved," I said. "The program is run like an emergency room in a hospital. We're always racing against deadlines. It's not as if anyone's going to die if I take three days—work days, not my weekend—to grade these papers."

"Right. So why are you giving your life to it? I don't see it getting better anytime soon, do you?

"No."

"Then let's take off. You can retire in June on your sixty-second birthday, and we can finally find our place on the planet," he said with his most endearing smile.

"But we've tried so many times and we still don't know where that place is," I answered, just barely containing the panic that had begun shooting from my toes to the top of my head. Tiresome research papers were at least a known and paid-for quantity.

"Shouldn't we finally spend time together without the constant stress of your job?" he asked. "Let's live and enjoy each other while we're still relatively young and healthy. We can live simply and in beauty if we search hard enough outside the U.S.," he continued. "We already know there's no amenable, affordable place in this country, no right climate, no right community."

"But how do we know if my early retirement income is enough to live on *anywhere*?" I asked. Visions of living in poor, developing countries alongside weatherworn, sunbaked, and leathery-faced expats filled me with dismay.

When a very generous friend volunteered his financial counseling, I proposed we take him up on it. Stretching farther into the realm of the practical than he usually ventured, Philip grudgingly agreed to an in-depth assessment of my retirement benefits and our overall finances. In the end, and somewhat to my surprise, it was agreed that we should be all right in a country with a lower cost of living.

"You're not going to be swimming in money by any means, but it's good enough for the simple life you're hankering after," our friend concluded.

That was all Philip needed to get our suitcases out of storage.

But the growing exhaustion of my job warred with fear-laden images of endlessly wandering the third world, perpetually homeless. I tossed and turned through the nights. Philip, on the other hand, was newly energized, and began his research.

"Don't worry, my love," he assured me. "We'll find a place. And when we do, we'll be happier than we've ever been here." I listened and tried to let go of fear and hesitation. Maybe he'd be right this time. Maybe I should embrace the idea that life is meant for living, not for clinging to security.

We did what online research we could from a distance (which, after so much travel, even Philip knew can be sadly far from what one finds upon arrival). We had long since adopted a raw fruitarian diet, mainly eating sweet fruit but also including avocado, squash, bell pepper, green beans, cucumber, and tomato (all of which are actually fruits, botanically). We also ate nuts and seeds, and—for me—some chocolate. So, looking for a temperate and sunny climate with an abundance of fruit, Philip took his finger and literally circled the equator on the globe in my office. He landed on the tiny Portuguese island of Madeira, a volcanic jewel set in the Atlantic Ocean about seven hundred miles south of Portugal and six hundred miles west of Morocco.

"It's described as 'the island of fruit and flowers.' What more can we ask for?" he said, beaming.

He read to me from websites and guidebooks. "Average temperature is seventy-five degrees year-round. Sunshine most days. Natives of Portuguese descent but with their own history and culture. Cost of living is lower than in most of Europe, but the culture is distinctly European. And lots of tropical fruit! It sounds perfect, don't you think?"

"Yes," I said. "Possibly too good to be true?"

"Ah, come on. . . . Come here and look at these pictures."

Trying hard not to think of all the other "perfect places" we'd been perfectly disappointed by, and trying very hard to get into the spirit of adventure one more time, I smiled my agreement and held my doubting Eeyore's tongue. *No point in predicting, dooming, or negating future possibilities based on past failures,* I coached myself, calling on my best New Age philosophy.

By the end of May 2014, I'd cleared out my cubicle, eaten my retirement cake, and we were headed out—Winnie the Pooh and Piglet on yet another adventure. (With Eeyore secretly buried and quietly moaning at the bottom of my suitcase.)

The problem with idealists is that they tend to crash hard against the unforgiving, adamantine walls of reality. For all his enthusiasm for discovery, Philip was not a good traveler. Fixed and stubborn by nature, he set out knowing what he was looking for, and when he was met with anything else, could neither adapt nor adjust.

We landed at Madeira's airport, a single runway jutting out into the sea on one end and nearly touching a highway on the other. Closing my eyes as we landed, I refused to think what would happen if the pilot couldn't stop before the runway ran into the highway.

As we soon discovered, the capital city of Funchal was yet another city undergoing major construction. Parks were surrounded by cranes and construction crews. Jackhammers clattered against concrete, and the incessant din was nerve-wracking. Construction dust coated the flowers. Shoreline walks were blocked off. Where one had once sat on a bench looking out to sea and contemplating life, now one looked at advertisements for the casino plastered on a prefab wall.

Many pedestrian streets in Funchal's Old Town were closed. This clogged the remaining narrow streets with ice-cream-cone-licking, Bermuda-shorts-wearing tourists sporting fanny packs, baseball caps, and running shoes. The airport had changed the nature of life on the island in the same way that Corfu's airport had changed it. Tourism: good for the economy, bad for us.

Even the fruit and flower market turned out to be more of a tourist attraction than a living marketplace, shooting prices up astronomically. We found two small health food stores in the entire city, neither of which carried produce. Philip became disconsolate.

One day, we took a local bus that climbed steeply from the shore to the hills above town. The hills seen from below were picturesquely covered with small, flower-bedecked houses. What appeared colorfully quaint from the distance, however, was very different as the road climbed and twisted precipitously upward. At one point, it seemed we all might have to get out and push. As we passed those quaint houses, we saw that stepping from one's front door meant either stepping in an immediate and sharp ascent or a dizzying descent. Retiring to a place where one needed to be more of a mountain goat than a senior citizen didn't seem quite the thing—even to two people who still had no conception of themselves as seniors.

We eventually made our way to smaller towns outside of Funchal, on the other side of the island. There, in lieu of construction noise, roosters waked us at 4 A.M. I, the suburban girl, remembered from Corfu that these dandies of the bird world do not simply greet the dawn with one quaint cock-adoodle-doo, but continue their crazy clamor throughout the morning, giving the weary wanderer no chance of rolling over and going back to sleep. The 4 A.M. rooster alarm clocks were preceded by barking dogs—one bark inspiring a neighboring bark throughout the night. These dogs were tied up outside to serve as guards against what, I wasn't sure. There was even a resident madwoman held captive by her family in one of the houses below our rental house. Her wailing intermittently invaded the relative quiet of the afternoons, distressing us but apparently not the now-napping roosters and dogs.

There was minimal public transportation, so our idea of living without a car was unrealistic. Isolated, economically challenged villages with one small general store carrying five shriveled oranges, bins of ancient onions, and a few wrinkled potatoes hardly seemed like viable retirement spots for two fruitarians.

"I think we should go back to Funchal and find a real estate agent to help us," I said. "We can't just give up and leave."

"But it's hopeless," Philip said. "Even if we find a place to live, where will we shop? What will we eat? And do you really want to live with what looks like at least a few more years of construction and chaos everywhere?"

I sighed in defeat. One more paradise lost. We, feeling equally lost after three weeks on the island, booked a flight out.

We spent the next month seeking and despairing throughout southern France and northern Spain. (Though there was much that was beautiful and intriguing while traveling through remarkable countryside and spending days in medieval villages and towns.) The following month led us north, to Copenhagen's historic pedestrian streets. Copenhagen was tempting with its renaissance castles, luxuriantly green and spacious parks, health food stores aplenty, and the best berries we'd ever tasted.

But, as Philip reminded me, "Summer is short here, winter long, cold, and dark."

We spent three weeks trying and failing to come to peace with our last resort: the hugely touted San Miguel de Allende, a small Mexican city that had become an expat magnet. I reluctantly agreed to try it, but my prejudices were confirmed—it was noisy, chaotic, and definitely third world. Philip was admittedly of the same mind and cursed the deceptive descriptions of the vibrant, green World Heritage site portrayed in *Condé Nast Traveler*.

Next, we went back to the States, exploring the deserts, canyons, and mesas of Arizona and New Mexico. Reminiscent of our first frantic trips made across the U.S. in search of our place on the planet thirty-six years earlier, each place, once again, failed Philip in one way or another. Increasingly disheartened, watching money pour out on motels, and weary of making and shaking salads in plastic bags to eat sitting next to streams in Santa Fe, Flagstaff, and Prescott, or dangling our legs over cliff edges in Sedona, I was ready to throw in the towel.

"Let's just go back to Fort Collins for now and regroup," I said. "We're exhausted. Our ideas are getting crazier by the minute. Money we don't have is rapidly turning into debt, and you're spinning through town after town crazed with road fever."

Without another idea to pull out of his hat, Philip reluctantly agreed.

"But I'm not going to spend the rest of my life in Fort Collins, in snow and winter, paying for expensive housing to live next to noisy, drunken college students," he insisted.

"Fine," I said, "but surely you see, we have to stop for now."

PART II

Standing by an Impossible Person

to the ant
that walks
on my guitar
the end
of the string
must seem
awfully far
and the reason
for stringing
a little obscure
and the man
who strums it
strange
I'm sure

—Philip Heiman

18

Standing by Him

In mid-November 2014, two weeks before we were planning to fly to Costa Rica for less expensive dental work and another retirement home exploration, Philip started running fevers in the night. He struggled through disturbing and disturbed sleep, sheets and blankets drenched with sweat as the fevers broke every night for a week.

Then there was the worsening of the annoying little compulsive cough we'd learned not to hear. That had begun a few years back, in the final of three years of nonstop unfiltered air-conditioning in Abu Dhabi. This also interfered with sleep, leaving him—and therefore both of us—exhausted each morning. Moreover, the cough began to exude a disturbing and pervasive odor.

"Do you smell something odd? Like burning rubber?" I asked one day.

"I think that's coming from me," he said. "When I cough."

"What in the world?"

"Sorry," he said. "Awful, huh?"

Everything became awful. Already thin after nine years on a raw fruitarian diet, he was now dramatically weaker, thinner, and increasingly more fragile, physically and emotionally. And yet he continued to believe that this was all just one more of his "strange afflictions." He'd had so many peculiar symptoms and mysterious ailments over the years that we'd both become accustomed, inured, hardly alarmed.

While in the past we'd attended to his symptoms with care and concern, consulting one holistic and alternative healer after another, reading up on all the latest hard-to-diagnose ailments and wondering about "highly sensitive people" and conditions like Asperger's, we had gradually come to believe that nothing was "seriously" wrong; that whatever was wrong could ultimately be healed via diet, lifestyle improvements, mental hygiene, loving compassion, and, now, perhaps, dentistry.

We even laughed (rather than cried) about his body being a barometer that somatized emotional distress in a myriad of arcane, doctor-confounding physical symptoms.

"Just love me," he'd say. And I did.

However, a few days later, a dramatic attack of pain that knocked the breath out of him alarmed us. On an unseasonably warm day for November in Fort Collins, I looked up from a picnic lunch in the park to see Philip bent over and leaning heavily against a tree. When I reached him, he was gasping for breath, unable to speak. I held him and repeated over and over again—to both of us—the yogi's mantra: "Breathe . . . Breathe."

Taking deep breaths, we tried to chase away the panic with inane humor as we hobbled toward the apartment, normally a seven-minute walk away.

"Want to stop for fried chicken?" I asked. The café behind our building was the bane of our existence, generously filling the apartment of two vegans with wafts of frying chicken.

"Yeah," he gasped with a roll of his eyes. "With fries and a Coke."

"That sounds good. Should we run?" I asked.

"Aren't I running?" he panted.

After thirty minutes, we finally made it home. We somehow managed to climb the longest flight of stairs in the world to our second-story apartment, where I eased him onto the futon that doubled as a couch.

Even this episode, unnerving as it was, didn't shake Philip's long-held and stubborn resistance to doctors, conventional or (in recent years) alternative. They'd all repeatedly failed him.

"I know you won't want to, but maybe you should see a doctor," I said. "This kind of pain could mean something serious, don't you think?"

"What good would it do? And what doctor?"

"There's that holistic healing center next to the bank. Maybe someone there would know what's happening?"

"No one's going to understand," he said. "They'll tell me I'm eating all wrong,"—*Maybe you are*, I thought—"say I'm much too thin,"—*You definitely are*—"or prescribe herbs or Ayurveda or something else I don't believe in."

I sighed.

The following morning, we looked out at a world that had changed. Temperatures had dropped below freezing, and the ground was covered with snow. After an agonizingly long, pained, and sleepless night through which he could neither lie flat nor get comfortable propped up against pillows, I tried another approach.

"What about that chiropractor whose office is on the way to Whole Foods?" I asked. "We can hobble over there in five minutes. You know, usually chiropractors have a more holistic perspective. And they know basic physiology, so he or she should be able to identify which organ or muscle is causing this."

I offered this as casually as I could, knowing that any note of fear or insistence would throw him into resistance. Much to my surprised relief, he agreed. He was obviously in more pain than he knew what to do with, and could no longer hold out with his usual "let's just wait and see" strategy.

At the chiropractor's, Philip described a gripping pain under the right side of his rib cage. "Maybe it's my liver? Gallbladder? Or just extreme muscle tension?"

"Muscle tension?" asked the chiropractor. "Did you lift something heavy, or . . . ?"

"Well, we're packing to move, so maybe."

The chiropractor listened, poked, and then promptly, and most unhelpfully, flew into a panic. After weighing Philip and finding a five-eleven man weighing 104 pounds, and after hearing the location and intensity of the pain, he reached near hysteria.

"You have to go to an emergency room for X-rays, a CT scan, or both . . . right now! Your gallbladder could burst any minute!"

This, not surprisingly, brought on panic in Philip, but the panic predictably caused him to dig in his heels, fortifying his commitment to deal with this in his own all-natural way. He couldn't get out of that examining room fast enough, and was buttoning his shirt on his way out the door before I'd finished paying.

This was all so familiar—Philip vehemently insisting and clinging to his beliefs. *But what if he's wrong this time and the chiropractor is right?* I thought, trying to control a panic of my own.

"No to hospitals, no to emergency rooms, no to X-rays," he said under his breath, chanting to the rhythm of his feet crunching through icy snow as we made our way back home.

Oh my god, I silently responded.

Any other professional help was rejected out of hand, the idea of X-rays and CT scans snorted at in disgust. My suggestion that we might, perhaps, delay leaving for Costa Rica until he felt stronger only further intensified his determination to go.

Looking at him hobbling along, slightly hunched over and breathing heavily, I wondered but didn't say, *How are you going to carry your suitcase, wear a heavy backpack, or walk through the airport? What if your gallbladder bursts on the plane? Or after we're in Costa Rica?*

I didn't know what to do. *Do I put my foot down? Refuse to go?* I googled "if the gallbladder ruptures, does a person die?"

The hysterical, "overreacting" chiropractor only added to Philip's backlog of years of suspicion, disappointment, and, finally, disbelief in doctors and healers of all kinds. It combined with a strong—some would say fanatical—belief in and adherence to the simple philosophy and practice of health known as Natural Hygiene. Natural Hygiene purports that the body has innate wisdom and can heal itself if given the needed conditions and support.

Depending on one's perspective, bias, and philosophy, Philip was either the most pigheaded and stubborn fool on the planet, or he was remarkably courageous, to be admired for his willingness to hold steadfast to his beliefs and convictions even in the face of pain and dire threat. I had chosen the latter for all our years together and chose to do so now. With his health hanging in the balance, he was once again fighting for what he believed, and I could only respond with awe, fear, and the intense hope that he was right.

"No medicine, no medicine men, and no delay to our plan to leave for Costa Rica," he said to all my alternate proposals.

My choice, then, became a non-choice: stand with him, or . . . stand with him. I found myself wishing for a miracle, but in lieu of a miracle, I strove desperately for increased inner fortitude. Talking both of us off the ledge of panic repeatedly, all I could do was be there.

As I proceeded to pack up the apartment, he sat propped up on the couch. "I wish I could help you," he said.

"You are! Just remotely," I joked. "Now tell me what you want to take and what you want to leave."

"But how can you manage everything?" he asked.

"What choice is there? You want to leave, so I need to manage. Besides, this is my chance to be in control, chief!" I winked at him and got a wry smile and that endearingly familiar tilt of an eyebrow.

Trusting his sense (which I was sure others would call *non*sense if we'd shared what we were not sharing with anyone) was my choice. I was frightened, edgy, nervy . . . but resolved. I decided not to voice feelings that might inflame our fears. I leaned into my love for him, along with the remarkable capacity I'd learned from him throughout the years: the capacity to hope beyond hope. As so often before, I decided in favor of him, incrementally becoming a tiny bit more like him: willing to face fear; crazily courageous when faced with doubts.

I continued packing the apartment we'd only moved into and minimally furnished four months before, following our defeated return from Madeira (and France, Spain, Denmark, Mexico, Arizona, and New Mexico). Philip apologized repeatedly for his helplessness, reassuring us that he was going to be much better as soon as he got to a warm climate. With the generous help of a remarkably kind and strong student I'd been tutoring, as well as two loyal and competent friends, I got rid of almost everything we'd accumulated. I transported a few final boxes and three beloved Oriental carpets to one of those friend's houses for storage.

Throughout those final days and hours before our departure, Philip was unable to stand for more than a few minutes at a time, let alone lift, bend, or carry. I look back at that time and see myself and my student walking back and forth in front of him—first in slow motion and then in high speed—lifting and carrying boxes and bags to the van. With each passing, the man upon whom I'd depended for thirty-six years seemed to grow older and frailer.

Nonetheless, the process carried on, moving us inexorably closer to the departure date and a plan that cared nothing for debilitation or fear. I was so preoccupied and busy with details, so intent on juggling my roles as nurse, cheerleader, household manager, and mover, that I barely felt how frightened I was.

December 2 arrived, and we were on our way to the airport. My friend dropped us at the curb, hugged each of us, and drove away shaking her head. I drew a last deep breath of clear, early morning Colorado air, gave a farewell nod to the mountains, and then headed into the airport. I was on my own now with this shadow of the man I'd known, depended on, and loved since he first "recognized" me in front of the meditation house in Denver so many years and another lifetime ago.

Philip asked for and was pushed through the airport in a wheelchair—my preview of a beginning surrender. Even after the attendant referred to Philip as my father (our eyes meeting in shocked dismay as we confronted the aging we hadn't seen), we carried on. I rushed to buy extra blankets to wrap around him as he coughed and shivered while we awaited a delayed takeoff on an icy, fog-bound winter morning. We carried on. If things weren't exactly normal, Philip was still recognizably the personality—if not the body—he'd been in all our years together: whimsical, stubborn, vulnerable, and, indefatigably, still hoping.

19

Costa Rica . . . The Beginning of the End

This had to be one of the craziest things we'd done yet. Who would uproot themselves again only 120 days after a failed, expensive, and months-long attempt to find an affordable retirement refuge? Who would hope and hope some more to find peace and a safe haven in a world that rarely offers it, much less on the cheap? Who would, yet again, dispose of all their worldly belongings to "travel light" and start anew? And finally, who would get on a plane to Central America with all their earthly belongings whittled down to fit into two suitcases and two backpacks when they were more unwell than they had been in years?

Who? Philip . . . and me, alongside him.

"I just need to get to a place where I can eat plenty of organic, tropical fruit, rest, be warm, find peace, feel safe . . . and have these painful teeth fixed," he said.

"Right," I answered with as much conviction as I could muster. I felt like we were walking a tightrope over a chasm of insanity.

So, two days after we landed in Costa Rica, Philip and I were sitting in the waiting room of a dental clinic in well-to-do Escazú, a suburb of the capital city of San José.

"It might even be this need for dental work that's caused these latest health problems. Dental infections can affect the whole body, poison the whole system," Philip said with a characteristic swing into optimism.

Sitting in that dental clinic, we were both wildly hoping this to be so, hoping it would explain everything that had inexplicably gone so wrong with his health in the past two weeks.

Following an exam that was constantly interrupted by Philip's now-irrepressible cough, however, the dentist said he would delay work on Philip's teeth. He suggested Philip rest for a week and then come back, asserting that it was unwise to use anesthesia when Philip was in such a weakened condition.

"After one week resting, if stronger, then I try one extraction and we see how goes, sí?" the dentist proposed. "You have blood work at local clinic," he added, not knowing who he was advising. "This give information for what wrong with health."

"Could it be dental decay that's making Philip this sick?" I asked. "You know, maybe it's an infection that's spread to his body?"

"No, not dental problems cause Señor Heiman's health crisis," he answered.

So much for that, I thought, staring disconsolately at Philip and our collapsed house of cards.

Back at our Airbnb, Philip, not surprisingly, rejected the blood work idea.

"What am I going to do with a diagnosis?" he said through a coughing fit. "Why do I need a name for what's wrong? I'm not going to a hospital, not having chemotherapy, not getting caught in the conventional medical model."

"But maybe a simple blood test would tell us what's going on, tell us if we need to be more worried, or better yet, that it's something—"

"What will I do with that?" he interrupted. "Am I suddenly going to cave in to the world of conventional medicine and treatments? No. Am I going to change my diet? Start eating meat and potatoes?"

The last question was purely sarcastic, as though eating meat and potatoes was as outlandish and offensive as eating raw sewage—which, in fact, it was to him. He ended the conversation with the Native American philosophy he'd always treasured. "I don't want a label that will suggest disease to my subconscious mind."

I understood. I always understood, mostly agreed. And yet now I was scared and so was he. Was he dying? Did I want to know? Did he? Did he simply need the rest and nutritious food he kept seeking? Was there no one to turn to?

We decided to leave our guesthouse when we realized our hostess had become increasingly uncomfortable with Philip being there.

"I don't want to interfere," she said, proceeding to do exactly that, "but you should get him to a doctor. He should get blood work and a diagnosis."

One week into our stay, I couldn't blame our hostess for getting nervous. Philip was spending all his time shuffling between our bedroom and a daybed in the guest lounge. When I wasn't reading to him, he coughed and dozed, wrapped in blankets in perfectly mild Costa Rican temperatures. How could other guests use this common space? His coughing was nearly constant and disturbingly dramatic, and he hadn't showered since we'd arrived—he was unshaven and disheveled. Why would any host want him lying there making her guesthouse look like a hospital ward?

Hoping to improve his appearance, I urged him into the shower. I helped him get shampooed and soaped up while he clung to me and I struggled to keep him upright.

"I can't hold myself up much longer," he said, soapy from head to foot.

"Just hang on," I said, futilely trying to avoid showering in my clothes.

He was already leaning more and more heavily on me, slippery and wet. I struggled to rinse him off while keeping him upright.

"How can someone so thin be so heavy? You're like a two-ton slippery seal," I teased while inwardly groaning under his weight. He was about to slide to the floor of the shower.

I didn't know whether to laugh or cry, and began to do both when I saw his look of befuddled vulnerability combined with a more familiar puckish amusement. Keeping a brave face on, I joked and even got a few laughs out of him as I got totally soaked. Somehow, I managed to control my rising hysteria.

I knew I'd never get him up if he slipped all the way down, and the thought of having to call our host for help was horrifying. She'd made it quite clear how relieved she was that we were leaving tomorrow, moving to a hotel closer to the dentist, we'd diplomatically told her.

I hated her, and even though I understood where she was coming from (a dead man in your guesthouse shower is not exactly good for business), I hated her even more. In fact, it was probably my red-hot anger that gave me the strength to keep Philip upright and get him rinsed, dried, and back on his bed, where we both collapsed.

Each time someone from the outside saw what Philip and I were blind to, with each well-intended recommendation (or interference, as Philip called it) to get a medical diagnosis, I became more dismayed. The dentist, our Airbnb host, friends back home—everyone talked to me, not to him.

"He's no longer rational . . . he's too ill to make wise decisions. You're the one who has to take control and act," they insisted.

Are they right? What exactly am I supposed to do? Put Philip in a burlap bag and drag him down the street to a doctor? I asked this inwardly, and eventually, aloud.

I'd stood by Philip and honored his choices for as long as we'd been together. Why would I—how could I—change now, even in the face of him possibly dying? I was terrified: there we were, on our own, far from home (whatever that meant anymore), and I was watching Philip grow more debilitated by the day. I would've given my own health in exchange for someone Philip would trust to really help him. But who?

20

What to Do in Escazú?

We moved to a hotel the next morning. Waiting in the hotel courtyard for our room to be readied, we listened to the roosters while sitting on our suitcases in a spot that ought to have had lounge chairs, fountains, and tropical birds and plants, but was, in fact, a parking lot and junk depository for the hotel. Philip started talking about leaving the dental work not for a week, but for six months.

"If the dentist says I should rest, why don't we head out for Panama? It's not that far. We can get there by bus in a few hours."

Just before leaving for Costa Rica, we'd read about a small highland town in Panama called El Valle. Grasping at straws, he was suddenly proposing this as the answer to our predicament.

"Panama's even better than Costa Rica," he said. "The guidebooks say El Valle isn't *too* remote, but is still peaceful. In the hills with lots of farms. Organic fruit. Remember? There's a market every day!" he reminded me. "And there's a large expat community, so that means English is spoken. It's also where Panamanians go on retreat—that must mean something good. And Panama has a lower cost of living than Costa Rica."

His eyes were bright with enthusiasm (or delirium), his energy up. If I agreed, he'd head for the bus station right then and there. Had he gone crazy altogether? I didn't know whether to laugh, scream, or cry. My head threatened to split open. My heart was racing; the cool early morning air had turned stifling and oppressive. We had to get out of the sun.

With Philip propped up against a pathetic palm tree, perched precariously on his suitcase, a rooster crowed and called me back to sanity.

"Are we really going to travel to Panama when you can barely walk to the bus stop?" I asked. "Do you think I can hold you up while carrying two suitcases, two backpacks, and a laptop in my eight arms?"

Putting this to him was like pulling the plug from his last vestiges of energy. But what could I do?

Shrugging, he handed the predicament back to me. "Well, where are we going to stay until I get well enough to go back to the dentist? You know it's going to take more than a week. We can't afford to keep staying in hotels."

Just then, a maid came out to tell us that we could move into our room. I helped Philip into the hotel and sat him down on the bed. Then I went to the front desk to handle the payment.

I met the hotel owner, and within minutes I could hardly believe where the conversation had gone.

"What wrong with husband?" he asked, and quickly called me crazy for not forcing Philip to a lab for testing and a diagnosis. "Yes," he replied to my burlap bag response, "dragging in bag, if necessary."

Where do people get off being so interfering? I thought.

When I got back to the room, I was glad it was shadowy so Philip couldn't see my burning cheeks. I was frustrated, angry, and frightened. He'd already collapsed on the bed, so I suggested a nap. He fell into heavy breathing within minutes.

I, on the other hand, was so agitated that I couldn't sit still. I paced the room, racking my brain and calling on every ounce of patience, courage, and inner resourcefulness I could summon.

Were we supposed to be learning something grand from this? How had we put ourselves into such a desperate situation? Teetering on the brink of despair while feeling I needed to maintain a hopeful face for Philip, I coached myself to breathe.

When had I become competent?

The responsibility for making wise decisions had suddenly fallen entirely in my lap. As unwise as we'd often appeared to others, in our little universe of two, we'd always made decisions together. I looked to him for strength and security, strange as that may sound. Now, however, I had to be the grown-up, had to grow up . . . right now.

Up against a very thick wall, discouraged, disheartened, stomach churning, tears brimming, I quietly let myself out of the room to try to clear my mind and ease my heart before Philip woke.

Sometimes an idea sleeps, incubates, and then, thankfully, emerges just when it's most needed—offering new clarity and resource. Philip, sitting up from his nap an hour later, remembered Richard Longman and his wellness and fasting center. Longman was known for his work with Natural Hygiene.

"The Highlands Retreat Center is here in Costa Rica! Why didn't I think of it sooner?" he asked.

"Well, we weren't this desperate," I said. "It's a good idea, I think. But you're already so thin . . . do you think fasting is feasible? I'd be afraid for you to fast, wouldn't you?"

"I don't know. Yeah. Maybe. But Richard knows so much about health and healing. Maybe he would just talk to me and give me some ideas."

Though not a medical doctor, Longman—in his many YouTube videos—had always struck both of us as intelligent, informed, humane, and committed to Natural Hygiene. He also supported the all-natural, raw, vegan diet we'd practiced for the past nine years. His holistic philosophy went beyond diet to include the basic principles for a simple, healthy way of living lightly on the earth.

One of those primary principles was fasting. Natural Hygiene recommends fasting as the first step to clearing the body of toxins so it can begin to heal itself. Richard had supervised fasts for thousands of people over the past twenty years.

"He won't insist on testing, diagnoses, doctors, or a steak dinner," Philip said. "He won't freak out about my weight. He won't freak out at all, actually, because he sees what we call illness as the body's call for help and healing . . . not as a dreaded affliction. He's healed himself and has been a part of the healing of so many others." He was enthusiastic now.

"Okay," I said, ready to jump on anything he was open to trying. "Let's find him." I opened my laptop and quickly found his website and a phone number. While I was dialing, Philip had a coughing attack and, falling back on the bed exhausted, asked me to do the talking.

Richard was available, and I explained our situation. He listened, asked questions, and then described what he could and could not do, what he would and would not promise.

"There's no question that Philip is ill," he said. "Of course, I can't know what's possible until I see him, but if you both feel like you're at the end of the road, he's got nothing to lose and possibly much to gain by fasting."

"But we're afraid that he's already too thin to fast—104 pounds, and he's five eleven," I said.

"You'd be surprised. It's safe and beneficial for people to lose much more weight than we imagine. I've fasted men down to seventy pounds and seen incredible healing of all kinds of conditions."

"Well, if you think it's worth a try . . ."

"Listen, Joan. I'm not promising a cure," he said. "It would be unethical and unkind for me to make promises. I'm just saying that it sounds like Philip's in need of something soon, and something radical. If he doesn't trust conventional medicine, then why not come here?"

There was one room left for the four-week session that had just begun at the center. With Philip nodding in the affirmative from the bed, where he'd listened to my side of the conversation, the decision was made. A driver would come for us in the morning and take us the four-and-a-half hours into the mountains. While most people in the program fasted for twenty-one days, Philip would probably do a shortened, ten- to twelve-day fast.

And that was that.

Even though we wondered if he wasn't already much too thin to fast, anytime Philip tried to eat anything, the horrible coughing intensified, his intestines objected, and his energy plummeted dramatically. So, maybe a fast was what his body was asking for. Proponents of fasting explain that 50 percent of our energy goes to digesting food, so if we fast, all the energy goes to healing. If we "get out of the way" (via fasting and resting), they say, the wisdom of the body takes over and we begin to replenish depleted reserves.

After years of failed medical treatments, Richard had healed his own debilitating intestinal diseases via fasting twenty-five years ago. He had continued to experience excellent health, and started helping others with what he called the "optimal diet" (raw, fruitarian, and often including meals consisting of just one item) combined with lifestyle changes related to sleep, movement, meditation, hydration, sunlight, healthy communication, and honest relationships. He successfully treated people with heart disease, high blood pressure, diabetes, eczema, psoriasis, digestive disorders, depression, anxiety, drug and alcohol problems, and more. Why couldn't he help Philip?

I described the location of the Highlands Retreat Center to Philip as I explored the website further.

"It looks beautiful. It says it's in a remote and peaceful setting in the northeast highlands of Costa Rica, not far from the Pacific coast."

"Yeah . . . what else?" Philip asked.

"Well, it'll give us the chance to be in the Costa Rica most people come here for . . . not the polluted city of San José with its graffiti, overcrowded suburbs, strip malls, and dental clinics."

"Right." He smiled.

"And it says the center's focus is on providing a place of peace, rest, and beauty where people can heal—something we haven't found in all our searching. It says rest is as important as fasting. That should mean quiet, eh?"

"Yeah. But do you think there'll be a lot of group stuff? I don't want to be in some kind of New Age community right now."

"I think you can choose what you want to do. After all, we're paying to be there."

I didn't trust that Philip wouldn't change his mind by morning, so I focused on the good points, repeating that Richard understood and agreed with Philip's resistance to conventional medicine.

"What a relief to be with a person you can trust to guide you through ten to twelve days of healing," I said.

"Yeah." He squeezed my hand as I curled up next to him. "And you? Do you trust him?" he asked.

"Yes, I think so. He sounded intelligent and kind."

"Imagine being with other people who won't think we're weirdos. People who don't run to doctors every time they're a little sick," he said.

A little sick? I thought.

I was already breathing more deeply at the promise of being supported and assisted, and, as Philip said, being with like-minded people who wouldn't call me crazy or accuse me of negligence. I wouldn't have to shoulder this nightmare on my own. Richard had invited me to rest, learn, eat simply and healthfully, and, of course, go on supporting Philip. I already felt as though a heavy weight had lifted from my shoulders.

After a while, stillness settled over the room. Even the beds and chairs seemed to understand that something good had finally been given. We lay nose to nose, looking into each other's eyes as we both digested this new turn of events. A shared smile rose, warm and golden, moving up from frightened, weary hearts, shining through grateful tears. He turned and I curled around him, spooning in our favored cuddling position. We both sank gently, gratefully, into the first peaceful sleep we'd had in weeks.

21

Now, We Just Have to Get There

Getting to the retreat center was an odyssey—mostly mountain driving for over four hours. The first thirty minutes were smooth sailing on a multilane highway, but from there on, we wound through mountains, valleys, jungles, and tiny villages on two-lane roads, often slowed by trucks and the long lines of traffic that couldn't pass them. Our driver, Maximillian—a man in his sixties with kind, chocolate-colored eyes—spoke next to no English, but his compassion and my little bit of Spanish were what we had to get us through.

"¿El servicio?" he offered after the first hour. *Los servicios* are public bathrooms. On this road, they were third-world experiences at roadside cafés or market stands where we paid dark-eyed, life-worn, unsmiling women for a few sheets of toilet paper and the permission to take said toilet paper into structures where I wanted neither to sit, stand, nor breathe.

Meeting oneself in situations like these is revealing. I've never been especially rugged (a three-month cross-country camping trip in a Volkswagen station wagon with a college boyfriend and a 120-pound dog seemed to cure me of roughing it for the rest of this life). However, I'm not a princess either—I've stayed in many less-than-Ramada-like motels, lived in roach-infested apartments on the seedier sides of Denver, and so on. But somehow, making our way through corrugated iron and scrap structures to squat gingerly over toilets, finding our way back out of these cobbled-together tin shacks and wooden sheds filled with so much stuff I couldn't see what I was seeing was disquieting, disorienting.

The chaos in the buildings and the resignation in the people conflicted starkly with my first-world sense of roadside rest stops. We were suddenly in a developing-world country very far from the tropical paradise described in our Lonely Planet guidebook. The combination of not understanding what people were saying and my ever-present fear for Philip—who held onto my shoulder as we threaded our way through mazes of stuff in shadowy buildings—was quickly undermining my confidence. Perhaps in another time I would have seen the "colorful adventure" side of these admittedly insignificant moments, but worrying about how Philip was managing in his toilet stall, swatting at flies in mine, and wondering what diseases, snakes, or spiders were about to pounce, I felt an unnerving sense of the ground underfoot being a lot less solid than I liked.

Should it take so little to unhinge me? I thought.

These small moments revealed just how thin the layers of my constructed, civilized certitudes were—a humbling and disturbing awareness. Suddenly, what had seemed like a great plan while sitting comfortably in our clean hotel room in suburban Escazú had me shaky. I wished for magical transport back to familiarity, even to our much complained about, noisy and aromatic apartment behind the fried chicken café in Fort Collins, or, for that matter, to any apartment in any U.S. town. However, there was no turning back; Max stood smiling, patiently waiting for us to get back in the car.

Farther down the road, Max pulled over again, this time at an incredibly colorful row of thatch-covered fruit stands—probably ten on each side of the road. At any other time, my fruitarian partner would have thought he'd gone to heaven.

"Fruta," Max announced.

Our eyes took in the abundance of colors, textures, sizes, and shapes. My nose twitched at the scents of sweet mangos and ripe melons. As we approached the stand, I was puzzled by a loud humming sound. A few steps closer revealed hundreds of bees swarming around enormous, ambrosial pyramids of golden pineapples. We stood in front of cornucopian piles of mamey sapotes and sapodillas, bright-orange papayas and persimmons, soursops, huge stalks of red, green, and yellow bananas and plantains, green and golden guavas, fuchsia dragon fruits, and still more. Even though Philip felt queasy, his eyes landed on the mameys. Much to the annoyance of the *vendedor de frutas* who obviously expected a bigger sale from the gringos, we bought two small mameys and nothing more.

Back on the road, Philip halved his mamey lengthwise with a paring knife. We admired the long, shiny black seed nestled in the dense orange flesh of the fruit. The taste of mamey is a heavenly cross between pumpkin and yam sweetened with maple syrup. However, after eating less than half, Philip's cough exploded with frightening intensity. We were finally and irrefutably convinced that, for whatever reason, his body was rejecting food. The horrible, acrid odor of the cough was so off-putting and pervasive that Max opened his window for relief.

"Lo siento, Max," Philip apologized.

"No hay problema, Señor Felipe." But when Max's eyes met mine in the rearview mirror, my eyes pricked with tears at the pity and concern I saw reflected there. The remainder of the uneaten mamey was dropped back into its bag.

The final forty-five minutes of the trip took us onto rough dirt roads, passing through forests interspersed with emerald-green pastures. Tiny hamlets of five to ten small dwellings and occasionally a small *tienda* (shop) would have looked poorer and more desolate if not for the effusion of fuchsia and bougainvillea that poured over walls and rooftops in rivers of crimson and white blossoms. As we drove on, shanties and shacks made of corrugated iron, as well as some more "affluent" cement-block houses, could be glimpsed through the flowers and dense foliage. Peering more closely, we puzzled at how every building was covered in barbed wire and roofed with razor wire. Each one its own little fortress.

"In the middle of jungles, in these tiny, rural settlements hours from the city—why barbed wire? Why this fear?" Philip asked.

The contrast between the innocence of the natural world and this seeming paranoia (or was it necessity?) was disturbing and depressing. I was frustrated not to have enough Spanish to question Max about it.

We passed immense fields grazed by horses and white, humpbacked Brahma cows. There were banana and coffee plantations, teeming rivers, waterfalls, and trees abundant with mangos. Small brown monkeys crossed above the roads, using the power lines as bridges (or trapeze wires). Taking it upon himself to be our personal ambassador to his remarkable country, Max proudly pointed out the sights.

Enchanting as it was, by this point, the trip had become interminable. Philip's eyes were shut as we bumped along at a snail's pace with Max trying not to jostle him too much. We created clouds of dust, both inside and outside the car, and swerved regularly to avoid enormous potholes, stray dogs, goats, and people piled on horses, donkeys, and scooters. Mechanical and animal vehicles were laden with every kind of goods and people—from families with as many as four small, doe-eyed children squeezed between father and mother, to building materials and burlap sacks stuffed with rice, beans, fruits, and vegetables.

At one point, a scooter laden with bags and people bumped too hard over a rut in the road; Max drove carefully around the man and his family as they alighted to gather up oranges that rolled and scattered in all directions. Even this temporary disaster was lightened by the laughter and shouts of the children and adults.

"Are we ever going to get there?" Philip asked plaintively.

"Soon . . . surely, soon," I answered.

I made reassuring noises, held his hand tighter, straightened him up from the slouch he was too weak not to slip into, and moved nearer so he could lean more heavily against me. He was exhausted, face colorless, hands icy on this warm and sunny tropical afternoon. Looking down, I saw with horror that his bare feet and ankles, sandals kicked off hours back, were swollen to twice their size.

Meanwhile, my mind raced between fears. We were traveling farther and farther from "civilization." I wondered what we'd find when we finally arrived. I suddenly remembered waking eye-to-eye with a black, hairy spider the size of a silver dollar on the wall directly above my pillow in a *cabina* in Guatemala years back. Clouds of ravenous mosquitos and phalanxes of biting black army ants penetrated my memory.

Worst, though, were my endless speculations regarding what in the world was wrong with Philip. Thoughts and fears grumbled through my head, echoing the rumbling of the howler monkeys that growled with lion-like roars from their treetop perches. *Choose a fear*, I chided myself.

"When will we be there?" Philip asked again with a whimper.

22

Relief and Release

After hours of driving, we finally arrived at the Highlands Retreat Center. The car door opened, and a welcoming hand reached in to take mine. Stepping out, I was gently drawn into an embracing hug that smelled like sunshine and felt like home.

"You're here. It's okay. You're okay," Richard Longman said.

Wondering why he was offering such heartfelt sympathy, it took me a moment to realize I was sobbing, dripping tears of relief and release onto his sun-warmed T-shirt. His arms offered solid support for the first time in more than a month. Richard's voice was warm, filled with care and reassurance. After so much that had been foreign on this endless, anxiety-ridden journey and the past long month of holding Philip together, hearing my native tongue spoken in the well-known cadence of an Eastern accent was like coming home. Hungry for comfort and strength, I leaned into this fellow countryman—a stranger who was instantly familiar. When he gently released me and moved to help Philip out of the car, two small, smiling women took my bags and my arm, leading me gently toward the building.

"Hey, Philip. Long, crazy journey, eh?" I heard Richard say as he pulled Philip to him in another welcoming hug. He held Philip around the waist and gently walked with him, nearly carrying him. His voice was comforting and reassuring.

"It seemed to go on forever," Philip answered. "Glad to be here. So tired."

"Your room's ready. It's right through here. We'll have you lying down and resting in no time."

We passed through a large indoor/outdoor room cooled by ceiling fans. People quietly lounged on couches. A few rose and took my hand, greeting me with kind, welcoming smiles. The room opened on two sides to the surrounding landscape, and the cool, deep shade felt heavenly after the long, glaring, and dusty journey. My shoulders relaxed, sinking down from the tension I hadn't known I'd been carrying. Tropical plants, hammocks, and pillow-softened chairs and couches created a sense of ease. A glimpse of glittering turquoise at the far end of the room came from a pool glinting in the afternoon sun, drenching my thirsty eyes. We walked as in a soft dream, everything hushed and tranquil.

We were ushered into our room by what seemed like a flock of small, graceful birds fluttering around us—women with liquid eyes, glossy dark hair, and sweet smiles. They pointed out extra towels and blankets and showed me how to operate the strange shower mechanism. Pointing and miming, we all giggled when we got a sudden cooling spray of water on our upturned faces. Though playful and childlike, I sensed a strength and confidence to be relied upon. Relief washed over me as I saw Richard gently lowering and laying Philip back on the pillows of a bed covered in clean white sheets and blankets. At long last, care for him was to be shared.

A few minutes later, alone and looking around our room, Philip and I quietly admitted to some disappointment that ours was the only guest room that wasn't a separate cabina. Then we remembered that the center was full, this was the only vacant space, and we'd been taken in at the last minute with no reservations.

"Richard said this room was specially designed for people who need easy access to that main meeting room we just walked through," I explained.

"Why do we need easy access?" Philip asked as he lay collapsed on his bed.

The room was clean, simple, rustic. Plants, wood furniture, and terra-cotta tile floors complemented the white of the bedding and touches of primary colors in the curtains and blankets. If not for the fact that the windows looked into the main room rather than outdoors, it was lovely. But we were disconcerted to have no direct daylight and very little privacy. The windows and door were our only source of air, and these opened into public space. Even closing the curtains left us feeling less than private and inclined to whisper.

I sat down next to Philip, placing my hand on his heart and letting the quiet soothe and surround us. My whole being began to sink into ease. Listening to Philip's breath deepen (he was already slipping into sleep), my ears picked up the sounds of birdsong and an unfamiliar clicking, which I later learned was made by geckos skittering across the ceilings.

Richard returned to explain that Philip's fast had begun with his arrival, and, it would seem, none too soon. His most recent coughing bout had fully exhausted him. He seemed too done in to be frightened—frightened of how poorly he felt, frightened of being out of control, frightened of facing days on end without food. Those were my fears at that moment, but he was just relieved to be out of the car, off dusty roads, and lying down in cool, shaded peace.

He was surrendering to a level of helplessness I'd never seen in him before. I didn't know that I liked it.

The instructions for Philip's fasting days were simple. Rest as much as possible, speak and socialize very little. Drink two to three liters of pure springwater per day, sit for a little while in the gentle morning sun, watch the many-colored birds that swooped and skimmed the pool in search of insects, listen to lectures (from his bed if he preferred, since Richard's voice could easily be heard through our open door and windows), meditate, sleep between sundown and sunrise, and fast. A do-nothing, be-still prescription.

"A human being—not a human doing—prescription," I said.

He smiled.

The day after our arrival, Philip's vital signs were measured and recorded: weight, blood pressure, temperature, body mass, muscle mass, body fat, hydration, and blood sugar levels. The circumferences of his arms, waist, and legs were measured and written into the record. We were both shocked to learn that he weighed ninety pounds. Two weeks earlier, with the confounded chiropractor in Fort Collins, his 104-pound weight had been alarming. But now he'd lost fourteen more pounds in as many days. Richard's eyes took in Philip's body, quickly landing on the swollen feet and ankles. His hands probed gently, his face expressing concern.

"How long has this been like this?"

"There's been a little swelling in the past weeks, but this is the first time it's been so bad. Wearing sandals is probably impossible," I said.

"Going barefoot here is a good, grounding thing to do," Richard said, smiling down at his own bare feet. "We may shorten the fast to seven or eight days, instead of the ten to twelve days I initially proposed. That may be all that's safe. But we'll play it by ear, see how it goes day to day."

This willingness to let Philip fast, even at this unbelievably low weight, was surely a testament to Richard's unwavering trust and belief in fasting as an effective healing practice. Even in this admittedly dire situation, he still believed it was the best thing to do. He'd been coaching people regarding health since 1987 and had been supervising fasts since 1993. I trusted him to know what he was doing. And, more importantly, Philip trusted him implicitly.

"Philip, you should be able to work your way back to health first via fasting and then by resuming a diet even simpler than the one you've lived with for the past nine years," Richard said. "Right now, you just need to rest and treat your body, mind, and spirit with great care and respect."

"It seems that anything I eat goes wrong," Philip said.

"Well, that's a clear message from your body," Richard explained. "If half our energy goes to digestion, when we stop eating for an extended time, all the energy goes to healing. That's what you need right now."

"Well," I said, "Let the healing begin."

23

A Place of Retreat

"Holy cow. . . . It's like a huge marching band drumming and parading on our heads!" Philip said in the middle of our second night.

"I thought the idea was peace and quiet," I said and dove back under my pillow.

Wind roared and rushed through trees; thatch-covered metal roofs clattered as though horses were stampeding across them. The wind was, at times, so fierce and furious that I feared trees, roofs, and possibly even whole buildings would blow down. Flowering bushes, palm trees, and all the thick, rubbery leaves just outside the open non-walls of the main room added their clamor to the tumult and cacophony as the wind battered and beat relentlessly throughout our first nights. Complaints issued from bleary-eyed guests who'd also been disturbed in the night by the rattling din, the rubbing and swooshing of enormous banana-plant leaves, and the clanging, clattering, and crashing on the roofs.

"This is a seasonal phenomenon. It will pass in a few days," Richard assured us all. And thankfully, it did.

Following the windy season, the rainy season meant sun all morning, torrential downpours between 2 and 4 P.M., and the sun returning around 4:30 to light up the day again until sunset. As the sky shifted from dark, silvery gray back to brilliant azure blue with the return of the sun, we all oohed and aahed at the single and double rainbows.

Daylight this close to the equator was from approximately 6 A.M. to 6 P.M. with very little variation. Sun and heat got increasingly intense between mid-morning and late afternoon. We sweated even while sitting still in the shade. When I realized we were this warm in December, having left the frigid temperatures and piles of snow behind in Colorado, I was all the more grateful to be here, even with the wind. Nights kindly cooled down to perfect comfort, allowing us to curl up under light blankets.

Ebony night skies displayed a phantasmagoria of stars. The constellations and planets were more brilliant and abundant than any I'd seen since that astounding night in the Rockies—now a lifetime ago. Full-moon nights were so bright that it was easy to walk outside without a flashlight, even when all the lights were out.

Glass pitchers were placed conveniently on tables all around the main room so guests could easily refill their glasses without having to leave their couches. Water was the only substance they took for twenty-one days, and they took a lot of it. Philip and I quickly grew accustomed to, and soothed by, the sound of water pouring into glass. It became a constant and comforting base note to the days, and in the hush of the afternoon, I could even hear the guests sipping. I joined in, regularly topping up Philip's glass and sipping from my own.

There were two resident cats at the center—a black male, Diablo, and a white female, Blanquita. Diablo yowled and caterwauled in the early morning until I got up and let him into our room, whereupon he'd curl up against Philip's legs and purr himself to sleep. In my grouchier moments, I clapped my hands and stomped my feet to chase him back out into the dawn light. He was the bigger of the two cats, more robust and glossy, and more aloof, except when he deigned to curl up in someone's lap to be stroked and petted.

Blanquita had a more plaintive cry. She was delicate, tiny, and looked more like a stray waif. She also sought out Philip, curled up next to him on his bed, and followed us out to the lounge chairs to sit in his lap by the pool.

"What's so cat-attractive about me?" he asked.

"Cats often seek out those who need healing," one of the guests answered.

They've certainly found their mark, I thought.

These two feline members of the community were half wild, half tame. When the morning staff ladies arrived, they wound themselves sinuously around legs, yowling urgent needs for breakfast. During the heat of the day, they stretched out on the cool tile floors, sleeping off nighttime adventures. In the dark of night, pupils dilated, bodies tensed, they hunted moths, geckos, mice, small snakes, and anything else that moved.

The two provided moments of hilarity. Moving from languorous lounging to sudden, inexplicable madness, they chased each other, careening wildly around the large meeting room, leaping over couches, streaking up poles and over tables, furiously wrestling in black-and-white flurries of kicks, bites, and howls. In calmer moments, and so endearing to watch, they assiduously licked and groomed each other with the deliberate concentration of two devoted lovers.

Outside, green parrots squawked raucously as flocks flew in formation over the grounds. Little birds I couldn't name—brilliantly colored flowers on wings, flashes of metallic blue, red, yellow, orange, and silver—flitted in the sunlight, each fluting a distinctive song. Mourning doves cooed and fluttered into the trees just outside our bathroom window. An occasional owl gave its archetypal hoot in the night, sounding either eerie or soothing depending on my mood and Philip's condition. Hummingbirds—tiny jewels of color—seemed to hold still as they hovered to sip nectar, when in fact, as I was told, their wings flapped up to seventy times per second.

Gardeners and workers moved slowly and rhythmically across the grounds during the day, their feet crunching across gravel paths that led between the cabins and the main room. The men were mostly short, dark, and agile. Working methodically, they built new cabins, repaired thatch, made sure the water tank was full and the pump operating. Constantly digging, planting, and tending the permaculture gardens, they filled baskets with an abundance of mangos, bananas, avocados, and tomatoes and delivered them to the kitchen. Their deep voices, rich and reassuring, sometimes sang, occasionally rose to meet a crisis or need for cooperation as the men would join to lift and carry the heavy sawn tree trunks used for construction.

Over time, we smiled or nodded in greeting, but an unspoken, agreed-upon distance of respect and privacy was maintained. I began experimenting with my elementary Spanish. "Buenos días, señor. ¿Qué tal?"

To which I received a good-humored lifting of a straw hat and the flash of a gold tooth in a white smile. "Bien, señora. ¿Y cómo estás?"

It was a comfort to have them about, and all the more so when, a few days into our stay, Philip fell, and neither he nor I could get him up from the ground.

I ran for help.

"Por favor! Es Felipe. Ayúdeme, por favor!" (Please! It's Philip. Help me, please!)

Responding immediately, they ran back with me and effortlessly lifted Philip. One in particular, the handsome husband of one of the sweetly smiling staff women, became our guardian angel, always keeping an eye out for Philip and often appearing exactly when we needed help.

The rhythm of each day started slowly and carried on that way throughout the day, so utterly different from the hectic energy of the city. Moving their brooms in smooth, rhythmic sweeps, swaying gracefully, and working at a leisurely pace with their mops, the staff women returned the main room to order after the night's wind and dust created a disaster area of dirt, leaves, and small branches. This ritual was practiced meditatively every morning; the wind and the havoc it wreaked an accepted part of life.

Each morning, I opened our curtains and door and exchanged greetings with the early shift of staff ladies.

"Buenos días. ¿Cómo estás?" they'd ask.

Following a difficult night, I learned to answer, "No está mal . . . no está genial." (Not bad . . . not good). This got me a sympathetic smile or squeeze.

"¿Cómo está Felipe hoy?" another asked with her compassion-filled, dark eyes. "Que quieres para desayunar?" (What do you want for breakfast?)

To which I learned to reply, "¿Cuál es mejor hoy, sandía, papaya, o mango?" (Which is best today, watermelon, papaya, or mango?) I based my breakfast choices on a carefully considered opinion about which fruit was ripest and sweetest that day.

Each morning, Richard met and greeted his staff with hugs and warm handshakes while listening attentively to needs and suggestions from all. They worked out plans for the day in good-natured tones of cooperation,

Richard implicitly relying on and trusting these young people with the responsibility of a smoothly run operation.

Richard was a constant and reassuring presence, his voice deep, resonant, confident, and moving between serious and playful as he checked in with his staff. He spoke fluent Spanish, but as though it were English—he had no ear for the accent. In fact, when I teased him about this, he said he'd never formally studied Spanish but had picked it up through need, exposure, and a fearless disregard for making mistakes. His only goal? Communication. How different from my careful questioning and checking with my patient staff-lady teachers, looking up words in my dictionary and checking for correct grammar and pronunciation. And . . . never getting beyond a rudimentary level.

Richard stopped at our door each morning, offering a warm greeting accompanied by a request to check Philip's vital signs. Temperature and blood pressure were measured every morning; more extensive checks were done weekly. Inquiring each morning into how each of us had slept, how we felt, and what our concerns of the day were, he listened and responded solicitously.

After his second night, Philip complained of the bed. "It's so hard, and I'm so bony."

Richard rubbed his closely shorn head, thought for a minute, and then said, "How about I get you a mattress pad? I'll search around for a piece of memory foam."

Philip, still lying in his too-hard bed, looked up with gratitude and nodded his agreement. By the time we returned to the room later that morning, his now-more-comfortable bed had been made.

Richard listened, soothed, advised, and encouraged; a comforting cross between life coach, philosopher, healer, and comedian. He was an endless and reassuring source of optimism without sugarcoating the struggles ahead. Within just a few days, the three of us developed an ease of warm humor and genial communication that felt natural to such an intimate situation.

Emerging from the shower each morning, towel-drying my hair and pulling on a T-shirt, I'd find him lounging comfortably on my bed, talking and often laughing with Philip. He told us his stories, as well as his dreams for the future of the retreat center and the extended utopian community he hoped to establish. His challenges and adventures—past and present—were inspiring and often hilarious. Laughter came easily, but so did serious attention and care for Philip's day-to-day condition and needs. Philip and I both felt we'd fortuitously landed in the hands of a competent and trustworthy healer and brother.

We were amazed at the depth and breadth of his knowledge related to food, nutrition and diet, permaculture, movement, addiction, psychology, secular spirituality, and communication. Richard's tendency to use humor to maintain balance and perspective was a wonderful antidote to the serious conditions people brought to the center. He was proof of how healthy and whole a person could be; he was stronger and more flexible than most of the guests, many of whom were twenty years younger than him. Strong, vibrant, vital, and intensely curious and alive, he was an inspiration to all of us.

While Philip was fasting, he actually felt better than he had in a month or more. It seemed the fasting theory was right. Without spending energy to digest food, the intrinsic healing capacity of his body was helping to lessen the cough, if not fully eliminating it yet. We grew hopeful. By the second day of fasting, he was no longer hungry and spent long periods resting. We walked slowly out to the pool in the early morning and again in late afternoon. Sitting in lounge chairs and shaded under palm trees, we watched hawks catching rides, floating on wind currents. Right next to us, swallows swooped and dipped into the clear blue water of the pool.

We kept our eyes out for the resident iguana couple, who routinely emerged from the space they'd made home under the pool. These two mini-dinosaurs slowly positioned themselves for a daily sunbath and barely moved unless one of the cats appeared, in which case, they would suddenly skedaddle with remarkable speed and agility. Later in our stay, we were tickled to witness the emergence of a new member of the family. Even iguana babies are cute.

Guests moved without hurry from seat to hammock, couch to poolside, their bare feet whispering over the tile floors. In the first week of their fasts, energy was low, and they, like the iguanas, were disinclined to move or talk more than necessary. They dropped into lounge chairs in the early morning sun, moved into the shade as the day and heat progressed, napped in hammocks, fell asleep with books unopened, wrote briefly in journals until heads nodded and pens fell to the floor unheeded. It was like being in Sleeping Beauty's castle where everyone had fallen under a spell of calm repose. The overall mood was mellow and quieted, perfect peace.

There were sixteen guests in addition to us, an intriguing group from all over the world. I counted ten countries: Germany, England, Austria, Finland, Norway, France, the Ukraine, the Dominican Republic, Canada, and the U.S. Philip and I were by far the oldest—even Richard, at fifty-two, was ten years my junior. The guests ranged in age from nineteen to about thirty-five. The only times we all came together were at 11 A.M. for Richard's daily lectures and in the evenings for meditations, poetry readings, music, films, and quiet conversation.

During the question and answer sessions that followed the lectures, they shared little bits of who they were and why they'd come so far to pay so much not to eat. They represented a variety of ailments, including digestive disorders like irritable bowel syndrome, colitis, and ileitis. Others spoke of autoimmune struggles like eczema, psoriasis, asthma, chronic fatigue, and fibromyalgia. More serious ailments were also represented: heart conditions, diabetes, high blood pressure, even cystic fibrosis. Still others had come to detoxify from drug or alcohol abuse, others to find freedom from compulsive and unhealthy eating habits. One nineteen-year-old wanted to restart his life on a better, more life-affirming path and saw cleansing his body of toxins as the way to commence.

As I listened to each person's story of struggle, I was honored and awed to be among these honest and truth-seeking people. When I spoke during morning discussions, whether for Philip—who lay on his bed with the door and windows open so he could participate—or for myself, I felt empathy and authentic goodwill coming toward us.

We were quietly content. Sometimes I read aloud, choosing from the center's large library of books. Occasionally, one or another of the guests pulled up a chair and we spoke in low voices, telling our stories, sharing ailments, and exchanging hopes in moods of warm, slow dreaminess. The feelings of frenzy and fear from the last weeks in Colorado and the week in Escazú quickly melted away; the center's slow pace and the simple daily routines were soothing to body, mind, and soul.

Philip felt more secure than he had in quite a while. Richard was always available; I was always within reach. There was nothing to do other than rest. No hurry. And, best of all, no one disapproving or doubting. What a relief to be among like-minded people, to feel less like crazy, eccentric outsiders than we'd felt in a very long time.

One morning, I found a song on YouTube called "No Frontiers" by Irish singer-songwriter Mary Black. It touched my heart immediately. I brought it to Philip, who'd been hungering for love songs, women's voices, harmony, and acoustic guitar. Lying together in the quiet hush of morning, we felt our way into the music. The lyrics evoked a deep sense of connection that was strong enough to erase fear. Replacing fear at long last, Black sang, was the sense of heaven found in lovers' eyes, a place where barriers of separation fall away.

Our eyes met and filled with tears as we read our love and his struggles with panic into these lyrics. Carried by the music and Mary Black's clear and lovely voice, I felt an aching, nearly heartbreaking love for Philip, as well as an ardent wish that fear might finally lose its grip on him.

24

Worries in Paradise

Some days, Philip slept so deeply that he didn't wake when I entered the room, made noise, or turned on a lamp. I began checking for signs of breathing—a strange, beyond-my-experience experience.

"Is he dying? Soon? Shouldn't I be able to sense, to know?" I asked Richard as we walked around the grounds one afternoon.

"Most of us have romanticized notions about dying and intuition or connection to the people we love," he said. "Philip is certainly weak and depleted, but—"

I began to cry, frightened and exhausted by trying to hold myself together.

Richard slipped a brotherly arm around my shoulders, drew me closer, and provided the safety I needed to let go.

"Honestly, I don't know which way this is going for Philip. The only thing I know is that when you arrived, he was as close to death as I'd want anyone to come."

"I can't seem to take this in," I said. "Will he walk out of here in a week or two and go on to slowly recover? Or is this really the beginning of the end?"

Richard didn't answer quickly, had obviously been wondering himself.

"We can only wait and see. Remember, when we first talked by phone, I told you what I could and couldn't promise. I promise now to do everything I know to do for Philip. The outcome is partly up to him, and, perhaps, mostly in the hands of something larger."

"I'm so unprepared for this," I said, looking up at him through tears.

"Yes, I know. We are—most of us—totally unprepared for this most important event of our lives. Whether it's about our own dying or the dying of the people we love most in all the world." He hugged me again and went on, "But let's talk a little about how we can take care of you."

"I'm not interested in taking care of me," I answered, impatient with concerns for me when Philip was so clearly in need of attention. "Besides, taking care of Philip . . . keeping him alive *is* taking care of me." I paused to cry painfully, feeling as though I was begging Richard to save the man I loved more than my own life. "I think he and I still believe he'll come through this—at least most of the time. But is this just because carrying on with life is familiar, while death is unknown?"

Richard smiled down at me wistfully as we circled back to check on Philip.

He was nearing the end of his first week of fasting, and he now weighed eighty-seven pounds. Richard still thought the fast could go on safely for a few more days. From the Natural Hygiene and fasting perspective, he explained, the longer Philip could maintain the fast (but not move into starvation), the greater his chances were for healing . . . as long as he had what Richard called "reserves."

"As soon as he's at the edge of his reserves, we'll stop the fast. I'll continue checking his vital signs every day. At this point, I think he can go a few more days. But we'll see. The longer he can go, the better."

I looked over at my skin-and-bones husband and prayed Richard was right.

Philip's fast ended after the eleventh day. On the first day of eating, he was given a choice of papaya, mango, coconut water, or watermelon. He chose papaya. I had some too, and it was exquisitely delicious. Unlike the papaya imported into the U.S. that costs a fortune and almost always tastes like nothing, papaya in Costa Rica tastes like a heavenly maple-syrup pudding. He was given a total of ten ounces of fruit divided into four tiny meals throughout the day. That was so little to someone—me—who'd been eating two pounds of fruit at each meal. His plates held silver-dollar-sized bites of fruit. But that was all he wanted.

On the second day, there were five small meals. In the morning, he chose watermelon, hoping there would be less coughing; he'd had an extreme coughing reaction to the papaya. We'd so much hoped the cough was going to be gone after fasting, especially since it had diminished so much during the fast. On day three, he was given four meals, but now the amount was increased to sixteen ounces of fruit at each meal. He tried papaya again for breakfast, but decided to switch to watermelon (which was outrageously sweet) for lunch since he'd coughed for hours after breakfast.

Much of our consciousness and our days now revolved around his food decisions . . . and his body's unhappy reactions to those decisions.

"What is this coughing and endless mucus about?" he asked Richard. "Before we got to Costa Rica, I'd had a dry, hacking cough for years. I guess it's good that I'm eliminating phlegm by coughing it up now, right?"

"But *why* is he producing it, and continuing to produce it now, after fasting?" I asked, unable to hide my exasperation.

"Mucus is one way the body eliminates toxins, and fasting has made this elimination more possible," Richard said. "Once Philip's body gets rid of all the toxins—and he continues drinking a minimum of sixty-four ounces of pure water every day for the next week or so—his body's need to create the mucus should cease. His fat reserves should increase, and then muscle will rebuild. Over the next year, I think Philip will go back up to about 135 pounds."

"Won't that be wonderful!" I exclaimed, looking over at my emaciated man with a hopeful smile.

Philip returned a weak if doubtful smile and whispered, "Yeah. Great."

Physical pain narrows consciousness down to a pinpoint. At the same time, there's an endlessness about it. The bed was too hard again (even with the foam topper). He couldn't sit up in a chair for more than a little while without getting tired. The seat was too hard; he was sitting on bones, after all. Richard cut out foam donuts of different thicknesses and sizes for Philip to sit on. Peeing was constant, waking both of us throughout the nights, and then it became painful.

Coughing continued to exhaust him; we went through rolls of toilet paper and boxes of tissues for all the mucus he spat into them. Each morning, I picked up the snowstorm of tissues he'd flung wildly during the night. They landed everywhere but in the trash can I'd placed—futilely—by his bed. His long, delicate feet were still swollen. The complicated, but apparently not unusual, issue of post-fasting constipation was becoming increasingly troublesome.

In addition, I was quietly falling into fearful thinking about money and what our lack of it meant; trying to breathe and let go, certainly not wanting to add to Philip's distress . . . but falling again and again into anxiety. We had planned to be here for two or three weeks. Richard continued to give us a generously reduced rate. However, we were beginning to see that Philip wouldn't be strong enough to leave for a good while.

So, where was the money to come from? Would I max out all our credit cards? How and when would spending beyond our budget end? Or would it not end? Would I declare bankruptcy? Would I have to get a job now that I'd retired? Who would want a sixty-two-year-old with multiple degrees and experience when they could hire someone younger and pay less? Who would take care of Philip if I had to go back to work? Should we go back to the U.S.? But how could we go back, when we'd left because we couldn't afford to live there on my meager pension and our social security? Where would we go, and how would we afford it?

Thoughts buzzed around my head relentlessly as soon as I awoke.

I considered asking Richard to help me think more clearly about all this. He'd achieved, lost, and re-created his life more than once. He'd lost everything in Panama when the Panamanian government decided to deny his proposal to buy the land and the center he'd been renting (and improving) for seven years. Not only did they deny his proposal, but they claimed the land and confiscated every stick of furniture while Richard was conveniently out of the country on a lecture tour. When it was clear that all was lost, he came to Costa Rica by bus with two hundred dollars and two suitcases. Started over. Created this remarkable place. And in just two years, it was already filled to capacity with guests, booked for the whole year to come.

I sat outside one afternoon, watching four buzzards as they floated on wind currents in a cloudless, bright-blue sky far above my head. The freedom and non-effort of their flight was magnificent . . . inspiring. I wished to join them; they made it look so easy to drift away from worry, fear, and illness. Such horribly ugly birds up close were so lovely in flight—or rather, in float. I should have focused on this positive attribute, but the more probable reason for their flight grabbed me: they were searching, always searching, for death.

25

Misery

Philip was utterly miserable, adding constipation to the list of other complications that hadn't ended with fasting as we'd hoped: coughing, weakness, body aches, and painfully swollen feet. Instead, he'd lost another six pounds.

Richard explained (again) that for some people, it can be very difficult to get the intestines active again at the end of fasting. When you start to eat again after fasting (eating only water-dense foods like the watermelon, mango, papaya, and pineapple and tender leafy greens he was served), the water from those foods will eventually stimulate and support elimination. In the first few days following an extended fast, however, there can be a digestive slowdown as the body's other essential organs absorb the water from these foods first. This means that the intestines may have to wait a few days before the newly eaten food is eliminated, causing bloating and extreme discomfort.

"There's no danger. But it's not always easy," Richard said, offering assurance from his twenty-one years of supervising fasts.

"That's an understatement," Philip groaned.

It was now Christmas, and it was all about poop . . . or not being able to. We were up all night with Philip in more pain from intestinal cramping than he could bear. Attempts to get to the toilet, attempts to get off the toilet . . . everything was difficult; everything took more strength than he had.

Who knew getting on or off a toilet takes strength? I thought.

Getting to the toilet became impossible without leaning on me to get there, to get up, to get back to bed. For two fastidious people, this level of intimacy was discomforting. My first attempt to give him an enema was unsuccessful, not to mention humiliating for him and distressing for me.

"At this point, I'm desperate," Philip said. "I've stopped caring about pride or humiliation. All I want is for this pain to end."

As I stood by, helpless, I whispered, "I feel awful."

"Not as awful as me," he said.

It made me think of what my parents must have gone through in my dad's last two years with colon cancer and a colostomy bag. I'm sure my mom was much more confident and capable than me. But how did she feel? And how did he feel? Mortified, I imagined. They were always, as far as I knew, even more private and modest than Philip and me.

We stayed yet another week. Philip couldn't possibly travel, nor could I imagine our being on our own. He was so weak with lack of sleep, coughing, and the endless, painful waves of intestinal cramps. At least he'd begun partially eliminating again, but that too caused pain. Urinating was also causing severe pain . . . pain that took his breath away. What was going on?

His appetite was spoiled by pain. Weakened and not wanting to eat, he was unable to sit up long enough to finish a meal. Each meal was a misery. He stared resentfully at a plate of melon that once would have lit up his face.

"You have to regain your strength," I said, echoing Richard.

"I don't want to eat. Have no room inside for more food that'll only get stuck there," he answered.

"But you must. Don't you see? You need to get stronger if we're ever going to get out of here. And Richard says it's only by eating that you're going to get your intestines working again."

"I don't want to cough all morning thanks to this melon. And I can't hold myself up in this chair long enough to eat it," he said.

"I can read to you while you try just a few bites," I said.

"Please, just let me go back to bed," he begged from his now eighty-four-pound body.

He could barely get from the chair back to the bed. So, I stood in front of him, held him under each armpit, and we counted, "One, two, three." We combined our strength to get him standing.

The bathroom now seemed miles away, far too hard to get to. Richard brought us a urinal and diapers. I was putting diapers on my previously proud, private, and romantic husband! The nights were a constant relay of disasters, discomforts, and disruptions.

So, there was no question of leaving . . . not anytime soon. If only there were some slight improvement to raise his spirits and hopes. If only he would return to eliminating naturally and painlessly (for the sake of his integrity, as well as his body). If only every day and night weren't spent in intestinal pain and coughing. If only he would begin to gain some weight. If only . . . if only . . . if only.

Minutes passed like hours, hours like days, days like weeks.

His face grew gaunt, cheeks fallen in, making him frightfully skeletal. His teeth were now too big for his mouth. His once mellifluous voice and particularly pleasing and articulate speech became garbled, muffled, hard to understand. Richard and I were continually asking, "What?"—which, not surprisingly, frustrated him to no end. The look on his face when he saw—once again—that one or the other of us hadn't understood was heartbreaking.

His feet and ankles went on being swollen with edema. I ended each day, sat up in the middle of most nights, and started most mornings rubbing his feet to relieve the constant aching and pressure—rubbing upward, trying to convince the fluids to move up his stick-skinny legs.

The smell of excrement and urine was omnipresent. I smelled it all the time; it was stuck in my nostrils. Changing diapers, giving enemas, cleaning him, emptying the urinal—I never dreamed of doing these things. Neither of us ever dreamed of his becoming so completely helpless. It was humbling and horrifying, even more so, perhaps, as I watched us adapting to each further move into decline.

26

Spiders and Snakes

With a drinking glass quickly flipped against the wall and a postcard slid deftly between cup and wall, I became an expert at capturing and removing hairy, thick-legged spiders from our room. *I* did this! But it was with fear and loathing.

Center instructions went as follows: a) capture spider in special spider cup provided in each room, b) carry spider outside, c) throw spider back into jungle.

The first time I saw one, I just couldn't; I had to ask one of the staff ladies to capture and remove it. But in just a few short weeks, I was better at it—better at spiders, better at private bodily functions. Better at being afraid.

One afternoon, I was attacked by a weird and fearful fantasy that a spider could hide inside the toilet paper roll in the dark of night, and when I reached to use it, there she'd be, horrifyingly skittling up my arm.

Only hours after this surely paranoid fear surfaced, it manifested. The beam of my flashlight only just caught sight of the wriggling movement of black legs sticking out from and then drawing back into the roll as I reached for it. Precognition? Or the law of negative attraction?

"I can't explain my fear and dread," I told Philip and Richard the morning after. "These innocent creatures have more right to be here than I do."

"But they're harmless," Richard said. "Not poisonous or even inclined to bite."

"Yes, that's all very well, but I can't rationalize the feelings away," I said. "In the middle of the night, I don't think, and I'm not rational."

On another evening, just as Philip and I were about to go bed, Richard rushed in with a camera around his neck and a flashlight in hand. He took hold of my hand.

"Joan, come see the snake!"

With curiosity, fear, and a tiny bit of courage because Richard was in the lead, I took one quick look at Philip. He grinned from his bed and nodded.

"Go . . . go!" he encouraged.

Most of the lights were out, so I watched the ground carefully. "Your snake could have slithered anywhere, but it'll probably be exactly where I step," I muttered.

Laughing, Richard led me to a far corner of the main room. Mostly relieved at seeing nothing but the large potted plant that inhabited this corner, I watched Richard. Undaunted, barefooted, and in shorts (which, I noted, would offer small protection from a snake), he was down on hands and knees, gently tapping at the pot. I gasped when the snake slid out from the other side. Thrilled, Richard managed to snap a few photos before the slinky night visitor circled the pot and found its way back into hiding.

"Well, it wasn't very large," I said, exhaling with relief.

"It's one of the few poisonous snakes in Costa Rica," he said with what seemed to be a bizarre glee. "Those spots and that coloring are the way you identify it."

"Oh . . . well, where will it go now?" I asked in growing trepidation.

"It'll probably find its way back out to the jungle during the night. Here, I'll light your way back to your room. Isn't it amazing to live in all this nature?"

"Hmm . . ." I managed. I was already resolving not to sit on any of the couches tomorrow morning without checking under and behind the pillows first.

Having recounted our adventure to Philip, who was already falling into his first exhausted stupor (if only he would sleep through the night the way he disappeared into the first hour), Richard wished us sweet dreams.

I closed the door and began my routine pre-bed spider patrol. I looked under the beds and up the walls. Sending the ray of the flashlight up and down and around the room, I noticed for the first time that there was a one-inch gap between the door and the floor. Definitely a space a snake could easily slink through. I was horrified. Searching for something solid to block the gap, the only thing I could think of were the extra blankets and towels. Feeling foolish but knowing I'd never sleep otherwise, I stuffed as much material as possible into the gap, all the time wondering how much strength the snake had to push these aside.

Lying stiffly in my bed, I thought, *You can take the girl out of the suburbs, but apparently you can't take the suburbs out of this girl.*

On yet another night, just before lights-out, a sudden clamor of shouts and screams arose from the main room. The few remaining guests who were on their way to bed were suddenly jumping up on tables and chairs.

"It's a tarantula!"

"Quick! Someone, *please*, catch it!" a female voice pleaded, veering toward hysteria.

"Where's my camera?" an excited male voice added to the uproar.

Richard showed up with a large glass, but just before he captured it, I caught a glimpse of the dark, grapefruit-sized creature skiddling across the middle of the room. The glass clinked down on tile, the card was slid beneath.

"Got it!"

"Oh my god," I whispered to no one in particular.

A few days later, I nearly stepped on a two-inch-long scorpion when I sleepily walked barefoot into our bathroom in the middle of the night. It had pincers and a long stand-up tail with a stinger barb at the end of it.

"There's no way I'm going near enough to capture that!" I said. I rushed off to find Richard. Of course, by the time we got back, the creature was no longer where I'd left it.

"I'm sorry, Richard," I said, grabbing his sleeve, "but you're not leaving here until we find it."

"We'll find it, Joan."

We looked behind the toilet, and I shuddered to think of it climbing up behind me. *Here's one more place to check at night,* I moaned inwardly.

We checked under the sink and on the pipes, but no scorpion. Then Richard slowly moved the shower curtain. "Here!" he said as the scorpion fell from the curtain to the floor and sped toward the door. Richard, moving quickly, trapped the creature under yet another glass.

"Got it!" he announced, and carried the monster out into the night jungle.

"Oh my god," I uttered . . . yet again. My next mental note: *Check and shake shower curtain before showering each morning.* I did for the remainder of our stay.

In truth, I wanted to escape—not just from spiders and snakes, but from the tropics entirely. My desire to flee was instinctive, reflexive, powerful. But Philip continued to insist that the temperate year-round climate, the abundance of fruit, and—if we could ever actually move into an apartment here like we'd planned—the lower cost of living all made it the most reasonable place for us to retire.

Unable to come up with an alternative, I resolved to keep pushing this insect, snake, and scorpion fear aside as best I could. *You need to learn to be afraid, and trust that you won't die of fear. Not a bad thing to learn*, I thought. Besides, dealing with Philip's immediate and many struggles had the one (and only one) benefit of distracting most of my attention from my terror of all the creepy crawly things.

27

Patience

One night, after weeks of constantly interrupted sleep, I fell into such a deep early morning nap that Philip couldn't wake me when he called my name. It frightened him so much, he flung his pillow at me. This was the second time this had happened in a week.

I was beyond exhausted. Every night was an endless round of coughing, massaging, and emptying the urinal. After a couple of accidents that soaked him and his bed in the middle of the night, I'd realized it was best if I got up to empty the urinal each time he used it. He was so exhausted that he'd actually fall asleep before replacing the full urinal on the floor. So, we'd agreed he should wake me each time he needed to pee—seven, eight, nine times a night.

His waking me out of the deep sleep I'd finally collapsed into brought up a resentment I hadn't yet felt. I was startled . . . then indignant.

"Sleep and disappearing into it is such bliss—how can you shake me out of it?" I felt grouchy, wronged, ready to weep with frustration.

"I thought you were dead!" he replied. His answer instantly erased my annoyance.

People at the center kept remarking at how patiently I responded to Philip's calls for help throughout the days.

"I'm so in awe of you. I don't think I could ever be so patient," said one young woman.

"It really doesn't feel like being patient," I answered. "It's simply what has to be done, probably similar to what parents of newborns feel. It's the only way I have left to show Philip my love."

The woman looked back at me with moony romanticism that made me laugh. I'd forgotten how old we must have appeared to her, and remembered looking—from my twenty-year-old eyes—at "old people" with a certain condescending affection.

Love—expressed in all the little and big ways of caring for Philip—was really all I had to give him. And the love manifested in acts of caring actually deepened and extended my love. Love given generates more love.

Now that's a lesson I wish I'd learned a lot sooner, I thought.

It was hard to fathom how the smallest setback discouraged, how the tiniest improvement meant so much. What barely looked like improvement from the outside made the difference between hope and despair, between feeling as though he was moving forward or sinking. I was so emotionally fragile, vulnerable, and easily frightened that my reassurances alone were no longer enough; perhaps this was because I was so caught in my fear.

Philip asked for Richard, asked to be told again and again that all was well, that what was happening was still within the range of normal. Thank heaven for Richard—his patience, his faith in healing, his overall optimism.

28

Saturday Night at the Movies

Movie night was held in the main room each Saturday, and the speakers were right outside our windows. What a dreaded weekly nightmare it turned into.

Philip's nerves couldn't stand the noise. Richard suggested the old "if you can't beat 'em, join 'em" idea, but sitting through a movie when he could barely keep awake after 7 P.M. was torment. Sitting up was torture; people were torture; noise was beyond torture.

"How about moving one of the reclining chairs into the dining room?" Richard suggested. "Then you can just rest while Joan reads to you."

We tried it one Saturday evening, but quickly found this equally wretched. Philip's sacrum had been rubbed raw at the base of the spine after months of lying flat on his back because lying on either side brought on more coughing. The tilt of the reclining chair made the pain on his sacrum worse no matter how many pillows I used to soften it.

Then, he had to pee constantly and couldn't do it easily from this kind of chair; he was now entirely dependent on the urinal. *When had he last used a bathroom?* I wondered. Even drinking less than the recommended sixty-four ounces of water left him constantly having to pee; water in . . . water out. By evening, in fifteen- to twenty-minute relays.

His pants got soaked on the first try and had to come off, so there he was, sitting half-naked under the blanket. He would eventually have to get back to the room minus pants, but one problem at a time. Then his bowels filled up, and again, the chair was not a feasible place for the manual technique I'd learned to assist him. (He couldn't eliminate on his own anymore—not in a diaper, no less a toilet.)

Adding to all this, the sounds from the movie, although not nearly as intense as in our room, were nonetheless still quite audible. He grew distressed and disturbed. In his pain and wretchedness, and by this time in the evening when any tidbit of energy he'd had during the day was utterly depleted, all he wanted was to disappear into sleep. Normally, this was the time he fell into a first deep slumber that temporarily covered him in a blanket of hypnogogic fog. Now, too uncomfortable in the chair to slip away, he became increasingly agitated and irrational. *My poor, poor boy.*

On the next movie night, Philip thought we should go stay in one of the guest cabins, out of earshot of the movie. Two kind women welcomed us to use their cabin. Richard was leery of the plan, not sure Philip would be able to walk the distance (a four-minute walk for a healthy person, but farther than Philip had gone in weeks).

Nonetheless, Philip insisted, so off we went—equipped with books, diapers, urinal, and extra pillows. We made our way very slowly but, reaching a slight incline just in front of the cabin, Philip had to stop. We stood in the dark with him leaning heavily on me and both of us trying to breathe in the strength and courage to go the final steps. A nearly unnoticeable incline was a mountain. We finally made it, and he collapsed onto a bed whereupon he fell into his stupor-sleep almost as soon as I began reading. He slept for the next hour and a half.

When the film was over, Philip made one attempt to stand but collapsed back onto the bed. I ran for Richard, who returned with me. He lifted Philip in his arms like a baby and carried him back to his own bed. *How have we come to this?* I thought. *And worse yet, how are we to go on from here?*

I knew we had no right to ask Richard to stop his movie nights or reorganize his program. He chose these films—all in one way or another depicting personal triumphs—to be inspiring for the guests. Yet I couldn't help feeling resentful and wishing for more consideration.

Philip was increasingly edgy, anxious, and utterly dependent most of the time now. Life had narrowed down to little more than pain, bodily functions, and constant attempts to achieve some minimal and temporary ease. *Is there no end in sight?* I wondered. *And what do I mean by an "end"?*

29

Good or Bad?

I'd hardly written anything in our month at the center other than one long letter to my mother to explain more completely what was going on—a letter sent over a week ago and still, my brother emailed, not received. *Why had we put ourselves in such a remote and out-of-the-way . . . out-of-the-world . . . place?* I thought.

It was now mid-January, and caring for Philip had become increasingly demanding. Witnessing his continuing decline, increasingly disheartening. The weekly weigh-in (that he had come to dread) said he was now seventy-eight pounds. He was skeletal, literally nothing but skin and bones.

"He just has to get through this final elimination of all the old, stuck, and toxic fecal matter," Richard said again.

"But he just goes on and on and on eliminating this 'old stuff,'" I said. "It's awful, filled with hard pieces . . . gallstones? Kidney stones? Old, dried fecal matter? When will it ever stop?"

And how will either of us survive my being this intimately involved in such an essentially and formerly private act? I wondered. *Can romance survive this? Self-esteem?*

"When this cleansing is finally complete, Philip will gain weight, the coughing will stop, the urgent and painful urinating will end, strength will build, and health will gradually be restored," Richard continued to reassure us.

We hung on to this hope more desperately every day.

While he'd been fasting the month before, which felt like years ago, life was easier for both of us. He was weak but hopeful, and not so needy—resting, dozing, listening to music and audiobooks throughout the day.

In those days of fasting, I could leave him for an hour to eat my fruit or salad meals peacefully and alone. I sat in the little screened dining room looking out at gardens, banana trees, and the azure-painted sky. Three times a day, I looked forward to these little breaks. As I ate wonderfully sweet plates of fruit, I watched the metallic-blue-and-green hummingbirds attracted to one of the flowering plants just outside the screen. They were so close, I could hear their tiny wings moving faster than I could see. The cats, Blanquita and Diablo, would wander past, intent on cat missions, stalking geckos or mice. The staff, too, would pass by, sometimes nodding or tipping a hat, some carrying jugs of water, others with piles of neatly folded and laundered sheets or towels, all held inside a purposeful-but-calm meditation in motion. I could even take some extra time after eating to sit under the shade of the enormous mango tree. The solitude was heavenly.

But that time had long gone.

Beautiful, loving messages came via email from family after I'd finally written to tell them what was happening. We had an email from Philip's oldest nephew, Phil. We were moved to tears as I read it aloud; he expressed such a depth of love and empathy. He tentatively suggested that in some cases even conventional medicine could help, and offered us his home to stay in if we wanted to come to New York.

But how could I explain Philip's adamant opposition to conventional or even alternative medicine? How would I begin to explain to anyone who stood outside Philip's intractable convictions? I asked Philip this, and he agreed to put it in his own words. He dictated the following note for me to send:

> Dear Phil,
>
> Please, trust that what I am doing here is a wonderful thing for my healing. I believe it is the only thing that may save my life. This place and the director are good for me, and I continue to trust that if I can come through this collapse (physical and emotional), it will be in this way and with Richard Longman's help. I don't believe I can heal in a hospital or even with other alternative approaches.

> Remember when I read to you years ago from D. H. Lawrence? He said, "The wounds to the soul take a long time to heal." Any other healing approach would separate my body from my soul, treat and suppress symptoms, require my taking substances or doing procedures I cannot believe in. In the end, they would leave me further away from my soul than when I started.
>
> It's all so difficult to put this into words, but I wanted to try for you. I hope you understand.
>
> Thank you so much for your loving concern and generosity of spirit.
>
> I love you deeply.
>
> Philip

If only Philip would have shown even the tiniest indication of healing via this radical approach. Even I'd begun (silently) to wonder how he could stay so committed to this one way when every day he continued so debilitated and disheartened.

How does he go on believing this is "good for him" when everything continues to be so bad?

30

Nicholas

Later that month, Nicholas, a twenty-eight-year-old man from France, showed up. He'd come on his own to Costa Rica and hitchhiked to Highlands from a banana plantation somewhere in the south. He'd spent the past month working in exchange for room and board; board, however, meant he'd eaten essentially nothing but bananas for a month.

Thin as a rail, he nonetheless shouldered a heavy pack with ease, was full of vitality and enthusiasm, and expressed childlike delight with his adventures and the kindness of people all along his way. His eyes—huge globes of light—and his laughter filled the room. Philip and I were charmed by his French accent and his vagabond energy.

"I'll bet he's got an interesting tale to tell," Philip said, eager for the company of this hippie Frenchman.

"Well, we're about to hear it," I said as Nicholas approached with an engaging grin.

I pulled over a chair and got him a glass of water. "Welcome, Nicholas."

We soon learned that Nicholas had cystic fibrosis—a hereditary, degenerative disease that used to kill most children before they completed elementary school. There's still no known cure, but treatment has improved so that the projected survival age has increased to around forty.

Richard, having pulled up a chair, explained what he knew about it. Something about a mutation of a gene that results in a buildup of mucus in the lungs, and often in the pancreas as well. Breathing and digestion are severely challenged, ultimately impaired, and finally cause death. (Richard didn't say this last part until Nicholas was elsewhere.)

"Both my parents are doctors," Nicholas said somewhat ruefully. "They've been sending me from one specialist and clinic in France to the next since I was a kid." He was totally fed up, ready to try any alternative he could find. "Cystic fibrosis makes assimilation of food more and more impossible, and that leads to weight loss." He pointed down at himself. "Like *haricot vert*—string bean, oui?"

We laughed along with him and pointed to Philip. "Two string beans," Philip said.

"The doctors fed me a super-high-fat diet. Butter or cream with everything, meat with every meal." Richard and Philip cringed. "So, more and more mucus," Nicholas said.

"That's how the body desperately tries to clear the fat," Richard said.

As a result, Nicholas's entire life had been dominated by incessant, body-wracking coughing and the spitting up of literal cups full of phlegm. And despite having existed on this incredibly high-fat diet, he showed up at Highlands as thin as Philip and wanting to try fasting as a final resort. While Richard wouldn't agree to a twenty-one-day fast (for the same reason he wouldn't allow Philip: not enough bodily reserves for the full fast), they settled on a day-by-day plan with careful monitoring each day.

Sitting with Nicholas by the pool during his first mornings, he was full of energy and dreams of the utopian community he hoped to start. This was despite the death sentence hanging over him—one that, statistically, gave him about a decade to live. He told us stories of his illness. It started in childhood, and his parents blamed him for something that was clearly not his fault. He described countless and futile medications along with their debilitating side effects. These conversations were continually interrupted by his alarming bark-like cough, but he reassured us that he was accustomed to both the cough and the mucus.

"This has been part of my existence for as long as I can remember," he said.

He and Philip shared some dark humor as they compared their coughs and cups of phlegm. We learned to deal with conversations punctuated by coughing.

In the latter days of his fast, Nicholas was so weak that Richard carried him from his cabin to the pool each morning, piggyback style. We became accustomed to the sound of his terrible bark as a new, if less harmonious, addition to the morning chorus of birds and staff ladies going about their chores.

When we sat with him, we enjoyed his wit and keen intelligence. He was convivial, eager to share and listen. An elfin spirit, his heart was wide as the sky and warm as the morning sun.

However, after ending his fast and beginning to eat again, he stayed—chose to stay—more and more alone in his cabin. After a few days, Richard moved Nicholas into his own apartment to be able to care for him more easily—and to mitigate Nicholas's tendency to want to isolate himself.

Nicholas stopped sitting out by the pool in the mornings, and then stopped coming to group meetings and lectures. We still heard him coughing from Richard's apartment but stopped seeing him except very briefly, and then, not at all.

After a few more days, I asked Richard about Nicholas. He grew grave and told me Nicholas was having a very hard time psychologically. He'd become very needy and frightened and refused food or drink.

When Nicholas finally came to use the computer in the office, I was shocked at the change in him. He looked like a fierce desert mystic—eyes wild, long hair matted and flying free of the ponytail he'd kept it in. His face and body were frightfully emaciated, eyes enormous and a little crazed. He looked right through me when I greeted him.

He started telling Richard he wanted food with more fat . . . then, that he wanted to go to a hospital. In his fear, he was reverting to the ways he'd known with his parents.

Richard tried for a day to reason with him, predicting that as soon as he went into a hospital in this state of emaciation, they'd start him back on a high-fat diet and undo all the cleansing from the fast. Richard feared this could kill him—that his organs wouldn't be able to deal with the drastic change back to a high-fat diet. But Nicholas continued to insist, so a ride was arranged for him to leave first thing in the morning.

The night before his planned departure, an hour or so after we'd fallen into a first sleep, we were awakened by an eerie, animal-like howling and then the desperate calling of Richard's name. I was up, out of bed, and at Richard's door before I knew what I was doing, but when I heard Richard's voice responding (Richard had given his bed to Nicholas and had been sleeping in a hammock on his patio for the past few nights), I went back to our room to comfort Philip, who'd panicked in response to the disturbance.

The next morning, the head gardener drove Nicholas to a nearby hospital used largely by expats. Less than a week later, we learned he'd died in the hospital.

Would he have died had he remained at Highlands, stayed calm, and continued to slowly reintroduce and eat the recommended water-dense fruit diet? We'll never know. Was Richard mistaken to allow Nicholas to fast at all? Again, there's no knowing. But whose responsibility is it when an adult man comes and asks to fast? Was Richard responsible even though he'd clearly presented the pros and cons, possibilities and risks; even though he'd explained what fasting had done for others but clearly made no promises? And who was responsible for Nicholas dying in the hospital?

Richard, the staff, and all of us who had come to know and care for Nicholas were distraught. My last sight of him was with the morning sun lighting up his long, unruly hair as Richard carried him—piggyback and shoeless—to the car that was waiting to take him to the hospital . . . and to his death.

31

A Twelve-Hour Nightmare

District health officials showed up two days after the news of Nicholas's death and asked to interview Richard, the staff, and all the guests. Each interview was basically the same; only the ailments differed.

"Where you from?"

"Norway," one guest answered. "You know Norway? Very far north. North Pole? Very cold. Here it is warm. Beautiful. Your country is beautiful."

"Why you come here?"

"I want to clean my body of all toxins. Want to improve my digestion."

"Why not go doctor?"

"I tried doctors for years. Not one helped me."

"What you do for health here?"

"Stop eating. Drink lots of springwater. Rest."

"Pay this man for no eating?"

"He's helped thousands of people get better from all kinds of sicknesses with no eating. He is very knowledgeable, very wise, very kind. He is a good man doing a good thing. Look how beautiful and peaceful it is here. Wouldn't you like to take a holiday here?"

At the end of their two-hour visit, the officials had found nothing blameworthy about the place, the treatment, or Richard's position, role, or behavior. They inspected the premises and found a spotless kitchen, perfect cleanliness and order everywhere. So that was that.

But perhaps Nicholas's death spooked Richard more than he realized. For the first time, he strongly encouraged Philip to go for diagnostic tests at a nearby clinic.

"An antibiotic might be worth taking," he said. "If your prolonged inability to regain strength and health after fasting is due to a lung infection, then an antibiotic would knock it out."

The infection theory was what Philip had long hypothesized as the possible reason for the persistent cough—the result of our three years in Abu Dhabi, living in constant air-conditioning in an apartment building where the air filters were never cleaned or changed, windows never opened.

"Is that what you would do? Take an antibiotic?" Philip asked.

"If it were a matter of my health or my life versus taking an antibiotic, and if I'd fasted without results, yes, I'd take the antibiotic, clear up the infection, and then return to natural ways of living and healing."

Feeling utterly discouraged at his lack of progress, as well as being shook up by Nicholas's death, Philip agreed.

I was surprised. Surprised by Philip's concession, surprised by Richard's about-face, and surprised by my feeling slightly disappointed in both of them. Yes, I was relieved, maybe even hopeful—with more information, some new piece of the puzzle might fall into place at last. But I was also disconcerted, wondering where their conviction and belief in natural healing had gone. What had become of their vehement disdain for antibiotics?

Is the risk of dying their line in the sand? I wondered. *Where is my line?*

All this and more swirled round my exhausted, overheated mind as Richard talked on about arrangements for the next day.

"All testing—a chest X-ray and a few blood tests—can be done at a local clinic in the nearby village of Nandayure," he said. "My driver will take you first thing in the morning. If we get you there right at opening time, you can see a doctor, take whatever tests, and get back here, possibly with an antibiotic in hand, by noon. No big deal."

"No big deal," Philip repeated. But his eyes, seeking out mine, were questioning, apprehensive.

The next day, we arrived at the clinic to learn that it was only equipped to do limited blood testing. Yet for a reason we couldn't understand (since no one spoke English), they kept us waiting for three hours in an open area with four temporary beds, upon one of which Philip was nervously perched.

The room was frigid with air-conditioning. The bed was hard, according to Philip's bony bottom; there was no blanket, no privacy. After about a half hour, I asserted myself in my pidgin Spanish.

"Por favor, mi esposo está muy frío," I said to one of the five green-clad attendants who sat chatting at the reception desk, ignoring us. At this, one handed me a single flat sheet.

"Pero mi esposo está muy, muy frío," I said with more determination.

So, they brought a second sheet. Apparently there were no blankets. In the entire three hours we were there, no one asked if Philip needed a drink of water or to use a toilet. The fact was, he wouldn't have had the strength to walk to a toilet if they had asked. Thankfully, I was toting the trusty urinal in my pack, and under cover of the sheets, he peed right there in his public bed. What else to do?

What kind of health clinic is this? I thought. *What kind of clinic shows no concern for the basic needs of a sick person?*

When a coughing episode exploded, one of the attendants rushed over with a face mask, shoved it at Philip, and gruffly motioned to him to put it on. Apparently they feared contagion, and of course this only added to our fears. Ten minutes after the attendant left, however, Philip ripped off the mask and stuck it under his hard, flat pillow. Tiny acts of defiance were all he had left.

The clinic doctors were convinced that *something* was very wrong with Philip. Other tests they were not equipped to do needed to be done. They insisted on Philip going to the hospital, and—for a reason that probably had more to do with money than anything health-related—said he must go in their ambulance.

The ambulance was nothing other than an empty van into which they finally rolled Philip on a stretcher. There was none of the other apparatus I expected to see in an ambulance: oxygen tanks, IV bags, an attendant other than the driver. The ambulances I'd seen in movies came a lot more equipped with medical people and paraphernalia.

The driver took off, Philip slipping and bumping as I tried to hold onto him while at the same time sliding on and off the narrow bench next to the stretcher. Philip rolled his eyes at me, looking like a spooked horse. It was a look I was to become increasingly familiar with throughout this interminable day.

We arrived at the public hospital in the small city of Nicoya after a twenty-five-minute ride. Philip was jostled and bumped out of the van and rolled on a gurney through the emergency-room doors. He was left in a hallway while the driver took me by the arm to the registration desk.

When I got back, the wild-horse look was in Philip's eyes again. The emergency room was a cavernous space with patients lying on gurneys. Again, no privacy, no blankets, and minimal attention. The whole situation was devoid of kindness or warmth, literal or otherwise. Doctors and nurses rushed about and had to be grabbed to gain their momentary attention. Patients lay on beds, uncovered and out in plain view, awaiting care.

Apprehensive and increasingly horrified, I rubbed Philip's freezing hands in mine, which were barely much warmer.

About a half hour after he'd been poked with needles by nurses and stared at by a succession of silent, serious doctors, I trotted beside him as he was quickly wheeled through a winding maze of dark hallways to the X-ray department. The door shut in my face with a metal clang.

I waited, suddenly wondering when I'd last taken a breath. Focusing on a single ray of sunlight that somehow made its way through a dirty skylight, I worked hard to quell panic.

How could healing happen in an environment like this? How have human beings who call themselves healers come to treat those who are most vulnerable and unwell so inhumanely? Is it the modern-day shift in consciousness away from care and toward cure that's created places such as this one?

When the door opened and Philip was wheeled out, that look in his eyes was even more pronounced. "The table was hard and so cold," he said. "No one looked me in the eye or smiled. I don't feel real or human." Then he asked the question I'd been trying not to allow into my mind. "Why did we agree to this?"

I could only look the question back at him through the tears stinging my eyes.

In late afternoon, just as we were hoping for the end of this ordeal, IV drips of saline solution with electrolytes, protein, and we didn't know what else were ordered. *Is it too much to ask that they tell us what they're doing, and why?* I thought.

Philip was utterly exhausted, physically and emotionally. Two English-speaking doctors finally took me aside and showed me a dark spot on an X-ray.

"Something serious wrong in lung. Maybe tumor. You say he lose many weight quickly and before this fasting."

"Yes," I said. "You're not sure it's a tumor then?" The word "maybe" was something to grab onto.

"Not sure. Need more, better tests. Just see dark spot in X-ray. See?" They pointed to the film that all looked dark to me, maybe darker in one place.

"So, you don't know it's a tumor . . . cancer. Right?"

"Don't know certain. But—"

"Could it be an infection?" I was still clinging to Philip's theory.

They looked at each other, then back to the X-ray. "Maybe . . . abscess from fungal infection."

I couldn't tell whether this was just appeasement, a softening of the blow, but I clung to it.

"You need go home U.S.A. right away for more tests," they continued. "MRI, CT scan."

"You don't do those tests here?"

They explained that to do them would require Philip being admitted to the hospital, which would cost a thousand dollars a night just for the stay. They didn't know how much the tests would add to this amount, and stressed that the technology in the States was superior.

Philip had heard none of this. He lay on the bed ten feet away, watching my face.

Why are they telling me and cutting him out? How am I going to tell him? Their uncertainty left their non-diagnosis nearly as blurry and vague as the X-ray looked to my unpracticed eye.

The kinder doctor led me to the payment desk on the other side of the hospital. Before going, I explained to Philip what I was going to do and where I was going, looking into eyes that were growing wilder again, pupils dilated with increasing distress. His teeth were chattering, his hands like ice.

"Don't leave me here," he said.

"I'm not leaving you here or anywhere, my love," I said. "I just have to go pay for your wonderful stay here. I'll be back soon, and then we can go home."

I squeezed his freezing, bony hand, leaned over the rail of the bed to kiss him, and turned to the doctor who had walked briskly to the door and was waiting to accompany me.

The bill was two hundred and fifty dollars, which sounded reasonable enough. I took out my credit card, which no longer held much reality for me—the balance due had gone blurry weeks back. Before I could hand it over, however, the kind doctor and the less-than-kind woman behind the desk entered into a heated conversation in Spanish. The result was a corrected bill of four hundred and fifty dollars, ostensibly because Philip had occupied a hospital bed for more than four hours (*But possibly because we're gringos,* I thought). Apparently, he had to pay by the hour to lie on a hard bed in an open room without a blanket.

In the middle of what felt like a never-ending negotiation (bless that doctor for trying so hard on our behalf), I saw that I'd been gone for what might be to Philip an alarming twenty-five minutes. I raced back through the halls and found him in full-fledged panic. He spluttered through tear-filled eyes as he clung to my hand.

"I called out the words you told me for 'help me'—ayúdeme," he said. "But not one of the doctors or nurses stopped. I didn't know where you'd gone. I can't take anymore."

"My darling boy, breathe. I've been trying to pay the bill. The doctor who speaks English is trying to help us."

"Look," he said and pointed to a new patient lying next to him, a young woman.

"What?"

"She's pregnant. Blood on her pants. She needs help. She needs a blanket," he said. Then he broke down altogether.

I tried, and failed, to reassure him. A few minutes later, I had to leave him again to deal with the absurd paperwork and bill-paying process.

By the time I finally finished and returned he was hysterical, and still no one had stopped to attend to him. He gripped my hand as an attendant rolled him out to the car where our driver, looking like an angel, was faithfully waiting.

When we finally got back to Highlands, Philip collapsed on his bed and fell instantly into a stupor. I sat on the edge of my bed, watching him through tears of relief and emotional exhaustion. It took me a few minutes to realize I was clutching the large envelope with the dreaded X-rays to my chest.

It was now after 8 P.M. We'd left Highlands at 8:30 A.M. for our "no big deal, you'll be back in time for lunch" visit to the clinic. Our simple morning in search of an antibiotic had turned into an all-day nightmare—and utter physical and emotional misery for Philip.

Round and round in my head, I repeated the unenlightened, unenlightening mantra, *What now? What now? What now?*

32

Seeking Forgiveness

On February 15, one week after our fateful trip to the hospital and just over two months into our extended stay at Highlands, Philip asked me to get in touch with his family.

"What do you want me to say?" I asked.

"I want them to understand why I withdrew from all of them after my mother died."

"That was twelve years ago."

"I know. I should've tried to explain sooner," he said. "But I couldn't."

"I know, my love. I tried for you a couple of times. But it would be good if you want to say something now."

As he thought this through, it struck me how people can live in the same family but have very different experiences or interpretations of the same experiences. It also occurred to me that we are all too often sadly unaware of—or unable to understand—the private hells the individuals right beside us are living through.

While his family (Misha, his sisters and brother, and his three nephews and one niece) may or may not have understood how Philip came to interpret and perceive life in the Heiman family as he did, and while his sense of his life in that family may or may not have been very different from theirs, he consistently told me the same stories over the years.

So, I honored his feelings and hoped that by speaking his truth aloud and sharing it with the people he had hurt but loved so deeply, he might take another step toward letting go of much of what had haunted him throughout his life.

This is what he dictated to me:

> I'm realizing today—very painfully—that my need to separate myself from the family has hurt all of you much more than I could understand it would. I was unable, at the time, to adequately explain why I was so desperately retreating. I feel that none of you could or should ever know how brutal and brutalizing Gale's relentless attacks on me were. His nonstop campaign to get me to be someone who he could accept—at the cost of who I was or needed to be—eroded my sense of joy, destroyed my nerves, and contributed to my inability to come to my life creatively and from the heart. Equally, Kate's [Philip's mother's] endless psychic demands that I save her from Gale were an enormous burden to carry—one that drained and sapped so much of my energy over the years—right up to her death.
>
> As a result, I threw myself into many mistaken and desperate acts and ways of being over the years. By the time Kate died, I felt I had lost my way entirely. I couldn't express to you how close to coming undone I felt at that time. And somehow, because you were all a part of the family, I felt I had to leave everyone . . . or go under. On the day of Kate's funeral, I was breaking down . . . going a little mad . . . right there in the midst of all of you. And you didn't notice.
>
> I never, ever stopped loving any of you, but I was too brokenhearted, desperate, and already sick to carry on. I felt like a wild animal—irrationally and desperately fighting for my life. But truly, I never wanted to hurt any of you in the way I did. I was just in such a disoriented and disintegrating state, I could only think to retreat. I was fighting to survive.
>
> I know that even prior to that time, I often asked you to be something and someone for me that I could not be for myself; ironically, this is what Gale had been doing to me. I know this was unfair, as well as impossible, and I apologize with all my heart.
>
> Sitting here today, having received the loving and forgiving messages I've received from you, as well as knowing how much pain I've caused

each of you—I see that what I've done to try to save my own life could only be perceived as heartless and incomprehensible to you.

Even while Joan has been here with and for me throughout the years, we were never able to find a place and a way to be in the world where I felt fully safe or nurtured. I have brought so much fear and need to our relationship. My sense of abandonment and the panics that have come from that have grown so overwhelming in the past years that I've continually—and wrongly—asked her to be my soul, my heart, my mother . . . my life.

So here I am—having faced death in these past weeks and still not sure whether life is possible—but more hopeful in the past few days. I am realizing—in the face of the love and forgiveness you have offered—that I must tell you and hope that you can hear me when I say—I love you . . . I love you.

Please, send whatever heartfelt healing you can. I can feel it . . . and it helps immensely.

With all my love,

Philip

33

Departure and Arrival

March soon arrived, with Philip continuing to resist everyone's urgings to return to the U.S. for testing. The X-rays lay dismissed at the bottom of my suitcase, brooding and dooming us like the disease they threatened.

Ever since we'd come to Highlands, Philip had hoped for the kind of transformation we'd been so surprised by when his father had faced his death.

Gale, who'd remained demanding and often arrogantly tyrannical until the day a doctor told him he had six months to live, was an unlikely model. For a man who'd always had a complex relationship with authority, the doomsday prognosis pulled the proverbial rug out from under him. In fact, Gale so trusted the words of that doctor that he died six months to the day from when the pronouncement was made.

"That's how powerful the force of suggestion from authority can be," Philip said just after Gale died. "Gale gave another man authority over his life and death. Don't ever tell me if something is fatally wrong with me."

Highlands was officially closing while Richard went on a lecture tour. We needed to leave, and since Philip's condition hadn't worsened dramatically, we decided to go back to the States to find a new retirement home closer to family and friends. We chose San Diego—its mild climate, ocean air, and health-conscious atmosphere all appealed.

Many of the guests stopped by our room to say goodbye. Pulling up a chair next to Philip's bed, they told him of their renewed hopes for health and wellness, their plans and next steps. He seemed to have taken on the dignity and compassion of a wise elder in their eyes. Often taking their hands in his, he listened and responded with heartfelt simplicity and care that moved most of us to tears. The energy in the room would become both lighter and denser, his love and tenuous hold on his own life creating a sense of meaning, connection, and valor.

When the farewell hugs and words had been shared and Philip and I were alone again, he'd look somewhat bewildered, as though not understanding what had just passed through him.

"You're turning into an angel," I said one day.

"But still so often a devil."

"Oh, my boy. Why will you not see your beautiful light and love?"

On the morning of our departure from Highlands, Philip was too weak to walk from his bed to the van. A one-minute walk was now miles across desert sands. We were finally leaving the same room we'd walked into three months and a hundred years ago. The staff women and the remaining guests gathered at our door.

Someone suggested getting Philip from his bed into the chair. "Then we'll all carry him in the chair," she said.

"He's King Philip," someone else said with warmth and humor as we all lifted him together. There was laughter—part simple humor, part nervous energy. Philip, too, was laughing.

At the van, Eric, the driver, lifted him in his arms like a father lifts a small child, as Richard had done numerous times. He placed him gently into the back seat. Each woman climbed in to hug and kiss Philip goodbye. Everyone hugged me. Everyone cried. Eric drove the van out of the gates, and the Highlands Retreat Center was left behind . . . after being the center of the universe for the longest three months of my life.

What's next? I wondered.

We'd arranged to stay at a little place called Mariana's Guesthouse, in a town next to the San José airport. We'd be there for four days before making the long trip back to the States. The four-and-a-half-hour drive was agonizing for Philip, the first forty-five minutes bumping along dirt roads. Each bump jiggled him farther out of his seat. He couldn't hold himself upright, and I couldn't stop him from slipping and sliding; his body was like a heavy sack of potatoes with a will of its own.

Seeing our distress in the rearview mirror, Eric pulled over and tried repositioning the seats. He placed pillows under and around Philip. His kindness helped, but Philip, weak and debilitated from the start, only became more and more enervated with each passing mile. Time and distance were endlessly cruel. But he held on, and I held onto him.

After an eternity of aching hardship, we arrived. Mariana and her husband met us at the door of the van with warm Tico hospitality and—the saving grace—a wheelchair. Eric lifted Philip out of the van and placed him tenderly in the chair. Philip was almost too exhausted to take in his surroundings, his eyes unfocused. But he pulled himself back, took Eric's hands in both of his, quietly thanked him for his kindness, and wished him well. I was touched, as was each person witnessing this tiny scene: Mariana, her husband, other guests sitting on the veranda. Gentleness, vulnerability, and gratitude brought a nobility to Philip's emaciated face and a sense of hushed, nearly sanctified awe to all who encountered him.

We were shown to our room, which was light and sunny, if somewhat eccentrically decorated with the Latin flare for vibrant reds, blues, and yellows along with plastic flowers and crosses. It was comfortable and welcoming. Philip collapsed on the bed with immense relief and fell asleep almost instantly.

A little while later, though, he was up and ready to try out the wheelchair, to explore new surroundings after having been limited to the same space for three long months. Once I got pillows under him and behind his back, he wheeled himself skillfully out of the room, taking to the chair like a pro. Delighted with his new mobility, he was like a teenage boy with his first car. A childlike pleasure—even a bit of reckless driving—took over as he navigated through the lounge, dining area, and out onto the front porch. What joy it was to hear his uncomplicated laughter bubbling up again.

I received an email from Tanya—Philip's ex-wife—that day. "You can't do this all alone, Joan," she wrote. "If Philip and you want, I will come and help. Just say the word."

I read her email to Philip and asked what he thought.

He looked at me through tears. "Please, ask her to come. And give her my love and thanks."

Even though we hadn't been in touch for nearly ten years, all past dramas and traumas were instantly forgotten. Tanya arranged to fly down to meet us at Mariana's. She was our rescue and support, familiar and reassuring after having been on our own and frightened for so long.

Misha had also offered to come, but he was raising his sixteen-year-old daughter, Malia, and pragmatically it made more sense for Tanya to make the journey. She even offered to stay with us in San Diego for a few days to help us look for an apartment.

In the meantime, Mariana was kindness itself. She shopped especially for Philip, finding soursop fruit at the market and making great claims for its healing properties. She didn't say so within earshot of Philip, but she was sure he had cancer.

"This fruit is the latest anti-cancer cure," she said.

She longed to feed and fatten him, was frustrated by his fruit-only diet. When she and I were alone, she questioned me, questioned the wisdom of fasting, and blamed it for Philip's debilitation.

"How can anyone get this emaciated?" she asked. "How can fasting—or this crazy raw food—possibly help build him back?"

Thankfully, she had the wisdom not to speak her criticism to Philip; with him, she was only gentle and mothering. I appreciated this, but I also wished she would spare me her suppressed wrath.

Here I am again, I thought. *The one who people speak to* about *him*.

Even though I was surprised that Richard recommended staying at Mariana's (he obviously had no idea how she felt about his approach to healing), there was mostly a sense of great reprieve and pleasure with being in new surroundings, being with different people, and having a wider variety of fruit options. Philip was also relieved that we were just days away from leaving Costa Rica. Much as he'd wanted to come three months ago, he was now equally anxious to leave. His hopes for healing and finding a home here had died a painful and disheartening death.

We anxiously awaited Tanya's arrival, and when she finally walked through the door, Philip and I breathed deep relief. The three of us hadn't seen one another in more than a decade, so there were some quick and subtly disguised adjustments to make between memory and current reality. We'd all aged, but no doubt Philip's emaciation and overall decline was the biggest shock. Tanya hid her dismay well.

We all relaxed together, lounging on the beds, talking and laughing like we'd done so long ago. She'd anticipated all kinds of contingencies for airplane travel, bringing warm socks, shawls, sweaters, and travel blankets for air-conditioned planes. She'd brought an assortment of inflatable cushions with soft handmade coverings.

We stepped right back into the warmth of close friendship—family—with ease and lack of reservation or self-consciousness. Surely this is what is meant by "grace."

34

Long Day's Journey into Night

At long last . . . departure day. At dawn, we rolled our suitcases out. Philip wheeled himself to the waiting taxi van and was pushed right in, the driver arranging to return the wheelchair to Mariana on his next trip back from the airport. We thanked Mariana and her husband for their hospitality, said goodbye, and drove away, hopeful and ready to start our new life in San Diego.

Tanya had arranged for a wheelchair to meet us curbside at the San José airport. An attendant expertly wheeled Philip through security and to the gate. There, two attendants lifted him from that wheelchair and onto one that was narrow enough to be pushed down the aisle of a plane. I'd never even noticed these before, but that's because we were now the people I'd never noticed—the people with special needs who board first.

When we got to our row, Philip was again lifted and gently placed into his seat. When his eyes met mine, there was sweetness combined with surrender as he bowed to each next step, each outstretched hand. The competence and tenderness of the attendants combined with my overwrought emotions and exhaustion had me tearing up. Philip was wearing an expression of bewildered submission mixed with gratitude.

"One step at a time, one breath at a time," I said, quoting a longtime friend of my father's.

Tanya handed me one of the inflatable cushions, and we busied ourselves with attempting to make Philip slightly more comfortable. We'd already talked and worried about how he was going to sit up for this six-hour plane trip from San José to Los Angeles, where we'd then catch another flight to San Diego. He leaned back and closed his eyes, already exhausted from the first leg of our centipede-legged journey.

For Philip, the flight entailed endless, enervating hours of never finding comfort. None of the cushions were soft enough to ease the pain as he was forced to sit on the open bedsores on his sacrum. The padded bandages I'd so carefully placed early that morning—hoping to protect and soften his way—were useless, quickly becoming bunched up under his constant wriggling and squirming in search of relief. He was hungry, but two bites of the fruit I'd packed made him queasy.

Our greatest concern, however, was what we would do when he needed to use the bathroom. And, of course, that time came.

I walked behind him as he leaned his weight on the backs of the chairs along the aisle. With my hand lightly resting on his back for courage more than anything else, we made our way to the toilet. I squeezed in with him. "I used to think there wasn't enough room in here for *one* person," I said.

"Now we're like one person," he said as we lowered him to the seat.

A moment later, to our combined dismay, he had zero strength to help me lift him back up. The one-two-three-lift method didn't work. My strength alone couldn't get him back onto his feet. *Where's that superhuman strength women find to lift cars off babies?* I wondered.

Meeting the anguish in his eyes, I once again covered my own distress. "Don't worry. I'll get help. You're not going to spend the whole trip in here."

"Help . . ." he said, looking entirely helpless.

Assuring him that all would be well, I squeezed back out and went in search of a male flight attendant. Fortunately, there was a strong young man close at hand. He looked so healthy.

"My husband . . ." I said, pointing to the toilet.

He reacted before I finished my sentence; apparently the look on my face was enough. I realized then that the attendants had been keeping a discreet eye on us. In minutes, he had Philip back in his seat with no fuss and a good deal of tact and solicitude.

After finally arriving in Los Angeles, we faced a layover of three torturous hours. We found a relatively quiet spot next to our gate and wrapped a shivering Philip in shawls and sweaters. I rushed off to buy another blanket and returned to find Philip slumped sideways, leaning heavily against Tanya.

"Strange to end up here—and like this—after all these years," she said, referring to finding herself propping up the man she'd divorced forty years ago.

But he was semi-delirious, and made what sounded to Tanya like a nonsensical reply. "A long life of abuse," he said.

Tanya looked her question at me.

I nodded. He was actually making sense, at least according to his uncommon sense.

"He's been one of the healthiest eaters on the planet for most of his life, at least according to some and certainly to him," I said. "All organic, only whole foods, no animal products, no refined sugars, no unhealthy fats, no alcohol, no processed anything—but he's still convinced he's paying the price for growing up on meat, dairy, sugar, and every kind of 1950s junk food."

He's always been a contradiction, I thought. *So optimistic in his idealism, so defeated in the stories he tells himself.*

All he wanted was to lie down, and there was no place to lie down. No way to get warm despite the extra socks and blankets in which we wrapped him. I went off again in search of a lounge, ready to pay membership in any airline club if there was a couch he could stretch out on. No such couch existed. Airport lounges are apparently meant for drinking and using computers . . . in upright positions.

"Isn't there an infirmary somewhere in the airport?" I asked at the check-in desk.

"No, there isn't," the attendant said. "We can call the paramedics if you want, but then he's not getting on that flight."

"No, don't call the paramedics," I said.

It's only a one-hour flight from LAX to San Diego. If we can just get there. If he can just lie down. If . . . if . . . if . . .

Tanya and I communicated nonverbally, our eyes meeting more than once, tears spilling over, hearts breaking. We watched him struggling and sinking, color fading, a jaundiced yellow spreading, eyes dimming throughout this eternal day of suffering.

Finally, the flight from Los Angeles to San Diego was announced. We were boarding. No one stopped a severely ill man from getting on the plane, though heaven knows why. With wheelchairs and continued assistance from kind, strong young men who lifted and carried him, we got through the next hour.

We'd passed through time zones and unending hours, from Costa Rica dawn to southern California night.

An angelic giant of a young man met us with a wheelchair in San Diego, talking us cheerfully through baggage claim. He picked up and effortlessly swung our two large suitcases onto his shoulders while pushing Philip and leading us to ground transportation.

Tanya and I ran to keep up with him. He hailed a taxi and tenderly lifted Philip like a limp rag doll, gently tucking him into the back seat of the cab.

Tanya and I took one look at our small and slight Afghani taxi driver and hated to let go of the gentle giant. Did he want to come with us, I asked? He smiled a shrug and waved a cheerful goodbye.

The Afghani looked as doubtful as we did.

"Will you help us get my husband from the taxi into our rental condo?" I asked him.

"I give my best," he replied with a nervous smile.

Finding the Airbnb condo in Coronado took searching, calling, and re-calling the owner. We drove up and down the same street in the dark; I even got out of the car to search while the taxi slowly followed me. We finally found the right address—a spot we'd driven past at least four times, the number entirely hidden by shrubbery.

Looking around, I noticed a medical center across the street. Tanya saw it too.

"Maybe we'll go there in the morning," I whispered.

She nodded.

The three of us carried Philip into the condo, the driver holding him under his arms while Tanya and I each carried a leaden leg.

Thank goodness it's dark, I thought. *Heaven knows what would happen if someone saw this scene.*

Philip was nearly unconscious as we lowered him onto a bed. He sighed, sinking into exhaustion and sweet, sweet reprieve.

It was all I could do to pull off his sandals and cover him with every blanket I could find. I sat with him, alternating between rubbing and wrapping his ice-cold feet in blankets and then shifting to the top of the bed to massage his neck and stroke his head.

As I whispered senseless encouragements and endearments he probably didn't hear, time stretched to its most surreal limits. Hours passed in minutes . . . in years. Mostly, he slept, but he occasionally stirred.

"In San Diego? Good to lie down," he whispered.

"Yes. We're in San Diego, love."

"Good. Love you . . . sleep."

"I love you, my honey. Yes, sleep."

A moment later, I realized he was snoring with his eyes open.

Did he survive this whole excruciating day only to slip into a coma now? My boy, my boy. Please . . .

35

Warm at Last

Just as I was wondering at this strange open-eyed snoring, Tanya—worry having obliterated sleep—came to the bedroom door.

Taking one look at him, she called his name. "Phil! Phil!"

Her voice, filled with fear and urgency, reflected the growing panic in my chest. I wanted her to speak more gently, was afraid she'd startle him. But he didn't respond at all.

"Joan, we have to call 911. We can't let him die in this empty condo with no more food in it than two oranges and a banana."

I stared stupidly at her.

"We'll have to call the police if he dies here. What will they think when they see this emaciated man in an empty apartment? I know he doesn't want to be in a hospital . . . I know you want to respect his wishes, but . . ."

"Okay. Call."

It was 2 A.M. In minutes, the condo was invaded by men in uniforms, all lights flipped on, destroying the night and the peace Philip had finally found. A policeman and a rescue team of five men rushed in and filled the bedroom; they were enormous, like a football team, yet they worked with coordinated confidence and grace.

I heard my voice from somewhere far away. "Is he dying . . . now?"

"I'm afraid so. But we're taking him to the hospital," the policeman said.

Suddenly, they'd wheeled him out. I turned frantically to Tanya. "We don't know where they're taking him. Or how we'll get there. Why aren't they taking us?" I spun around wildly, but the policeman's hand was firmly on my arm.

"I'm going to walk you both to the hospital," he said. "It's just a block away." He was gentle, reassuring, solid. The three of us walked out into a warm night as though we did this all the time, as though we were friends going out to dinner and a movie.

At the door to the emergency room, he handed me his card, took my hand, steadied me with his steadiness. "If you need help with anything, call me."

Even in my panic, I was momentarily stopped and awed by his kindness.

In the emergency room, Philip was already in a bed, surrounded by a team of doctors, nurses, and technicians. Everyone doing something. Machines all doing something. Monitors hooked up. Tests ordered. Everyone knew their part in this strange, brightly lit choreography.

Philip was alive. He was conscious. Tanya and I were invited into the room, and I stood by the bed holding his hand as everyone worked around me. They put him under a lightweight blanket that blew hot air on him.

"Warm," he whispered, smiling weakly.

A tall doctor moved and spoke quickly. In the midst of the madness, I was aware of his foreign accent and wondered where he was from. *Why do totally irrelevant thoughts flit through in the most relevant of moments?*

The doctor gently told us what was happening, what was going to happen. Tests, X-rays, scans. Then the questions began: "How has he gotten this emaciated? Where have you been? Why fasting?"

Everything felt "normal" as long as Philip was talking, smiling weakly, looking into my eyes, holding my hand in his live, now-warm hand. I kissed his soft cheek as he pressed it against my lips. He kissed mine, wetting his lips with the salt of my grateful tears.

With the resources of the rescue team and the emergency room staff, he had miraculously returned from death. And, hope against hope, he was still with me.

36

Questions, Choices, and Choices Questioned

For what felt like hours, or lifetimes, Philip was examined, wheeled out for X-rays and other tests, brought back freezing, gratefully put back under the warming blanket, hooked up to an IV, a catheter, and I didn't know what else. I answered countless questions and filled in even more forms.

Finally, a doctor came in to talk to us. "We're ready to take him to intensive care. It'll take a little while to get him set up there. Why don't you go home and rest, and come back in about two hours?"

I told Philip, "They're taking you to intensive care now. They say we should leave and come back in two hours. All right? Are you still warm? Are you comfortable?"

"Warm . . . all right . . . come back. Bring a book to read to me?"

"Yes, my love. Rest. I'll see you in just a few hours. I love you and love you."

"Love you, little darlin'."

I kissed him one more time. He pushed his face against mine, smiled quizzically, still not sure how this had all transpired, how he'd landed where he'd never wanted to be.

A famous line from Laurel and Hardy popped absurdly out of my mouth. "Well, here's another fine mess you've gotten me into."

He laughed weakly, squeezed my hand, squeezed Tanya's hand. Tanya and I watched the nurses wheel him down a long corridor and out of sight before we turned and walked outside.

"I guess it's Friday," she said.

"I guess we're in San Diego," I said. "And Philip is alive."

We hugged and cried our gratitude as we walked toward the condo in the first, soft light of a California morning.

Back at the condo, we were met with the aftermath of the rescue team's work. The bedroom was a disaster area littered with papers from packages torn open, used needles, blankets thrown from the bed. Philip's sandals lay forlornly where I'd dropped them from his feet just a few long hours ago.

I opened curtains and windows, let the morning sun and sea-softened air cleanse the room, and quickly disposed of the trash. If only the fear-filled images of the past few hours could be disposed of so easily.

"How about sitting outside by the pool and eating the oranges?" Tanya asked, standing in the doorway.

"Pool? Oranges? Sure." My eyes were gritty; a wave of exhaustion passed over me. I felt demented.

We found a table in a sun-dappled spot under a family of tall palm trees. The large courtyard—empty but for us at this early hour—surrounded an Olympic-sized pool, a kiddie pool, and a Jacuzzi. It was all beautifully landscaped with flowering bushes, palm trees, and manicured grass. Very California.

I peeled an orange without knowing what I was doing until the tangy, sweet scent of citrus touched my nose. Every sense felt heightened: light and shadows, aquamarine blue of the sky reflected in the water, my body in the chair, bare feet on warm ground, softness of the air on my face, mixed scents of flowers, grass, and citrus.

"Everything seems so real . . . yet surreal," I said.

"Trauma, sleep deprivation, and fear are coursing through our veins."

"The quiet is heavenly." Just as I said this, the whine and whirr of lawn mowers and leaf blowers started up. We looked at each other and broke into hilarious, stress-relieving laughter.

"Philip wouldn't like this," I said. "He'd get up and go back inside." We laughed, feeling grateful for life, oranges, noise . . . everything.

Back at the hospital two hours later, a kind woman escorted us to the intensive care unit. When we got there, I looked through the glass. Philip was awake, hands moving as they always did when he talked.

"He's hooked up to life support," a nurse explained, "and he's on blood pressure medicine—his blood pressure is dangerously low. He's also on oxygen, and the IV drips are for antibiotics, vitamins, protein, and minerals."

But he's alive. I realized I'd been semiconsciously chanting this.

With my hand on the door, the nurse said, "You need to wear face masks until we know more about possible contagion—going either way." She showed us how to put the masks on.

"This isn't how I'd choose to be seen by Philip on our first date after he died and came back to life," I joked nervously.

When we entered the room, Philip, still under his magic blanket, was propped up on so many pillows that he looked like a child-sized version of himself in a giant's bed. An oxygen mask covered his nose and mouth.

"I don't feel so bad about my little paper mask," I said to him. "We both look ridiculous."

He nodded in agreement. The mask squashed his nose and muffled his voice, but not enough to mask the annoyance in his tone. He had apparently been defending his dietary choices to a nurse who appeared equally annoyed.

"There's plenty of protein in avocados," he said.

"You are completely depleted of protein, albumin, vitamins, and minerals," she snapped.

I took his hand and shushed him. Tanya did what she could to soothe the nurse with a whisper of sympathy and commiseration.

Later, it occurred to me that this nurse and many of the others who were so competently caring for Philip were baffled, frightened, or angry, depending on their personality and defense mechanisms. It seemed they didn't often see people in this state of dilapidation in this private hospital.

"How did this happen?" the nurse asked me. "ER says you were out of the country. Where have you been?"

"In Costa Rica," I answered.

"Why were you there?"

"We went for dental work and to explore retirement possibilities. He was unwell when we arrived but suddenly got much worse. We went to a holistic healing retreat in the mountains."

I was still hoping I might not have to talk again about fasting. Based on the reactions I'd gotten in the emergency room, this would not go over well.

Three doctors entered the room.

"Why is he so utterly depleted?" one specialist asked. "He's so dehydrated that one kidney isn't functioning at all."

"He's totally devoid of protein and albumin, vitamins and minerals," another continued, echoing what the nurse had said a moment ago.

"His liver is damaged. His heart, weakened. Why? What kind of 'healing center' was this?" asked the third.

They all seemed angry.

Here we go, I thought. I looked the nurse in the eye and said, "He fasted for eleven days and then seemed unable to absorb or assimilate the food he was eating after the fast."

"Fasted? On what?"

"Pure springwater."

"Eleven days?"

"Yes. He couldn't complete the usual twenty-one-day fast."

"Twenty-one days of nothing but water?"

"Yes. Thousands of people have been through this protocol during the last nineteen years." *I'll impress them with the term protocol,* I thought.

"These are supervised fasts with a professional," I went on. "Plenty of people who've followed his program have healed from every kind of sickness."

"Is he a medical doctor?"

"No."

Eyebrows raised. They looked at me as though I'd deliberately tried to murder my husband.

"You said he ate food after the fast. What kind of food?"

"Fruits and salads."

More eyebrows raised.

A lot of people exercised their eyebrows that day. In fact, I'd never been so aware of eyebrows. On some, only one brow raised in question or skepticism. Others shot both up nearly to the hairline in surprise or disbelief.

On still others (like the angry nurse), both brows crunched together in frowns of disgust or puzzlement.

Here I was again—facing doubt, disbelief, and dismay.

Philip's eyes met mine over his mask. *Well, what can you expect in a place like this?* he telegraphed to me. His brow was lifted to the skeptic's position.

As the questions and comments swarmed the ICU room, Philip's eyes repeatedly met mine. Looking out from behind the oxygen mask, his eyes expressed disdain rather than fear. Even in this dire condition, and as unnerved as he was to find himself in a hospital, I could see he was still thinking that medical people were predictably wrong. They were overreactive and hysterical.

Lying there, totally at their mercy, he was finally, utterly incapable of choice—even the choice to reject their help. This was exactly what he'd fought against as long as I'd known him: not to fall into "that world" with its complete abnegation of all that he still doggedly believed to be right and true about holistic healing. Even on the edge of death, he was not in the least convinced that they were right and he was wrong.

That cynical look in his eyes combined with other nonverbal reactions—hand flinging out in disgust, eyes rolling to the ceiling. He had landed in this bastion of all he abhorred. I had landed him here.

Have I betrayed him? I wondered. *Should I have let him slide gently into the coma toward which he'd already moved so far before we called 911? Was it my selfishness that agreed to the call, wanting to keep him with me regardless of his pain or philosophy?*

"He has severe pneumonia," the pulmonary specialist said. "His lungs are filled with liquid. They also look like the lungs of a heavy smoker."

"I doubt Philip has ever held a cigarette," I said. *And he only smoked pot for a very short time more than forty years ago*, I didn't say.

"Has he had one or more heart attacks?" the cardiologist asked.

"No, why?" I asked in a growing blur of confusion and overwhelm.

"His heart has the scars of a heart that's had multiple heart attacks."

What in the world? Could this explain the many times he'd complained of "weird" pains in his arms, shoulders, and back? Pains that seemed inexplicable and then passed just as inexplicably?

"Has he had kidney problems?" yet another specialist queried.

"No!" I answered, suppressing a scream of growing vexation. I was teetering on the verge of overwhelm.

"He's nearing kidney failure. One kidney isn't functioning at all, the other one—just barely."

And on it went that day. When I tried to explain his thinking about the possible lung infection from the three years of uncleaned air-conditioning vents in Abu Dhabi, they looked doubtful at best. If I weren't so fatigued (going on twenty-four hours without sleep and pumping enough adrenaline and cortisol throughout those hours to fuel a race car), I don't know how I would have reacted. Frustration and fear coursed through my veins at about a hundred miles an hour.

But exhaustion and a small, growing doubt kept me from exploding.

Why had this happened? Why this utter collapse of all his organs? If he was made worse by fasting, what other options did we have? By the time we'd gotten to Costa Rica, he couldn't eat anything without violent reactions. And how had so many other people walked away from twenty-one-day fasts feeling more vital and healthy than they'd felt in years?

Meanwhile, Philip was comfortable in a bed that went up and down, was soft but firm, kindly supporting his weak and weary bony body. He was, perhaps, more comfortable than he'd been in months. Nurses, doctors, and specialists came and went. Countless more tests were done and endless questions repeated. Philip was awake and alert, wanting me to read to him, asking me to bring an organic juice from the health food store he was pleased to learn I'd already found.

When we were finally alone, I apologized for landing him where he least wanted to be. "We didn't want you to die in the condo. Didn't know if you were sleeping or dying. Oh, my boy."

"It's fine. I feel better. Everyone—except that angry nurse—is kind. I'll get out of here soon."

I spent the rest of the morning with him. When my head fell to my chest, one of the nurses realized I hadn't slept in more than a day.

"Philip," she said, "tell your wife to go get some sleep. She won't be any good to any of us if she falls apart too."

"Yeah, you go rest and come back later, love," he said.

I didn't want to be away from him, but I could barely stay awake. The nurse added that the best thing for Philip right now would be sleep, so I promised to be back in three hours and kissed him goodbye.

"Don't go anywhere without me," I said.

He smirked.

37

Most Difficult Decision

That evening, while Tanya and I were out having dinner, my phone rang. A man's voice introduced himself as a Dr. Green. He said he was the surgeon who'd been called in on Philip's case. He wanted to perform a microsurgery.

"I want to find out whether what we're seeing in the X-rays is a tumor or an infection in his lung. If it's an infection, it would be much better to know the kind of infection so we can use the most effective antibiotics. Presently, we're loading him up with everything—shooting blind."

So they are taking the infection hypothesis seriously after all! "But do you really think someone in Philip's weakened condition can survive surgery?" I asked.

"Well, Mrs. Heiman, here's the way it is," he said. "Philip has a 50 percent chance of surviving the surgery and saving his life. Without surgery, he has no chance and will die in the next few days."

This no-nonsense statement rang through my head while people strolled past me on their way to cafés, bars, shops. Tanya and I had found our way to an area on the bay where recreation and enjoyment were the name of the game. *And here I sit, receiving Philip's death sentence*, I thought.

"I'll talk with Philip about it when I go back to the hospital in an hour," I stammered. "Can I call you back in the morning?"

"Sure, but don't wait too long. He doesn't have much time."

Thanks. And you enjoy your dinner too. My mind reverted to cynical-wacky in response to the surreal cliff edge on which I felt myself to be precariously teetering.

Back at the hospital, Philip slept. I sat with him. Watched the rise and fall of his chest. Felt grateful for the rise and fall of his chest. Also for the warmth of his hand, the peace on his face. Even the low noise of the monitor was comfort. As long as it made noise, Philip was still there. *Make noise,* I told it.

I talked with the night nurse about my conversation with Dr. Green. She said it could wait until morning. "There's no need to disturb Philip now," she said. "I'll call the surgeon and tell him we'll be in touch in the morning."

I was temporarily content just to sit with him.

At midnight, I kissed Philip and wished him sweet dreams before heading out. The halls were quiet, empty but for an orderly passing me in rubber-soled shoes. He smiled, wished me a good night. How quickly I'd learned my way through this maze of hospital corridors where I'd been utterly disoriented only a few hours ago.

I'd fallen into another time warp—this day now felt like a month. Walking the one block back to the condo, I thought how bizarre it was that we'd just happened to find a condo this close to a hospital. We couldn't have found a more opportune location if we'd tried.

The streets were empty, the night soft and quiet. When I got to a darker stretch of the street, it occurred to me that I was walking alone in a strange city in the middle of the night. I felt oddly detached, free of usual fears. It's not that I felt unconcerned about possible danger, and it wasn't that I was flirting with some kind of nihilistic not caring if I lived or died. It was more that everything—*everything*—had shifted. Nothing else seemed important while Philip lay in that bed, halfway between life and death.

What a way to get a taste of the detachment I've been seeking—and mostly failing—to find in years of meditation, I thought. *I suppose there's an unexpected freedom in it, but it's not the kind of freedom I want.*

Saturday morning, I returned to find Philip awake. We talked about the surgery and agreed it was worth a try if it gave him a chance at living.

He wants to live.

I rescinded the noninvasive-procedures order and signed the paperwork allowing the surgery.

Tanya came, and the three of us tried to communicate through the face masks. Talking took more energy than he had. He was frustrated yet again at not being heard or understood, though thankfully there was a new touch of forgiving humor and surrender about him. I hoped I'd be able to remember the way he spoke in those moments—there was something endearing, funny, rhythmic about it.

He asked for pen and paper. Barely having the strength to hold the pen and unable to see without glasses, he wrote. I tore page after page out of a small pocket pad—the only paper I had—and he scribbled indecipherable words, one on top of the other. I got the gist: he wanted a story, his glasses, juice. He wrote the name of a healing juice mix—mangosteen, sea buckthorn, and açaí—that he'd wanted to try back in Fort Collins so many months ago, when he was still walking, talking, and choosing freely. We had never bought that juice; it was so terribly expensive. *Why hadn't we just bought it for him?*

In the early afternoon, he was offered (and, to my surprise, agreed to take) a sedative called Ativan. I warned the nurse that he hadn't taken any kind of drug in twenty-plus years, so the dose should probably be quite low.

"How long will he sleep?" I asked.

"About three or four hours," she said.

Five-and-a-half hours later, while Philip continued to sleep all the sleep he hadn't slept for months, the pulmonary specialist called me from the room. He had seen my permission to do the surgery and wanted to talk. He was the most sympathetic and communicative of all the doctors, and he seemed genuinely puzzled and distressed about Philip.

The more he heard about Philip's hypothesis regarding the cough and the possible infection that might have started three years ago, the more disturbed he became.

"If that's the case, this whole thing could probably have been avoided. If Philip had taken a course of antibiotics five years ago when the cough began . . ." He trailed off, possibly regretting this comment, realizing it was pointless conjecture going nowhere. Water under the bridge.

"What do you think of the surgery?" I asked.

"Well, the surgeon is right—the proposed surgery gives Philip a 50/50 chance of surviving, while no surgery means certain death. But did he tell you all the details related to the surgery?"

"Such as?" I asked.

"First, to do the surgery, Philip will have to be intubated."

"What's that?"

"Usually it's an oxygen tube inserted through the mouth and down the throat. But in Philip's case, we'll need to do a tracheotomy–a small incision here." He pointed to the middle of his throat. "The tracheotomy won't be removed, and after the surgery, Philip will need to have an oxygen tank with him wherever he goes."

I took this in, my heart beating faster as an absurd memory jumped to mind of Philip furiously kicking a suitcase across the road after it refused to roll or stay upright on a cobblestoned street in Lisbon. I could see him, in a moment of frustration, doing the same to his oxygen tank.

"And," he continued, "he may also need a feeding tube inserted. There's a risk that he may never eat solid food again."

"Strange details for the surgeon to have omitted," I said weakly. At this point, I was flat-out stunned. *Is this bizarre conversation really happening? About Philip?*

"In addition," he said, "this surgery will have no effect on his failing kidneys, his weakened liver or heart."

Is this guy trying to kill me?

"Can I wait for Philip to wake up so he can make this decision for himself?" I asked.

"Philip isn't going to get clear or awake enough to make this decision. You need to do it for him . . . now."

I looked from his face to the faces of the two nurses standing sympathetically behind his chair.

You're all joking, right? This is just a big, bad joke, yes? But no one laughed. They just waited and watched, expecting me to make the most difficult decision I'd ever faced.

Finally, I said, "I don't believe Philip would want a life of such impairment."

The doctor and two nurses agreed, seemed to exhale relief. So . . . back to the non-invasive position. I signed more papers, barely seeing what I was doing. The world had gone even stranger than it had been in the last seventeen hours.

Sound was different—as though coming from a distance. Sight had changed—everyone seemed very far away, even when they weren't blurred with tears. Feeling was numbed, muffled, dazed—I felt stupefied, unable to take in what was happening. But they went on talking at me as though I were perfectly present, cognizant.

"We will treat Philip as a hospice patient now," one of the nurses explained. "All the antibiotics, vitamins, and minerals now running through the IV will be allowed to run out, and they won't be refilled. An oxygen mask will keep him comfortable and morphine will keep him from discomfort or pain. We'll keep him in the ICU over the weekend and move him into a hospice room first thing Monday morning."

I nodded. Grabbed on and clung to "Monday morning." That sounded like Time.

"You can stay in the room with him if you want."

"Yes! I want."

A little while later, Philip began to stir after close to seven hours under the influence of Ativan.

I pressed my face close to his and spoke softly into his ear. "Can you hear me?"

Eyes still closed, he nodded yes.

"Show me with a nod that you know I love you."

This nod made me weep with relief, happiness, and (unfounded) hope.

"My boy . . . I love you so much."

He nodded again, our faces pressed together.

However, just as he began to return, the night nurse came in. "I'm going to add morphine to his IV," she told me.

"Why does he need morphine? He's just now coming back," I said, hearing panic in my voice and feeling it in my chest. "I want him to have a chance to open his eyes . . . want him to smile, talk, be here again."

"Joan, my primary responsibility is Philip's comfort, as surely yours must be." Her sympathy was scant. She was brisk, terse, matter of fact.

I felt desperate. “But I can’t understand why he needs morphine. He hasn’t complained of pain since he got into the hospital.”

“Philip,” she said, “are you in pain?”

He nodded.

“I’m sure he’s confused. Can I ask him again?”

“Of course.”

But again, he nodded.

So, that was that. I knew it was the nurse’s job to keep him comfortable, not me. But I hated that she was about to take him from me—possibly forever.

One nod, one nurse, one dose of morphine . . . and I’d lost him.

I held his hand, squeezed as close to him as all the tubes allowed, kissed and hugged and held and cried as he slipped back under a blanket of unconsciousness . . . and far away from me.

PART III

Losing an Impossible Person

Voices fade.

Finally
reverberations
taking years
to still,
ripples melting
to mirror smooth
water,
eyes looking into
eyes,
heartbeat of
love that does
not trouble—
awakens memory.

The journey
away
becomes
the journey home.

—Philip Heiman

38

End of Life as I Know It

When I returned to the hospital at 11 P.M. after two hours away, I planned to sit with Philip for a while, say goodnight to my drugged sleeper, and go back to the condo to lie down for a few hours.

"Does this plan make sense?" I asked the night nurse. "You said he would be moved to the hospice room on Monday morning, right?"

"Well, I don't think he's going to live through the night."

"I'm sorry?" I asked.

"I'm seeing the first signs of imminent death."

I was shocked. *Were you going to say anything? I'd like to impose imminent death on you for the calm, cold way you just announced this*, I thought.

Everything changed in an instant. I wasn't going anywhere. I wasn't leaving him to die alone—even if he didn't consciously know I was there.

Philip rested, unconscious and breathing with the support of oxygen. As he gulped rhythmically for air throughout the night, I matched gulps with him. As each IV emptied, it wasn't replaced. Midnight to morning, I watched him, watched the monitor, afraid to leave him even to go to the bathroom.

I talked to him, held his hand, kept my hand on his neck, his heart—got as close as I could. I kissed him, cried, whispered to him, told him everything I could think to say. I repeated constantly how much I loved him. I also railed at how I hated that he was leaving me behind; told him how stupid and stubborn he'd been to end up here so much sooner than either of us wanted. I waited, watched, wept, and, crazy as it sounds . . . hoped.

Maybe the nurse is wrong. Maybe they're all wrong. The talk earlier in the day of moving him upstairs to the hospice room on Monday must have meant they were expecting him to hold on.

So, even though the night nurse didn't think he'd make it through the night, I hoped. Hoped for consciousness. Hoped for his eyes to open, to meet mine one last time. Hoped for one more smile, one last word. Hoped against hope.

Tanya came at around 5:30 A.M. "I wasn't sleeping," she said. "I suddenly didn't know what I was doing there when I should be here. Are you okay with my being here?"

"Yes, of course. . . . I'm glad you're here. They say he doesn't have much time."

We breathed with him, sat with him in silence. Peace filled the room.

We watched the dawn light expand and fill the room. Listened to the monitor as it slowed, and flattened, and slowed, and slowed . . . and finally stopped.

Even when the monitor went fully flat, even when the nurse came in and switched it off, he was still gulping air. And I was still hoping.

Even when she said, "He's gone," I hoped.

"But look." I pointed to the rising of his chest, the continued gulping of air. "What's that?"

"That's just a reflex," she said.

Reflex? Who's still reflexing?

Even as those final reflexive breaths continued—dead but alive—I hoped. I wouldn't let them touch him while those weakening gasps for air continued.

Philip took a final in-breath and exhaled a final out-breath at 7:25 A.M. on Sunday, March 15, 2015. And then, there was no more. Just stillness and gone-ness as he passed peacefully beyond my reach forever. Peace . . . no more struggle, no more discomfort . . . but for me . . . no more him.

39

An Unceremonious Ceremony

In the minutes following Philip's final breath, life . . . or I . . . stepped back, much as he had stepped out and moved on from his body. My body and mind were wrapped and padded, my hearing oddly muffled. I could barely attend to what was going on around me. Everything was hushed and stilled, slowed down, even while figures moved purposefully all around us.

As Tanya and I walked out of the room where Philip lay, no longer inhabiting his Philip-ness, a new hospital face appeared amid all the gentle others who were busying themselves in the hushed efficiency that accompanies hospital death. She laid a kindly hand in mine, introduced herself as a supervisory nurse, and said she'd like to talk about how she might help me.

I vaguely took in and appreciated the emanating kindness but wondered, *What can possibly help me now?*

Through a quieting cushion, I heard Tanya's voice calmly responding. "Yes, thank you. We could certainly use some help."

We walked—*This must be what sleepwalking is like,* I thought—to a private room. She told me her name. I forgot it.

Sound, sensation, and sensitivity were all subdued, muted. I was in some calm underwater or cloud-covered place, as though on calming drugs. Slowly, this gentle woman, whose name I later learned was Diane, emerged from the mists.

"What do you want to do with Philip's body?" she asked.

As with most everything Philip, this was yet another complicated question. When Philip was alive and well (or not so well), our discussions of what to do with our bodies when we died were usually skipped through with a bit of joking and a lot of avoidance.

Both his parents had been cremated; that seemed like the simplest and least disturbing option to me. The idea of moldering away in a box in the earth held no appeal for me, nor did I like the idea of taking up needed land with gravesites and cemeteries. Moreover, cremation made the most sense for two people who'd been as transient as we'd been over the past thirty-seven years. We hadn't purchased plots and had no idea where we'd want them if we had.

Nonetheless, Philip had repeatedly objected to cremation on esoteric and ecological grounds.

"Bodies are supposed to return to the earth, spirits given their own time to rise," he'd say.

"But burial is ecologically disastrous," I'd reply.

"There are ecologically friendly ways now," he'd say. "Cemeteries without gravestones, just nice green parks. No embalming or lead-lined coffins, so your body goes quickly back into the earth. You return to the ground, your body nourishes the earth, and your soul or spirit has the time it needs to understand that it's no longer in the body."

"And where are we going to find one of these friendly places? And how much do they cost?"

"Well, google it, as they say," he'd reply, laughing.

". . . Philip, you're impossible."

"I'm hungry. We can bury ourselves later. Let's have lunch."

Of course we never did google it, nor did we ever make a plan.

Fortunately, Tanya had begun to talk to me about this yesterday—a hundred years ago yesterday, when Philip was still Philip.

I had googled ecological cemeteries near San Diego, my sight blurring with tears as I laughed ruefully with Tanya at the absurdity of searching the internet for eco-friendly burial sites.

"Okay, I found one out in Joshua Tree," I said. "About three hours or a hundred and sixty miles from here."

"Joan, do you know what it will cost just to transport his body there?"

"The range for burial is between $3,500 and $6,500. But no transportation included."

"Joan," she said, "I hate to be harsh, but be realistic. How are you going to pay for all that?"

"Yes . . . and even worse, who's going to visit this ecologically friendly site once I leave here?"

"True," she said.

"But what about his wishes?" I asked and burst into tears yet again.

"Even in his passing," Tanya said, "he's causing trouble."

We leaned against each other, our tears mixing in bittersweet laughter.

Of course, Tanya was right. A visit to the hospital's business office earlier had informed me that an $82,000 hospital bill was looming.

A hospital social worker had appeared at my side a little while later to talk through the options for Philip's body. *As if what to do with his body is exactly what I need to talk about in my last hours with him*, I thought.

I asked her, "How can I go against what he's clearly said time and time again, and what I do I tell him?"

She suggested simply saying, "I know what you want, and I will do my best. Your body will be treated with respect and love."

"That's it? Don't say, 'I can't manage to pay for a burial?' Don't say, 'I don't know where to put you?' Don't say, 'How can I bury you here in California with no one to look after you once I've gone?'"

"Nope," she said. "Just tell him that you love him, and that you'll care for him in the most loving way."

In fact, I never had the opportunity to tell him anything. He was never conscious again. And now here we were—he out of his body, me in mine.

I explained my quandary to Diane, expecting her either to laugh or sigh with impatience. Surely she had more important things to deal with than a crazy conflict between Philip's philosophy and my failing finances.

"When Philip and I argued about cremation versus burial," I told her, "I'd say, 'But we have no *place* to ecologically bury you.' At which point, he'd pause and tilt an annoying eyebrow. 'Well then, just put me in a canvas bag and drop me in the sea,' he'd say."

"Many of these conversations," I continued, "took place in Colorado, where there is no handy sea in which to drop a man in his canvas bag. I'd ask him, 'And where does one buy a canvas body bag?' But this was typically where the conversations would fall into laughing mini-wrestling matches and then conveniently move on to something more important, like lunch."

This angelic woman listened and didn't laugh or sigh.

"You know," she said, "there are plenty of us who share Philip's bury-me-at-sea fantasy. If you're willing to go ahead with the cremation, my husband and I own a sailboat, and I'm sure Greg would be happy to take you and Philip out on our boat. You could drop his ashes into the sea, and in that way, you'd be honoring his wishes . . . at least halfway."

Tanya and I looked at each other in amazement, and then all three of us burst into relieved and delighted laughter.

So this is the compromise, Philip. This is the plan.

Tanya and I went back to the condo, where she began calling to find the quickest, least expensive cremation services. She found one that was willing to take Philip's body from the hospital to the crematorium, do what they do, and then meet me back at the hospital in a few days with the ashes in their simplest urn. It would cost $822.

It all still made me very uneasy. The black and white of it was that I was having his body cremated when he had expressly said he didn't want to be cremated. That was going to be hard to live with. This wasn't a minor decision about whether or not to eat a chocolate bar; this was his body . . . and no one really knows, at an esoteric level, what cremation might mean to the spirit or soul.

Utterly uncomfortable as the decision was, and as much as I hated making it (and would likely hate it forever), it was done, couldn't be undone.

My job now was to keep calling and pushing all kinds of city and county offices to sign off on the death certificate. I also arranged a tentative date with Greg to sail at the end of the week.

The idea that I'd be sailing out into San Diego Bay with a total stranger to drop Philip into the sea was less unsettling than I would've imagined.

After all, at this point, I was still walking around numbly, wrapped in mists and clouds or swimming fathoms deep, surrounded by underwater creatures. I was nowhere real, solid, or familiar.

Perhaps this is what the body and mind do naturally in response to shocking sorrow, like the morphine that eased Philip's final hours, I thought.

My heart was doing a strange dance. It would step out for hours at a time, leaving me dazed or oddly forgetful of where I was or that this enormous life change had happened. Then it would re-emerge and I would go from numbly but outwardly normal to being suddenly clobbered by huge poundings of pain.

The problem with this was that I never knew when the punch would come. All too often it happened in a public place: standing in front of a pile of oranges in the health food store, walking down a sunlit, flower-bedecked street of boutiques and gelato shops in chic Coronado, stopping to watch children fly kites in a park overlooking the bay.

One minute I looked like everyone else out for a pleasant day, and the next I was catapulted out of "normal," flattened in a downpour of drenching emotion. The saving grace was that I didn't notice, or care about, the reactions of those around me. Grief brings temporary release from self-consciousness.

Tanya stayed longer than planned, not wanting to leave me alone to deal with my last days in Coronado, especially the burial at sea. But grateful as I was for her help, her shared grief, and the practical to-do lists she made for me each morning, I needed time alone. It turned out that I had four days in between her departure and my own plan to go back to New York to spend time with my mother and contemplate my totally uncontemplatable life.

There were bureaucratic delays in getting the official signatures needed for cremation, and much as I wanted it all to be done, I found some ease in the extra days and anonymity I had as I wandered aimlessly about Coronado.

It's a lovely place: perfect weather, friendly people; quaint, comfortable, and human-sized architecture. I even looked at rental signs. The idea of moving to a place where no one knew me was appealing. I dreaded dealing with the sympathetic faces waiting for me back East.

I went to a salon for a badly needed haircut and had a long, teary, and sympathetic talk with the stylist, who invited me to join her backyard yoga class that evening. More California kindness.

A few days after Philip died, I discovered that the holdup for the necessary signatures was at the hospital: the doctors either hadn't determined the final cause of death or hadn't agreed on what they would write down. They didn't know whether Philip had a cancerous tumor, an abscessed infection, or something else entirely. Without the surgery, they couldn't really know.

When it finally came, the death certificate listed the causes of death as

- septic shock;
- pneumonia;
- chronic obstructive pulmonary disease (COPD).

A life and a death summed up in bullet points, I thought.

Eventually, all was settled, and I arranged to meet the man from the cremation service at the hospital. About to leave the condo with only the key and a check in my pocket, I realized I'd have to carry the urn back with me. In what does one carry a funerary urn as one walks down a sunny San Diego street?

I started to giggle hysterically at the absurdity of it all, but my laughter quickly turned into tears. I emptied my backpack of the oranges, pineapple, and salad greens I'd just bought at the market and set out to fill my empty pack with a load the likes of which it had never seen.

The cremation man (*What are these people officially called?),* dressed in the proverbial dark, pinstriped suit, was waiting for me on a bench in front of the hospital. I looked down at my sandals and tatty sweatshirt and wondered if I should have dressed for the occasion.

"I guess you aren't exactly a good advertisement for the hospital," I managed to say.

"No," he replied. "I thought it would be better to meet outside." *Did he smile sheepishly?*

He was empty-handed, and I suppose my question showed on my face. He walked me over to his car and opened the trunk. At this point, a surreal fantasy flashed through my delirium: *This feels like a drug deal.* Feeling giddy and about to get hysterical again, I bit my lip, dug my nails into clenched fists, and ordered myself to get a grip while he rummaged in his trunk.

First, he handed me what he called the "necessary documentation." I signed some papers held out to me on a clipboard, and in exchange for the now-rumpled check, he handed me a gaudy red, fake-velvet bag weighing more than I would have imagined possible.

In response to the dumb incomprehension on my face as I stared down at the burden he'd deposited in my hands, he explained gently, as if to an idiot, "The box inside the bag is the urn."

His eyes, sympathetic, met mine momentarily, and he gave me a firm funereal handshake. I slipped the tawdry bag into my pack, waved goodbye, and walked away. With the late afternoon sun shining down on the burden I now carried on my back, Philip's heavy presence was oddly comforting, if somewhat unsettling.

Back at the condo, I placed the urn and its bag on the table amid oranges and salad greens. I was so stupefied that I didn't feel the tears on my face for a few minutes.

No one prepares us for this.

The next morning, Greg picked me up according to plan and drove us to his dock. He was a perfect blend of decorousness and matter-of-fact practicality. We boarded a sleek white sailboat and headed out into San Diego Bay in the direction of the bridge. He kept up a comfortable banter of small talk and boating information, which distracted me from what we were doing.

After about twenty minutes, we got to an open space near the bridge.

"Does this look all right?" he asked.

"Sure. But is this legal?" It hadn't occurred to me to ask before.

"Well, if it isn't, no one will be the wiser."

I took the box in its awful red bag out of my pack and put it into his hands. "This *will* sink, won't it?"

"I don't see why not."

We paused for a moment of silence, and then I dropped Philip into the bay. I was in one of those my-heart-has-gone-elsewhere moments when it hit the water. It went under . . . and then it surreally bobbed back up.

We stared at it, stared at each other. I hardly knew whether to laugh or cry.

I looked out at the row of mansions along the nearest shore. "Is Philip going to wash up in someone's backyard tomorrow morning?" I asked, walking a tightrope between hilarity and horror. "What do we do now?"

Starting up the engine, Greg slowly followed the bobbing box that was already being carried toward the shore. With a pole in one hand and his hat tilting crazily over his nose, he repeatedly and apologetically attempted to push and hold the box under.

"I'm so sorry," he said.

Down it went . . . and up it came. When Greg nearly fell into the water, my hysteria rose again. I buried my face in my hands. With irrepressible laughter shaking my body (*God, Joan, must you?*), poor Greg assumed I was sobbing. He was distraught.

When I realized what I'd done to the poor guy, I tried to comfort him as the misinterpreted tears rolled down my face. "Listen," I said. "We can either see this as horrific or absurd. Let's choose absurd. Philip would."

He nodded and made a few more failed attempts with the pole. "Would you mind if I drive the boat over it?" he asked.

"No, no . . . fine. Just sink it."

The box, by this time, had freed itself of its bag. *I knew Philip would hate that bag.* Greg fished the sodden red mess out of the water and discreetly tossed it out of sight below deck.

When we dared to move the boat, the box was finally under . . . and staying under. With a huge sigh of relief, Greg unfurled the sails and made me the captain, borrowed cap and all. Sunlight glinting off the water, the boat gliding white and soundless, we sailed companionably back to shore. What a most unceremonious ceremony.

Philip, my irascible trickster, you've had your last laugh, I thought.

40

Married . . . Without My Husband

Back in my childhood home on Long Island, everything was the same, very little changed. Every vase, lamp, picture, the whir of the attic fan, the click of the key in the lock was familiar. But I was not at home inside, not familiar with this new version of me who felt, at best, like half of me. Hollow, scooped out, pared down. Dry and parched.

As I wrote in my journal, I wondered how the tears continued to pour from an inner desert.

> You're gone. How could you leave me?
>
> I feel as though I'm constantly betraying you in every moment when I'm not thinking of you or feeling the loss of you. I feel terrible, strangely frightened, when I realize I haven't felt bad for the past hour.
>
> I also feel I'm betraying you in every act you wouldn't like, wouldn't agree with: eating cooked food, discussing our—now my—financial problems with my brother, sitting through a dumb musical the day after I got here. Thinking of going to North Myrtle Beach to explore living there to be close to Tanya, Misha, and Malia. Reconnecting with your family.
>
> Everything I do feels like treachery, selling out, double-dealing. Why am I choosing to act in all these ways you wouldn't have? Who am I when you're not here in your stronger, more defined personality? Have I been nothing other than a response to you?

> What will my life turn into? What or who will I be? Single, solo . . . on my own at sixty-two? A widow, for God's sake!
>
> If I know and have known myself for the past thirty-seven years as the person who loves you, who am I when you are no longer here in your body to love and be loved by me? I am married to you, but you are no longer here.

One afternoon, my mother and I saw the film *My Old Lady*. This was one more Philip betrayal, since, starting in the 1980s, he saw film as emotional manipulation, so we'd stopped going. As a result, I was in a movie time warp, knowing nothing of actors or films from the past thirty years.

In the movie, the main character, at age fifty-seven, is still caught—nearly paralyzed—by the sorrows of his childhood. He is an emotional failure. The continued pain and anger he feels toward his father, combined with the trauma of having seen his mother commit suicide, have eaten at his heart and defeated his soul. It hurt to think of Philip, whose life had also been so tragically diminished by never being able to free himself from the disappointment, anger, and damage to his self-worth that he'd suffered in relation to his parents.

At the end of the movie, the main character—finally somewhat psychologically freed (*Do people outside of movies ever really get free?*)—responds spontaneously to a woman who habitually walks along the Seine singing operatically. He sings back to her, and for just a moment, they connect through the beauty of their voices floating, meeting, and mingling across the water.

My mom said that scene reminded her of Philip; his romantic, always-singing self. It warmed my frozen heart just a bit to hear her describe a part of him I cherished, one I didn't know she knew.

I was afraid that if I didn't think of Philip enough, he'd start to disappear. *I wonder when and if I'll trust that you won't slip away from my heart*, I thought.

"I sometimes wonder if I told your dad I loved him enough," my mom said one day, tears welling up in her eyes.

He'd died in 2000, but years and years later, he still hadn't slipped away from her heart. How and why did I have this fear? Why would thirty-seven years of joy and sorrow, laughter and tears, stories, failures, and dreams melt away?

> This morning I caught myself chanting, *I don't care*. Don't care what I eat. Don't care whether I go to a film or watch TV. Don't care that I spend time with people you didn't want to spend time with. I don't care . . . don't care about anything. Except that I am missing and betraying you. Will this feeling of unfaithfulness and deceit fade? Surely there is a healthier, happier way to maintain my connection with you.
>
> Here without you . . . for the rest of my life. A never-ending absence. No more you to listen, to argue, to cuddle, to soothe. No more you to live a life that once seemed full of laughter and possibilities . . . and now feels empty, dead-ended.
>
> I'm sixty-two, about to be sixty-three. I could live another twenty to thirty years. Without you? Meaningless. A whole different life. Do I want it? Not really. I am married . . . without my husband.

41

Lessons in Grief

Two weeks later, in early April, I was sitting in the refectory at the Meher Spiritual Center in North Myrtle Beach. The late afternoon air and mellow light filtered in through the open screens. Surrounding evergreen trees shadowed the room, filling it with the clean scent of pine. I'd signed on for a week's stay at this beautiful coastal retreat, lovingly tended and set amid five hundred acres of virgin forests with freshwater lakes and paths leading to the sea.

I should have been grateful for the blessed peace and sanctuary the center had offered every other time I'd been there. Instead, I was uneasy as the recipient of too much sympathetic attention.

News of Philip's death had preceded me. I didn't want to be perceived as weak and wounded, even though I was and I would have liked to crawl into a cave indefinitely. Uncomfortable with people seeing me as needing sympathy, empathy, or pity, I simultaneously didn't want to be viewed as "coping well" and "being strong." I didn't want to cope or be strong. *Who does one go to for permission to officially break down?* I thought.

I also didn't want others to wonder at my heartlessness if they found me laughing, eating lunch, or just carrying on with the day instead of stumbling through a deluge of weeping. *Why so much pride, if that's what this is?* I wondered. I was afraid of being considered "wimpy" or asking for sympathy. And I feared being seen as insensitive.

It was preposterous to be so aware of others, concerned with their perceptions and opinions when this huge pain was dragging at me with ten-pound weights on my legs and lead encasing my heart. I was absurdly plagued with self-conscious cares—so different from those first days when I didn't notice others, when they were blurred and shut out by tears or numbness.

On my second morning, I walked right into a fellow guest I'd been avoiding. I'd evaded her for a day and a half with quick nods, eyes turned down—even unplanned, sudden turns off my intended path. It wasn't that I was put off by her; more that I sensed her desire to help, to ask and know more than I felt like sharing. I came here to be alone. But, even in the midst of grief, I was more concerned about hurting this woman's feelings than with protecting my own.

Good god! Will I ever feel justified in putting myself first? Is this a woman thing?

Finally, cornered and unable to extricate myself, unable to say thanks but no thanks, I invited her in and we settled into the dappled morning light that fluttered onto my cabin's screened porch.

We talked first about the plane trip from San José to San Diego; the painful and exhausting ordeal that Philip suffered and would have died of only a few hours after arriving had it not been for the hospital . . . or fate.

"I hate that he suffered that trip all for nothing," I said.

"Sometimes exhausting the body like that gives the soul a way to soften into letting go," she said. "A physical challenge at the end of life may exhaust the resistances of the body, making the move toward death easier for the soul."

"Hmm . . . maybe. I've certainly never thought of that. Still, I hate those pained and cruel twelve hours that he struggled through so bravely. Tanya and I literally watched his life-force waning by the hour . . . and could do nothing."

"You did all you could by being there and loving him," she said.

It wasn't enough! I wailed inwardly.

"If we hadn't called for help," I said, "he would have died in the condo, on that bed, without the drama and trauma of paramedics, the ambulance ride, the emergency room revival, endless testing, questioning, and the day and a half in intensive care. Wouldn't a simple, quiet slipping away have been kinder?"

"Hospital stays are not solely for the patient," she said. "Those extra hours may have been 'given' to you. The hospital relieved and released you—possibly more than Philip. For the first time in more than three months, you could just be there without having to nurse and care for his body. The nurses in the ICU are much more prepared, adept, and equipped to make people comfortable than we are."

"Well, yes. I'd never thought of that either."

She gently asked me to tell her what he'd given to and done for others in his lifetime. I supposed she was trying to show me all he'd completed.

OK, I can do that.

I thought of ways that Philip had shared himself and supported others, and it soothed my heart momentarily to remember and tell a stranger of all the good he'd done.

I told her that when his sister's children and Misha were young and needed an adult with a different perspective, he was there—emotionally and spiritually present. He was so *other*, so different from the adults in their lives.

This had been confirmed in their last messages to him: letters sent to me after he died, and their spoken tributes when we all finally came together to commemorate his death and life.

Misha had written, "Time spent with you has made such an impact on me . . . I love you so truly and deeply. The person I have become has been shaped and influenced by you."

Our niece wrote, "You will always be an inspiration and a guiding presence in my life."

Our youngest nephew said, "I can't tell you how comforting it was, even at a very early age, to have found you, to know that we were of the same tribe. You made me feel understood and free."

Our oldest nephew wrote, "You showed me a love for music, art, and poetry, and you taught me how to listen to the wind."

I told her how, even at the end of his life—seventy-eight pounds, weak, losing his hair, and barely able to stand without leaning on me—women and men at the retreat center in Costa Rica had come to sit, talk, and listen to him.

"I love to hear him talk," one woman had said. "I don't care what he's talking about. Everything he says is like a jewel to be explored in all its facets and then cherished."

It wasn't only what he said, but how he said it. He had the most charming speaking voice I'd ever heard—melodious, mellifluous, resonant.

Then I told her about the Australian nurse, another guest at Highlands, and how, to my surprise, he'd accepted her offers to treat his terribly uncomfortable bedsores. She had seemed happy to serve him and to teach me to do the same. He, in turn, was willing to surrender his control and expose himself so vulnerably—literally baring his bottom—to a kind and competent stranger with nurse's hands. He'd offered an astrological reading in exchange.

"Thanks, but no," she had said. "Astrology just isn't in my belief system."

A few hours later, she returned. "I can't believe I would be so closed-minded to turn down an opportunity like this. Without having had a reading, I've already experienced your wisdom, insight, and compassion. If astrology is your 'tool,' I'd be foolish and arrogant to let my ignorance prevent me from benefiting from what I can learn from you. Can I change my answer and accept your invitation?"

She left the center the following day. A few days later, she wrote to tell us that the reading and Philip's conversations with her had given her the clarity and courage to change her life entirely, to move to a different country and start over with the daughter she thought she'd given up on.

This turned out to be Philip's last reading.

I thought of others he'd touched deeply in astrological readings, in conversations, in stimulating and challenging, but always loving, friendships. I went into my cabin and brought out a letter from a friend that had just come in the mail. I read it aloud to her.

> Philip was a unique character unlike anyone I've ever known. He was brilliant, a romantic idealist to the nth degree, a gentle soul. He was always worth talking to, and that too made him exceptional. So many people, including myself, have really nothing very interesting to say, but

> Philip's wide reading and spiritual intuitions offered me new ways of looking at my world and myself. People were fascinated by Philip, as was I, and the fact that he did not take advantage of that is hugely to his credit. His ethical values and his sense of humor and modesty preserved him from doing harm to his own soul and others. Instead, he expanded people's horizons and made them see the stars. I could say that it was tragic that he wasn't more fulfilled, or his talents put to even better use, but I don't know myself if that's true. He was a poet and a spiritual seeker, which is a hard vocation in this day and age, but I think he lived it. I'm so very sorry he's gone, Joan, and grieve your loss with you.

Then, she moved me gently back toward considering that Philip's "spiritual work" in this life was complete. I'd heard and read this thinking before. In the abstract, it had made some sense to me—when I'd managed to transcend my agnostic reflex. But now she was bringing the abstract home. No longer philosophizing, I didn't know what I felt about it.

Had he done all he had to do in this lifetime? With all the limitations that prevented what might have been an even more creative, productive, and satisfying life, had he done all there was to be done?

"He'd gotten himself stuck," I said. "Stuck in a stubborn, neurotic state of mind. Stuck in inflexibility. Stuck with fear and panic neither of us could assuage. And finally, stuck with physical ailments neither his body nor his spirit could sustain. So in that sense, perhaps, one could say he'd gone as far as he could go in this life. Maybe."

"Had you done all you could do together in this lifetime?" she asked. "Was your spiritual work together completed?"

"No!" I said, nearly shouting. Knowing how much more there was in him—so much more love, creativity, beauty, poetry, I resisted.

"We could have loved more deeply, given more fully, explored more fearlessly," I said. "We might have moved more fully into our creativity, both independently—he in his poetry and astrology, I through writing—and by joining these gifts together. We could have shared them with others." Annoyed and defensive now, I continued. "Yoga and meditation could also have gone much deeper, much further—together and independently. We might have found that place of peace, simplicity, and sanctuary he so longed for. We might have created a simple home, planted a garden, grown fruit trees."

"What more?" she asked gently.

"We might have finally found a way to 'slow down' as he always wished—to feel safe, to find and create beauty in one tiny corner of the world, as well as in our hearts and souls. And we might have continued to evolve in relating heart to heart with increasingly fewer words and an ever more immediate communion of feelings."

"So why do you think this hadn't happened yet?" she asked.

Why am I submitting myself to this interrogation? What does she know that I don't?

"I don't know. If I acknowledge how stuck he seemed to have become, and if I acknowledge that I couldn't find a way to approach his fears or my own limitations, stuck in all my stuckness as well as his, then I suppose I can try to see that 'our work together' had gone as far as it could go in this lifetime. If what *is* is truth, then I suppose I might eventually come to accept that we had gone as far as we could go together in this life. But I hate this, and I nearly hate you for pushing me to say it."

She bowed her head and sat quietly. I became aware of birdsong and the far-off whispering of the surf washing up on the sand.

"He has gone away," she said.

Can I see everything as being exactly as it needs to be? I asked myself after she'd left. *Everything as necessary, or as given? No regrets, no judgment, just a loving surrender to forces much greater than my own?*

I woke up the next morning to angry disbelief and rejection of our conversation. I could *not* believe or accept that Philip and I had no further to go together. Nor would I accept or surrender to his death as my "opportunity" or "possibility" for continued growth. I hated this kind of thinking. I felt tricked and New Age philosophized.

I just wanted Philip back . . . stuckness, stubbornness, impossible-person-ness . . . all.

42

Moments

I understand now why my mother puts her television on as soon as she gets up in the morning—even when she's not yet in the room to watch it. I have been, largely without pause, moving from audiobooks to music to podcasts to the newly discovered and dangerously addictive Netflix.

The silence is so . . . silent. Something alive and vital, Philip's large and human presence, is so dramatically missing. Gone. No intimacy; no comfort; no "my person."

In later years and especially toward the end, when Philip was too weak to sit up or even hold a book for more than a few minutes, I read to him for hours, and we spent even more hours listening to audiobooks together. Now, I let the narrator of an audiobook read me into sleep as Philip once did. Literature still offers solace, nurturance, and inspiration, even in a home that feels achingly empty without Philip sitting here reading by my side.

But a voice inside says I must befriend the silence. My lost sense of inner peace will not be found in filling every minute with some kind of noise.

* * *

A date pit falls out of a notebook! Dates—his sweet temptation. I hold something that was in his mouth. Can't throw it away.

* * *

I catch myself hoping he'll walk through the door. I want to believe he's just gone off on an extended trip. That I'll wake from this impossibly bad dream. That I'll turn to find him beside me.

* * *

I'm disturbed by feeling so quickly depleted and drained after being with anyone for more than an hour or two. Every appointment, meeting, date, or even phone call forces me out when so much of me wants to stay in, quiet and alone. Lonely for him but choosing to be alone.

I look for the days on my calendar where there's nothing—not even a meeting with the financial consultant, a hair appointment, a need to shop for food. I breathe with relief and feel my heart expand into these solo days.

* * *

I walk in the early morning, talking on the phone with Tanya. We understand and accept each other effortlessly, find the same things funny, baffling, or alarming.

Oddly, back in the first tumultuous years of my relationship with Philip, when I was "learning" him (somewhat akin to learning a foreign language), it was Tanya who helped me acquire the needed vocabulary and syntax. Having their son, Misha, with us over summers and staying in touch throughout the early years via phone calls, handwritten letters, and visits, Tanya and I built the ground for what was to be a lifelong love and friendship. She and Philip were apparently more comfortable as friends, no longer caught up in the expectations and struggles of a marriage. So, most of the time, we made a good trio for Misha as he was growing up.

I recall long walks on the beach in South Carolina, just Tanya and me talking through my conflicted feelings of wanting the deep communion that Philip was forever seeking while also wanting to hold onto my independence. Unlike family or friends who didn't know and couldn't love him as Tanya had and still did, she listened with humor and spiritual perspective. While other friends questioned, doubted, and criticized the odd guy who seemed too emotionally complex and psychologically demanding, Tanya held my anger and resentments right alongside my growing love and deepening affection . . . judging nothing.

* * *

I was walking in the sun this morning. I felt a sense of well-being I've not experienced in I don't know how long. Then, a punch in the stomach came with the re-realization that he is never going to take my hand, walk beside me again in the Colorado sun.

* * *

A weepy day. I knew that listening to "No Frontiers" by Mary Black would reach into my heart.

"It's very brave of you to listen to music," a friend says. "I stay far away from it when I feel vulnerable."

"But I *want* to touch the place of connection," I reply. "I want to feel everything there is to feel, even if right now everything is pain."

When Philip and I had last listened to this song about the release from fear, it was only weeks before he died. We didn't know that death would be his release. Now, for me, there is monstrous absence. This appalling empty space he's left behind for me to try to inhabit.

How am I to go on day after day, year after year, without you? How can I live on in a life I don't love or want?

* * *

Hang pictures on the walls of a new home—without him. Find a comfortable reading chair, a lamp, a table. *Why? What's the point?*

* * *

I wake up early today, wandering aimlessly through showering, bed-making, turning my studio apartment night room into a day room. Now at 5:30 A.M., watching through the great gift of large, eastern-facing windows on the sixth floor above the treetops, I behold the minute-by-minute transformation as gray cloud cover tints into soft, unnamable hues. The only open part of the sky, resting low down and miles off at the horizon, shifts from pale pink to brighter coral to sun-kissed apricot.

On the sidewalk below, an elderly woman rides her motorized chair through shadows where all is still in near darkness. Dressed in black, she lifts her little black dog, drapes him in a white blanket and settles him in her lap.

Such sweet tenderness and enviable accord. *Do I want a dog? A companion?* When I gaze back up, the topmost part of the rising sun now gleams white-gold on the horizon, its light inching through the branches of the tree nearest my window. Farther out, mist covers the distant rise of the land beyond town, and as the sun touches the ground, it lights up soft, dreamy blankets of mauve, blue, and purple.

I sip tea and listen to *Wild* by Cheryl Strayed. She talks about her mother's unexpected death from lung cancer, and I cry into the first morning light. I'm grateful for the immediacy of emotion that brings Philip near, even while simultaneously bringing the immediacy of bereavement. How odd that these two seemingly contrary emotions now come together.

The sky above the clouds now turns a soft baby blue while the growing sun lifts to meet the lowering cloud bank. Will the sun be swallowed by clouds, or will it burn them off? The sun is more than half hidden now, lighting the clouds with beams of brilliant light. The blue sky momentarily turns bluer . . . and then both sun and blue disappear into a somber, slate gray.

Now, at 5:55 A.M., the sky is no longer extraordinary. Just quietly subdued . . . sober. If I had woken up and opened my curtains now, as I normally do, I wouldn't know what had transpired in the past twenty-five minutes.

In twenty-five minutes, hope can die. A person, too, can shift, change, and move from life into death. Philip, still alive at 7 A.M., was dead at 7:25. Throughout a long and never-long-enough night, he breathed his way toward his death—much as the sun breathed its way into cloud this morning.

7:25 on March 15, 2015. A minute on the clock; an inhalation, a final exhalation. I go on inhaling and exhaling without him.

I walk involuntarily into this unsought and unwanted life. Cheryl Strayed chose to walk the Pacific Crest Trail. Part of me wishes to walk as she did, to exhaust myself with physical effort, walk away from the past, brave the future, be enchanted by natural beauty.

Another part of me knows, however, that at least for now, I will sit right here, sit still into this journey.

* * *

Again and again, I berate a cruel fate: *Why was he taken from me?* We could have, should have had at least twenty more years together. Other older couples get to stay together. Even those who barely like each other.

* * *

I wake up from a complicated, multi-layered dream in which Philip has returned—confirming my continuing waking sense that he's just away on an extended trip and will come home any day now.

In the dream, he was unconcerned about dropping buttery crumbs on my newly purchased armchair. My therapist suggests that it might have been a playful message from Philip not to sanctify him in his death. It would be impossible to do so; a saint, he was not.

I suddenly remember a reading done by Liz Greene—renowned astrologer, Jungian analyst, and author living in London—back in 1982. She told me that our relationship, struggle-y as it was and probably would always be, would most likely survive.

"You have the capacity to see and love Philip with all his warts. And warts he definitely has," she said, laughing.

I didn't know whether to laugh or not.

* * *

Sometimes I can't help wondering if the joy and laughter I had with Philip were my lifetime's allocation; if that was it for this lifetime. A self-pitying and morbid thought, but grief is full of downward dives.

* * *

When my father was dying of cancer back in 2000, my mother and I stopped into a restroom in the hospital.

"Do you have, or are you now wishing for, some kind—any kind—of spiritual perspective to face this terrible time?" I asked the woman who had taught me agnosticism.

Her face softened as our eyes met in the mirror. "I wish I did. I envy people who have a religious or spiritual belief to carry them through times like this," she said. "But I can't put spirituality on like a coat just because I want or need it. If you don't have that kind of belief, you just don't have it."

Our eyes filled with tears before we went back to washing our hands and applying fresh coats of lipstick. Applying coats of lipstick is possible—coats of faith, apparently not.

* * *

I find scraps of paper stuffed in a pocket and realize they hold his last written words. I can't throw them away, so I add his nearly indecipherable and pathetic scribbles asking for juice and a story to his poetry file.

* * *

A young woman who works at the local food co-op—someone I hardly know—approaches me. Apparently she's learned of my grief from another employee whom I'd recently had the courage to tell about Philip's death; I couldn't bear to have her imagine we'd divorced, didn't want to wait for the moment when she might ask, "Where's Philip these days?"

This second woman approaches me while I'm studying the ingredients in a bottle of olive tapenade, wondering about trying something new.

"Can I hug you?" she asks. She holds me long and tenderly, then releases me. I feel like a tiny, fragile bird in her arms. Stepping back, she looks into my eyes with huge and beautiful compassion and says, "I am so very sorry."

The experience—both sweet and startling—shakes me. Life is so big and so small; so immense and so petty; so dramatic . . . and so mundane. So olive tapenade. So life. So death.

* * *

Other encounters with people in shops, at the bank . . . people who knew us as one. I avoid them for as long as I can. With the passing of time and on days when I've already cried buckets and feel relatively washed out, possibly pulled together, I begin to brave the conversations.

Sympathy is kind, yet so hard to take. There's no "good" way to deal with it. I am sorry to bring my news to a dear young man Philip and I both liked, a manager at Whole Foods; I want to apologize for upsetting him and disturbing his busy day.

But he stops, listens, takes me into his arms. "Let me hug you whenever you need," he says.

* * *

Two strangers are talking in a café as I pass their table.

"We haven't had time to grieve," one says.

I am tempted to pull up a chair, so fully do I relate to this. "Me neither," I want to say. And then I want to ask, "But would you know *how* to grieve if you were given the time?"

For a few moments, I feel related, connected, wish to sit and talk and explore these enormous unanswerable questions with strangers who become familiar in shared sorrow.

* * *

I look at three favorite photos that capture cherished aspects of Philip. In the first, he is reflective or possibly whimsical. In another, he toasts me, disarmingly charming. In the third, his face pressed against mine, we are laughing, joyful.

Six-year-old me stomps her foot: *Why did you leave me?*

I obsessively return to the image in my mind of him just after death—fallen slightly sideways, finally released, hopefully at peace, but more dramatically and radically gone, ended, more withdrawn than I can stand.

Juxtaposing this uncompromisingly final image with the early photos of him—young, vital, laughing, and loving—I struggle to incorporate all, to allow and accept . . . and love . . . all.

* * *

While I do all right on my own, life feels unreal, a stage set on which I must play an unfamiliar and unwanted role. I catch a glimpse of my face reflected in a passing shop window. A mask covers all that is uneasy, unsettled, and endlessly unhappy. The mask is brittle, less than alive, uninhabited by the warmth of my soul. My persona is less than real, the smile painted on.

Witnessing this contrast between what's going on inside versus what appears on the outside is unnerving.

* * *

Nothing holds interest. I attend a book reading and wish I'd stayed at home. I walk through an art gallery and see nothing of beauty; nothing touches my heart. I share a meal with a friend and the food turns to straw in my mouth. People on the pedestrian mall are one-dimensional cutouts, not living, thriving companions on the journey.

* * *

Sitting in my 450-square-foot studio apartment, I feel a wave of gratitude for the three remaining Oriental carpets that transform this 1970s high-rise space into a cozy nest where I continue to feel Philip's presence.

He loved simple and delicate folk designs, whimsical ethnic décor, and, greatest of all, Oriental carpets. When we moved to Abu Dhabi, we took five carpets *to* the Middle East. (Talk about sending coals to Newcastle.) By the time we returned, we had fifteen.

* * *

I feel angry with him for leaving me. Then guilty for feeling angry, then guilty and angry for having survived him.

Why did you die—why leave me to carry on?

Bewildered, disoriented, untethered, I go endlessly round and round in the hugely silent company of his incomprehensible, inconceivable absence.

* * *

I wait behind an older couple at a street crossing. As the light changes, they lightly, habitually link hands.

My left hand twitches as I feel that move, that accustomed, automatic reaching for Philip's hand. I feel our fingers seeking their familiar grasp, my hand folded into his, pinkies linked.

I remember always finding him on my left side when we walked, feeling oddly off-balance when we would occasionally end up on the "wrong" sides.

Laughing as we'd correct, wondering how we'd come to feel so "right" or "wrong" in these positions.

These are the little things that make up the growing tapestry of a relationship, the loving details of a life shared. I am exhausted with missing them.

* * *

A stranger in a shop tells me of the death of her husband nineteen years ago, followed by years of hardship raising three small boys alone. Her face wears the scars and lines of her sorrow and suffering. Her eyes fill with tears and anguish as she talks.

"No," she says, "the pain doesn't go away. It softens, becomes a companion, and aches like an old wound on a rainy day. But it has taught me to believe there must be something more and something better to live toward in this life . . . and possibly, in the next."

I walk away, tears turning icy on my cheeks in the winter air. I wonder if I will come to believe in that something more, something better.

* * *

I am not *in love*. I love, yes. But I am not *in love* with anyone or anything or life itself. My heart doesn't participate. I am not central in anyone's life; no one person is central in mine. I am missing an essential part of myself. But I carry on. What else is there to do when love and the beloved are gone?

* * *

Christopher Parkening plays solo guitar on the radio; music so familiar and often shared with Philip. I burst into tears as I get up to see what the song is. It's Bach's "Herz Und Mund Und Tat Und Leben."

With my miniscule German, I translate "Heart and World and Death and Love." And weep some more. Then I put the words into the online translator. No. I have it wrong. It is "Heart and Mouth and Act and Life." What lies deep within my affections must be spoken and acted upon . . . and lived.

* * *

Day follows day; I carry on. I am grateful for friends who care and about whom I care, grateful for this little aerie I call home, for days of solitude, for little interactions that bring or give a smile. I love the crusty old cowboy, Smokey, who sits in the common room of my building, nods as I go by, calls me *darlin'*.

I feel a deepening love for and from my mother. I'm tickled by two new buds opening on the mum plant I bought for my table last fall. I laugh aloud as two squirrels do their nutty dance, hectically scrambling and tumbling around the base of an old cottonwood tree.

* * *

A friend writes that people stay connected to loved ones who have died. She says, "They are absent but not gone."

Perhaps, but right now the live, warm, touching, laughing, meeting of eyes, lips, minds, and smiles are all gone. And I? I—left behind—am stranded, shipwrecked, bereft.

43

Therapy

After the first month of river-flowing tears, grief shifted into what I described as "emotional sneezes." Air-gulping tears erupted at odd times and places and then, just as quickly, subsided—leaving me unnerved and hesitant to go out. So, I decided to try therapy.

"What are you looking for from therapy?" the therapist asked at our first meeting.

"To do more than 'sneeze,'" I said. "To unplug emotionally and allow the flow of sorrow, and find a healthier way to retain my connection to Philip. I'm so afraid that I'll lose a sense of connectedness with him that I think I may be holding onto pain as the only way I know of staying close to him."

"Why did you choose me specifically?" she asked.

"Well, I understand that you practice body and energy therapies rather than relying solely on talk. I've habitually coped with pain by thinking my way into and through it, and I'm hoping your approach to healing will show me how to let my heart lead and the wisdom of my body be my guide."

We began and ended each session of body and energy work with a few minutes of talk. In between, I lay on her massage table while she held her hands lightly on different parts of my body while asking me to articulate memories, images, and emotions.

In our first session, I quickly felt lost and uncertain. "I don't know how to grieve, how to live with grief. I wander around not knowing if I want to sit or stand, go out or stay in," I told her. "I'm sure I'm not the first, last, or only person to feel this way. Why don't they teach this in school? I mean, who needs algebra when we don't know how to deal with death . . . or how to die?"

"These feelings, impressions, and puzzlings related to grief are unique to each of us," she said. "And apparently they're also universal. You're not alone, and yet you feel terribly alone."

I settled into the warmth of feeling seen and understood. "I need time, space, and so much solitude to feel and know how to be with myself and this unspeakable absence," I said. "I'm fortunate I'm not afraid of solitude. What I hate is feeling alone when I'm with others."

"When you're here, I'm here for you," she said. Her hands were warm and warming. "I feel Philip's presence standing by your right side," she said. "He can be with you whenever you invite him." I was struck by her sense of and comfort with the realm of spirit.

"I can't honestly say I feel anything spirit-like," I said as we ended the session. "But this hour has filled my heart. My sense of him is more awake and available than it's been in the past month."

"I'm going to leave you to rest now— take your time and call me when you're ready. Koda, come."

Koda, the therapist's dog, was still dozing peacefully on the floor, where he'd been throughout the session. His eyes opened and his eyebrows raised, but the rest of him remained on the floor.

"Koda?" she repeated.

Koda beat the floor with his tail but still didn't rise. She called him once more, but he didn't move. After being cooped up in a small room for two hours and watching his person walk out, I was moved by his choice to stay with me. His presence was surprisingly comforting, confirming my nascent longing for the wise company of animals.

I left her office, an easy fifteen-minute walk from my apartment. She worked out of a house that Philip and I had walked past regularly, only a few blocks from the little house we'd lived in another lifetime ago. I felt both released and exhausted, emptied and cleansed.

My head full of tears, eyes red and swollen, I hid behind rarely worn sunglasses. For the first time, I understood why so many people love dark glasses—beyond the coolness factor. With my eyes hidden, all of me felt more hidden, oddly protected. I felt less exposed, more privately held within my own psychic space. I appreciated this unexpected but simple means of psychological protection.

In our next session, and in complete contrast to my agnosticism, I found myself asking the therapist for help with a growing fear that belied what could be seen as an esoteric belief.

"By wishing and wanting Philip back, might I be selfishly keeping his spirit from going free?"

"Where does this concern come from?" she asked.

"Nearly forty years ago," I explained, "I talked to a psychic about my grief for Buddy, my dog. That was three years after he died, and I told the psychic that I was still falling into wells of sorrow. I was still regularly dreaming that he was alive, and waking from those dreams aching for his living, breathing animal warmth. I asked the psychic if it was normal, and if not, what I could do.

"The psychic told me that dogs go to a wonderfully free and unfettered place when they die," I continued. "A place far better than anything they know here—no leashes, no waiting for humans to let them out, no restrictions. But she told me that, in his loyalty and love for me, Buddy was holding himself back from going to that place. That's why I kept seeing him in dreams. He was responding to my need. She said he would do this as long as he felt me calling for him. The psychic asked me, 'Out of your love for Buddy, can you set him free? Do you love him enough to let him go?'"

"That was a powerful and challenging thing to ask of you," my therapist said. "Were you ready to hear it?"

"I guess so. When she explained it that way, her words propelled me forward, left me able—wanting—to release him from the hold of my sorrow. And shortly after our conversation, the dreams and my pain diminished."

"I think I understand, but tell me, how are you connecting this to Philip?" she asked.

"Well, I'm afraid I'll do the same to Philip—hold him back with my selfish and impossible yearning for his return. I don't know how to maintain a felt sense of connection with him if not through this pain and longing, but what if I'm keeping him from where his spirit wants to go? What if I'm stopping him from traveling on? Ugh . . . this is awful."

"It is awful," she said sympathetically. "But I don't see it quite that way. My sense is that the spirits of those who pass on *want* to be near us when we need them. The spirit world isn't black and white, not nearly as literal as this one. When people die, the love that we shared continues infinitely. People and animals move easily back and forth in spirit form, able to comfort those left behind while simultaneously inhabiting their new existence in the spirit realm—not one or the other, not here or gone, captured or released."

I was relieved by this alternative and possibly kinder way to look at death. I began to feel freed from the idea that I was selfishly holding Philip back with my wish to have him with me. But I also needed to let go of my anger at being so ill-prepared for all this.

"How is it that I am only now, at this late date, constructing a cosmology?"

"I guess without a religious or spiritual background, and without ever having a pressing, personal need to deal with death—except when Buddy died—you're just coming to it now . . . when you need it."

"But I managed to go through the deaths of my father and both of Philip's parents without feeling this bereft and lacking," I said.

"Losing and having to carry on without the most beloved person in your life is like nothing else, not even the loss of parents," she said.

Later that day, a radio show on NPR caught my attention. The narrator told of a survivor of the 2011 tsunami who had set up a phone booth in his yard with an old rotary phone connected to nowhere. He used this phone to "call" and talk to his lost loved ones. The narrator described how a growing number of others who had lost family, friends, and lovers to the tsunami continued to travel many miles just to use this man-made phone line to heaven.

Then the narrator explained that Japanese Buddhists believe the spirits of the dead may linger close to the living in the case of sudden death; they may be confused and unable to pass beyond, or they may be worried about those they've left behind. So, in some of the phone conversations, the bereaved gave reassurances to the dead.

"We're okay," one young man said to his father. "We miss you and love you, but we're all right. You can go on." Tears choked his voice and startled me into a bout of weeping.

Is this what I needed to say to Philip? These people seemed to have a cosmology that included helping to set the dead free.

Philip, my love, may you be free—but please know how my love longs to fly with you.

Another young man talked through heart-rending sobs. He spoke to his whole family; he was the only survivor. "Sometimes I don't know why I go on living," he said. "Without you, it all seems meaningless. I'm so sorry I couldn't save you."

Yes. Meaningless without you, Philip. I'm so, so sorry I couldn't save you, my love.

In our third session, another concern surfaced.

"I haven't experienced the tidal waves of grief described by some. I've actually wished for them," I said. "I've been rolling words like 'suppressed' and 'repressed' around in my mind. I've even questioned the depths of my love for Philip."

"Why that?" she asked.

"Well, why am I not devastated all the time? Was I less in love than I'd thought? Why doesn't grief jerk me outside of 'normal' and knock me down, instead of sneaking up and leaking out in surprise moments, only to sink back to wherever it is that grief hides in people like me?"

"Introverted people, which you obviously are, don't emote in an outwardly demonstrative way any more than they do anything else in an extroverted way. Does that make sense?"

"Kind of."

"The quiet, river-flowing sadness, the wish for solitude, the tender longing for his arms around you, even your 'emotional sneezing' attacks are an introvert's way of grieving," she said. "It's very different from the huge swells, upsurges, and wipeouts that a more extroverted person feels and dramatically expresses as they surf through grief."

"Introverted grieving," I said. "Who'd have thought of that?"

There was nothing wrong with me; I wasn't hard- or cold-hearted. Our love was not less simply because I wasn't expressing grief in the way it's portrayed in movies, with background music that tugs at our hearts.

As much as people say "there's no right way to grieve," somehow this new understanding of how different personalities mourn in different ways was more helpful than anything I'd been told thus far. Staying fully aware of and inside this grief, having the courage to stay with pain without sinking into maudlin, sentimental, or stuck states sat right beside my competently coping self.

And I was apparently very good at coping, even though I often felt like there was a civil war going on between carrying on and falling apart. I knew I didn't have to choose one or the other— cope or collapse—but more often, I instinctively coped. It was easier to present a strong front than to deal with the sympathy that threatened to undo me. I didn't want to dissolve into a pool of tears over the cucumbers at Whole Foods whenever I ran into a kind friend.

And yet, I wondered if my coping cut me off from my feelings, and hence, from Philip. We don't get to choose when or how we feel. Or do we? I felt that some subconscious defense mechanism was choosing coping over crying, but it wasn't what my conscious self wanted.

Crying with others was rarely something I did. Crying, period, hadn't been easy since my teens, when I had irrationally conflated the vulnerability of crying with admitting wrong or guilt.

After the first weeks following Philip's death, when control just wasn't available, my coping self began to pull me back together, said I could wait to cry until I was alone.

"In time," people suggested. "In time," I would find myself in a life in which Philip gently moved aside to allow for new friends, creative endeavors, new interests, and possibly, one day down the road, even a new partner. I hated this overused phrase in the language of well-intentioned but useless comfort.

A "sense of purpose," they also told me, was to be attained via volunteer work or a part-time job; by staying busy; by spending time with others; by getting a dog, a cat ("Why not a gerbil?"). Perhaps. But right then, all was flat, pointless, devoid of meaning or pleasure. I rebelled against the prevalent cultural messages that advised "moving on," "starting new chapters," and "letting go." When a ninety-six-year-old relative kindly suggested that I needed to be open to finding a new partner, I was appalled.

"You are too young, attractive, and intelligent to live the rest of your life alone," she said.

"How old were you when Uncle Len died?" I asked.

"In my seventies. But that's different."

"Why is it different? I'm in my sixties, not that far from seventy, not all that young. You were also attractive and intelligent. You've lived alone for the past twenty-plus years. Do you regret it?"

"No. But you're different," she insisted.

"Well, at this point, I don't feel different. And replacing Philip feels impossible, nearly nauseating." A momentary silence fell over the dinner table.

I felt as though people offering this kind of advice, though surely well meaning, must have no idea (or memory, in my aunt's case) of the pain that is not defined in clock or calendar time, cannot and should not be curtailed. I didn't want Hallmark-card sentimentality or saccharine memories. Nor did I mean to idealize or sanctify Philip; he was no saint.

Instead, I was looking to be true to myself and him as I lived in and through this complete reversal and change. I didn't want to "get by" or "survive" this period of grieving; I wanted an authentic metamorphosis that included all the mess and muddle, all the heartache, and with that, all the love.

In another therapy session, I asked if other couples had those (idiotic) conversations about who should die first. "We did," I said with a sad, wry smile.

"Tell me," she said.

"He'd say he should go first because he wouldn't be able to cope without me. He'd argue that I was stronger, that I would get over the grief in time, but he would not. He even thought I might be better off—less burdened without him. I knew he was right about the coping and strength parts, but not the being better off without him. I'd tell him I didn't *want* to cope or carry on without him, that he wasn't a burden."

The therapist nodded and made a sympathetic noise, urging me to continue.

"And now here I am, he having gone first, as he wished, and me coping," I said. "But this coping feels like playing a part—walking through my days and being with people but without a heartfelt sense of presence, meaning, or joy. I feel oddly separated from myself. Numb, nearly dead inside, except when I'm crying."

"You do know this is to be expected for a time—your time, right?" she asked.

"Yes, but in the meantime, how do I muster the energy and enthusiasm to get up in the morning? For thirty-seven years my meaning and pleasure were intermingled with his. Who and how am I to be without him?"

A few minutes later in our conversation, the therapist paused. "What would bring comfort?" she asked.

"I don't know. I don't know that it's comfort I want. I want people to acknowledge the pain, to be willing to talk about Philip—I sense people are staying away from 'the painful topic,' not realizing how much more painful it is to ignore it. I also want invitations complete with the explicit and implicit understanding of my choice to turn them down if I can't face turning up—that would be really good. In fact, I think this is my new definition of a friend. Someone who will understand if I cancel last minute, if I say, 'No thanks.'"

Later that day, I repeated some of this conversation to my mother.

"Philip's death and your loss is heartbreaking," she said. "No one can take that pain from you."

"Is this how you felt when Dad died?"

"Yes. It just has to be endured. I am so sorry, love." Her words were solace in their honesty, empathy, and love.

In addition to therapy, I turned to yoga—not in classes, but each morning, on my own at home. Yoga had been a friend since I was in my twenties. It's not that through yoga I'd found great relief from or insight into my grief, but I found comfort in the solo and inward space it offered.

I also looked to meditation yet again. I'd tried this so many times and in so many ways over the years, but now, in more desperate search of a center from which to carry on, the words of Pema Chödrön, Tara Brach, and others brought me more willingly to my mat most mornings.

I finished four sessions of therapy, and much as I would have liked to go on, I couldn't afford to. So, we parted with a hope that I might be able to return in time.

After just a few months, however, I found myself wishing again for someone to talk with, someone outside my daily world who would listen, reflect, and share insight more than advice. I felt the need for a response from someone who had worked with all the minute particulars of grief, all of which were still unfamiliar and took me into such strange and rocky territory.

I was also beginning to feel that to go on talking and writing to friends or family was burdensome and asking too much of them. So, I was pleased to learn that the hospice center in town provided grief counseling on a sliding-scale payment system. I made my first appointment.

44

Therapy, Continued

There were so many unresolved questions and lingering feelings of guilt and inadequacy that the sorrow seemed to be carving out a home for itself in the cave of my heart. I gathered these up week after week and brought them to the patient and insightful grief counselor at the local hospice center.

"Philip had become increasingly disappointed, disillusioned," I told her. "He told me he no longer wanted 'gurus,' that we needed to listen to our own voices. But he continued longing to feel more enlivened and enriched, and more at home and at peace. This longing began to center on finding that place on the planet where he'd finally feel at home."

"So this is why you did so much traveling?" she asked.

"Yes. In his last years, his overall dissatisfaction turned into an insistence on finding a place to retire outside this country. But it seemed to me that he wouldn't rest wherever he was—at home or abroad—because he hadn't found a place of rest within."

"Did you tell him this? How did he respond?"

"Not terribly well. He acknowledged the truth in it but continued believing that we had a better chance of finding inner peace when we were more in sync with our outer place."

"How did you feel about the retirement abroad idea?"

"I was ambivalent. I shared his desire for a more temperate climate, and I agreed that we needed to find a less expensive place to live on our limited retirement income. And I continued to share his sense of adventure and longing to live in different, hopefully less materialistic and more gentle, cultures."

"And the unshared part?" she asked.

"It was scary. Europe—yes. But Europe was less affordable than here. We knew we had to look elsewhere. Central America and Mexico I was a lot less sure about. I didn't feel an affinity for Latin culture. Didn't feel at ease with the poverty, the stories of crime and political unrest. I hadn't liked being seen as a rich *gringa*, especially since I was far from rich."

"Hmm." She nodded.

"And our history of moving to places only to be disappointed in one way or another also frightened me. I didn't have the confidence I'd once had—neither in other places nor in Philip's ability to compromise or adapt. We were no longer kids. And then there was the problem of his precarious health—both physical and emotional, neither of which he was fully willing to admit, except as the reason why we had to get to a warmer climate with lots of good fruit. And then, of course, there were my money fears. Would the cost of living really be lower? Would we be comfortable, happy?"

"You talked about all this with him?"

"Oh, yes. He agreed, but he believed we still had to try. There was really no choice, to him. We couldn't afford to live in the States—and certainly not in a town as expensive as Fort Collins."

"It sounds very difficult," she said.

"And worst of all, in addition to all these pragmatic fears, I felt hurt, then frustrated, and, finally, resentful."

"Because . . ."

"Why wasn't being with me—who he said he loved deeply—good enough wherever we were? Much as I know that no one person can or should be everything to another, it was and still is hard to feel like I couldn't fulfill his deep longings, that I'd failed him."

"Do you think that's what he would say? That you failed him?"

"I guess not."

"Do you think this chronic and debilitating unhappiness of his also contributed to his early—much too early—death, possibly creating an emotional and literal drain on his spirits and his immune system?"

"Yes, I don't doubt that."

"I can see how this whole situation would both hurt and worry you."

"I also hate to admit the resentment I felt. Many of his feelings—especially the panic and the dissatisfaction—caused him to narrow down the parameters of our life. One by one, more and more of what we'd once enjoyed lost meaning for him—film, art, walks through old neighborhoods. And people, too—nearly everyone was rejected as not being meaningful or real enough."

"This must have been very sad and difficult for both of you," she said. "He was the one who introduced you to so much beauty, culture, and enjoyment. He was the more extroverted of the two of you."

"One day, I said to him, 'Soon there will be no one and nothing left.' He said something like, 'I'd rather be alone with you than with people who are not kindred spirits.'"

"Sounds like he was in one of those rock-and-a-hard-place situations. And therefore, you as well," she said.

"People in his family who we both loved and valued dearly—even his son—were cut out. Things we'd enjoyed doing were no longer satisfying. When he sat there looking right at me saying he was lonely or that he couldn't find his sense of home, I felt lacking, not good enough—not sensitive or imaginative enough, not slowed-down enough, not free enough to love and meet him in this deepest communion he endlessly longed for."

"Hmm."

"In reaction to this rejection of so much we'd built our life around, had I begun to close my heart? Had I at times—yes, I had—imagined and fantasized a life of greater ease and freedom without him . . . oh my god."

I placed these painful confessions in the lap of my counselor, who listened with gentle care, never interrupting, never cutting me off, never judging, chiding, or dismissing me (as a reasonable friend might with a "don't be ridiculous!"). She just created the space for me to spill it all out, made a place for me to listen to myself.

"What if these wishes for release from his growing negativity and exclusivity were answered?" I whispered. "What if they . . . what if I contributed to his terrible and early death?"

Even these impossible questions were uncritically and empathetically received and held within the crucible of her acceptance of all it's possible to feel.

"How do I live with this guilt and heartache. How do I include these ugly pieces in the story of our life and love?" I asked.

She paused, sighed, smiled wistfully. "What would Philip say if he were here now?"

Looking up from a soggy mess of tissues and misery, I see him laugh and hug me to his chest. "'Oh, my darling goose.'"

She smiled.

I breathed again, forgave just a little, and felt held in a moment of grace large enough to contain all the pain, regret, and love.

In the long journey of a life shared, there are many hesitations, many mistakes made. Feelings are not constant. Love ebbs and flows. The ebb tides in a marriage are frightening.

"There were times," I admitted in yet another session, "when I felt as though he'd become nearly a caricature of himself."

"Tell me more."

"His habits and routines became annoyingly predictable. And once that started to happen, once I began to second-guess and judge, it was very difficult to reverse. My underlying love and compassion felt buried fathoms deep. He must have felt this."

"Was that the first time you'd gone through this together?"

"No," I said. "There'd been plenty of other times of struggle in the past. And at least in this last time, I had those other dry spells to look back on, to encourage myself and say, 'This too shall pass.'"

"Couples who are together for as long as you were go through these times," she said.

"Yes. But considering how it ended, it feels terrible now. It doesn't fit with my image of the bereaved widow." We laughed.

"In the months just prior to Philip's final collapse in Costa Rica," I continued, "I was falling into this terrible waning. I felt cut off from the spontaneous warmth and loving intimacy we were so capable of. He seemed increasingly rigid, self-absorbed, and fear-driven. In the three months of travel in 2014, and then back in the only apartment we could find and afford—but never love—in Fort Collins, I accumulated resentments, often felt exasperated and indignant. It's awful."

"Yes."

"But then, at that tree next to Spring Creek, when pain doubled him over and took his breath away—suddenly, in that moment, everything shifted. Love flooded back in. Did the beginning of the end renew my capacity to love?"

She smiled. I wept.

The concerns I brought to these therapy sessions seemed endless.

"I just want to be alone most of the time. Friends here who offer so much kindness and support are wonderful people. And it's not just that they're kind and supportive of me—they, each in their own way, are also seekers of meaning and a life well lived. I respect and appreciate who they are."

"Yes?" She encouraged me to go on.

"But after just an hour or two of being with anyone, I feel like I'm pushing, straining. When I get home, I'm drained. I'm forcing myself. I don't seem able to be myself in the way I almost always was with Philip, even when he drove me crazy."

"No one is going to come anywhere near to the intimacy you felt and shared with Philip. Maybe ever . . . certainly not for a very long time," she said.

Hearing this brought a bittersweet happiness for having been understood and accepted.

She continued, "Choosing to be on your own, to honor the longing for solitude for however long it nurtures you, is fine, necessary. Explaining to friends that you can only manage short visits is understandable—they'd understand, wouldn't they?"

I was relieved. She wasn't pushing me to move on. No timelines, no stages to pass through. Her acknowledgment of time—*my* time—was comforting. The encouragement to recognize and protect my boundaries, freeing.

To be with Philip was to be with myself—to be closer to and more fully myself. It was being home. Despite struggles and conflicts, his eccentricities rubbing up against mine, and all our stubbornness, there was a certainty, an unshakeable communion, a deep and abiding love.

I tried out a new philosophy on her.

"Maybe when a person is so much a part of who you have become . . . maybe when they die and are no longer physically with you, in some profound way, it's not such a big change because they're a part of you. They're still with you in the way that matters most. When this awareness settles around me, he doesn't feel so gone."

She smiled.

45

No!

On September 10, 2015, six months after Philip's death, I was walking through a golden autumn morning. Leaves, sunlit and celebrating, laughed and fluttered in cool morning breezes against a brilliant blue Colorado sky. My phone rang—as always, buried at the bottom of my pack. I scrambled to catch the call, answering on the final ring.

Tanya's voice reached me through choking tears. "Malia died on her way to school this morning, driving herself for the first time . . ."

"Oh my god."

"She must have been confused. When she called me she was on the wrong road, going in the wrong direction altogether."

"You were on the phone with her? When she crashed?"

Sobbing. "Yes. I was telling her she needed to turn around and head back in the opposite direction."

One of Philip's morbid fears about people getting into car accidents while talking on a cell phone had become a reality with Misha's beloved sixteen-year-old daughter, our granddaughter.

"What happened then?"

"I heard her say, 'Oh . . . ' And then the phone went dead."

"Oh my god."

Misha had suddenly, appallingly lost his only daughter. Malia, dead . . . gone . . . on this very same morning when leaves laughed against a cerulean sky.

I strained to take in Tanya's words, both of us—grandmother and step-grandmother—now strangled by shock and tears. My mind went white, simultaneously whirling at top speed and going deadly still, unable to comprehend the incomprehensible, bear the unbearable.

Not again . . . this feeling of being unable to fathom tragedy. Not again.

Back in 2004 or so, Philip and I had babysat for Malia; she would have been only four at the time. We came to the corner of a quiet street in Denver, ready to cross. She pulled away when I reached to take her hand.

"Not hold hands," she insisted.

She was a stolid, independent creature who knew what she wanted and stood stubbornly for it. Philip's whimsical eye met my questioning one over her curly little head.

I asked silently, *Do I take her hand, like it or not? What about safety?*

Without words, we moved nearer to her, agreeing to walk closely on each side but allowing her this budding strength. The three of us seemed to know she'd need it; she'd already lost her mother to alcohol in infancy.

We only saw her on rare occasions after Misha moved them to the East Coast. Years later, Philip and I spent another afternoon with fifteen-year-old Malia when they came on a rare visit to Fort Collins. She was quiet, observant, shy but present, and we were taken by her loveliness and delicacy. When we said goodbye, she folded herself into our arms, avoiding eyes or kisses. I managed to kiss the top of her head.

"She ducked under our wings like a tiny, vulnerable sparrow," Philip said as the car pulled away.

I learned later that Misha left that afternoon with the premonition that he was seeing his father for the last time. He was right; Philip died less than a year later.

Just five months ago, before any of us could've guessed at the fate that was rolling implacably toward Malia, and just a month after Philip's death, I'd had the opportunity to spend a few weeks with Tanya, Misha, and Malia. She was an ephemeral child-growing-into-woman, shyly reaching out to connect, to offer comfort in my grief.

Often watching rather than joining in around dinner tables of adults, she retreated into silence—perhaps into nothing more than a teenager's natural and necessary move toward independence and self-discovery. But Tanya, a fiercely protective grandmother, worried about her.

"Teenagers who don't participate, who don't know how to interact with adults, are in for a harder life," Tanya said as we walked the dogs one day.

"Maybe," I answered. "And for you, whose three children are all extroverted and at ease in the company of others, I can see how Malia makes you uneasy. But last night, I saw how talkative and goofy she is with her girlfriends. She laughed and teased along with the others, filling the bathroom with giggles as they styled each other's hair. She'll get better with adults in time." But I sensed I hadn't done much to allay Tanya's concerns.

Only months later, at the memorial service, Tanya told me she was surprised to hear how others had perceived Malia.

"I felt as though a different child from the one we'd known so intimately and worried about so often was being mourned," she said.

"In what way?" I asked.

"Her friends, teachers, and neighbors described her as kind, funny, playful, even outgoing. I rarely saw that side of her."

Now, Tanya lives with the regret and remorse of having missed whole parts of her granddaughter. Out of the golden goodness of her mothering heart, she couldn't stop wanting to protect this precious, vulnerable child.

Another part of Malia also became baffling to Misha and Tanya in her last year—Malia seemed to have become a sensitive, spiritual seeker, and a dreamer.

Tanya told of finding her in her bedroom crying just a few weeks before the accident.

"Oh, honey, what's wrong?" she'd asked.

"I miss my grandfather," Malia had said.

Tanya said she'd been momentarily stunned. She missed Philip, the grandfather she'd barely known?

At other times, found alone and asked what she was up to, Malia would answer, "Nothing."

Sitting or lying on her bed, she appeared to be daydreaming or thinking, or perhaps, in accord with Philip's philosophy, just being. Unlike my own teenage years, spent largely under headphones or out of the house, Malia's "doing nothing" was often without the teenage accompaniments of music, phone, or internet.

When Malia and I hugged goodbye at the end of my last visit, she cried in my arms. I was painfully aware of her too many losses. Her slight body trembled and my cheeks were wet with our mingled tears as she pressed against me.

"Love you. Come back, okay?" she whispered.

"I will, darling girl." She sounded hauntingly like Philip.

After her death, Tanya and Misha found pages and pages she'd written to God. Who was she, this quiet, lovely angel whose time on earth was so very short?

And now, who is Misha to be? She was an integral part of him and his existence for the sixteen years in which they'd lived together, much of that time just the two of them.

In the hours, days, and months since Malia's death, Misha's life was utterly upended, his heart and mind rejecting intolerable loss. Remorse for having given her the gift of the long-awaited car and endless questions and attempts at making sense of the senseless haunted his days and nights.

Having given his life to her, raising her as a single father in their rural, South Carolina home, sharing cats and dogs and starry nights, surfing and loving the sea together—what was he supposed to do with this hideous and shocking absence? And how could he begin to digest losing his father and his daughter within a six-month period?

I learned that grief counselors call this "complicated" grief, "cumulative" grief, or "grief overload." I wondered how, six months further down this road of insufferable bereavement, I could give love and commiseration across the miles of physical distance that separated us. I was now aware of the solitary journey of grief.

And Tanya, too, participating daily in the raising of this otherworldly and somewhat baffling child—what was she to do with this anguish? How do parents and grandparents survive and carry on from the incomprehensible death of a child?

I saw it in the faces and eyes of every person I told. There is something so abhorrent, terrifying, and devastating. In our attempts to take in this news, to swallow and digest it, we run into something that even non-parents intuitively reject. The response is disbelief and then outrage. "*No!*" repeats itself over and over in the heart.

In the days following this new loss, the pain of Philip's death came rushing back. I found myself right back at the beginning—up against the unfeeling, unyielding wall of soul-searing, heart-numbing, mind-boggling sorrow. I had nothing to say, nothing to give in the way of comfort except a profound and inexplicable longing to go on loving and living—wounded and wearied as we are.

The teachings and teachers I'd been reading and listening to seemed to be saying the same thing: have the courage to let the pain be there, to find (not, of course, painlessly) that ultimately, we survive even the intolerable. The pain does not go away, is not fixed or healed or forgotten, but changes, reshapes itself and us forever. Agony shifts and transforms into something else, something that potentially deepens our humanity, our capacity for empathy and kindness. We are changed, different, and, eventually, enlarged.

And yet, to do this—and to do it again and again as we face each next loss—asks so much of the heart and its ability to stay soft and open. It is so difficult, in fact, that I couldn't consciously choose the moments when I veered away, avoided painful emotions, encounters, memories. It just happened—taking me with it into one or another temporary diversion or distraction, into that hated numbness that left me less alive.

The morning after Malia's death, not sure how to sit still with myself or bear this sharp-edged, heavy stone that stabbed and weighed so heavily on my heart, I decided—absurdly—to go to my Spanish class. However, as I walked through the life on the streets, everyone around me acting like nothing tragic could or had ever happened, I stopped, stood still, unable to go on. I was baffled, wondered how this day could go on being so beautiful when so much tragedy had happened. How could the sun go on shining? Sorrow, always a possibility, lay just around the corner for any and all of us.

I walked on, but in the opposite direction of my class. I just walked.

46

Scars

A friend called to tell me that her dog-companion of the last sixteen-plus years had taken a sharper turn toward dying in the past few days. As I listened, an increasingly familiar dread settled over me.

I knew this gray, dark-river feeling, had felt it sweep through and turn into a flash flood too many times in the last months, threatening the normality of the day. Even though her dog may or may not die today or tomorrow, I was aware that he—like all of us—was going to die, and in this case, probably ahead of his person.

Ultimately, we go into these enormous and devastating life events on our own. At the click of the ended phone conversation, I felt helpless to reach her with any real comfort, as I'd increasingly felt helpless to reach Philip, even as I'd held his hand or curled up as close as I could beside him. Even as I felt when talking with Misha or Tanya now.

Life presents itself in this raw solitariness. No matter what I or any of her many other caring friends could say or offer, she was—when we hung up the phone—essentially alone. Grief is ultimately a solitary journey as we move into our souls and on into our remaining, ever-emptying, ever-changing years. We go through the hours and days of grief alone; no one can hold or carry our pain.

That thought was dark and sad—and real for me. But on that same morning, I found a blog post by Tim Lawrence about the "scars" of loss. In it, he made an eloquent, heartfelt plea not to try to change or reconstruct the scars of loss into something positive. For however long it takes, he encouraged, we must acknowledge the loss and the grief, allowing the scars to form, to be there. He continued by saying that accepting these scars allows us to ultimately admit and affirm that our life is forever changed. We are made more of who we are becoming as we traverse this rough terrain. More, not less.

His words helped me move toward loss in another way. I'd realized in these slow-quick, time-warped months that there was always another layer of the onion to peel away, another translucent awareness that shaped the next moment, bent my perception, and revealed yet another angle on death and surviving loss.

Grief, and coming to grips with it, presents a shifting-sands sort of process, ever changing, ever reforming. At times, I got the feeling that living with grief was enforced work on a spiritual jigsaw puzzle. There were an infinite number of pieces by which I might be befuddled for the rest of time. There were always more pieces, hidden pieces that would fall off the table and disappear into the dark corners of the room. All the time I'd be working on this Sisyphean task, a gray and disturbing fear would taunt me, whispering, "You'll never achieve wholeness." Yet, in time, another small piece would click into place, and I'd wonder if I'd moved just a little bit further.

But moved further toward what, exactly? Was the essential piece, the next critical move, the becoming somewhat comfortable with—or at least tolerant of—the not knowing and uncertainty? Living with a puzzle that will never be completed and finally being okay with that? While there are those for whom faith provides certainty, for many there are only questions. Where does the spirit go when it leaves the body behind? For many, for me thus far, this piece of the puzzle may only be answered after I have passed to the other side.

In Anne Lamott's funny, tragic, very honest, and delightfully eccentric *Operating Instructions: A Journal of My Son's First Year*, she writes about how one can never really get over the death of the people who matter most. She compares it to breaking a leg: you'll walk again, but always with a limp.

Surprisingly, I found—at least that morning—that I was beginning to accept the scar, the limp, not as purely burdensome and negative. As an open wound heals into a scar, or a broken leg into a limp, these horrible losses change life forever. There is no going back, no returning to the way life once was. I still hated this—how not? But I was also beginning to glimpse that the change promised a depth and resilience needed to face all that was inevitably to come on life's hard roads.

In fact, the scars may be precious. For one, they're always there to remind me of the impossibly beloved person I've lost—a token in my soul similar to his silver Swiss pocket watch, his amethyst pendulum, and the photos that sit where I look to them every day for contact and comfort.

The changes, and the scars, also present me with my own mortality, less and less to be denied or ignored. That he died right next to me, right up close, brings my eventual death nearer, makes my ending and finality more real. Might this deeper death-knowing inspire a more intentional and heartfelt living?

Finally, the scars bring me face to face with the fact that I'll have to—and will sadly be able to—brave the many more inescapable losses coming toward me: my beloved ninety-four-year-old mother, all the others whom I love and include in the story of my life.

In a sense, then, each scar becomes emblematic of a potential strength in our psyches—the way the skin grows over a wound, making that piece of skin somewhat tougher than the rest. It's the horrible strength we gain and keep gaining to face this loss, as well as the inevitable losses and possible other tragedies yet to come.

If this sounds morbid or gloomy, I don't feel it that way. If we must die . . . and we must; if we have to lose the ones we love . . . and we do; if we have to lose some of our own agility, stamina, or memory as we age . . . and we will; I want to be increasingly more aware and prepared. The scars and the limp may help in this, I think. I hope.

47

Joining Forces with a More Fearless Soul

Following Philip's death, I experimented, if uncomfortably, with new freedoms, making new solo choices for the first time in many years. I found myself doing this at the most mundane levels: what to eat, whether to drink coffee, whether and how to spend money, buying a book at full price, and so on ad nauseam. Each choice had me conflicted, wondering if I was moving against him, superstitiously fearing his spirit might forsake me and further the horrible distance between us.

Since Philip's death, I've been forced to realize yet again—from both subtle and not-so-subtle comments made by family and friends—that some people thought I was dominated by him. And regarding small (to me) issues of eating, drinking, and spending, I guess this was so.

I decided early on not to bother with issues that were relatively unimportant and easy either to give way on or to do when not in his company. *What harm did the chocolate do to him if he didn't know I'd eaten it? Which is more important: to do everything openly or to maintain peace and accord?* While I don't recommend a policy of dissembling to anyone entering a relationship, I see and accept that I chose to compromise on the small issues in favor of a marriage that meant the world to me.

Many of Philip's restrictive ideas reflected his idealism and his beliefs. So, my objections—"But I like chocolate, coffee, cheese, ice cream!"—were met by a genuine concern for my health, as well as for the environment and for animals. I never felt his motivation to spring primarily from a desire to control or dominate. On the contrary, he was trying to save my life. In his intentions, there was loving care.

He and I rarely differed on that which was real and essential. I shared in his ideals, principles, and hopes—they were what initially drew us together and carried us through our differences. It is true that without him, I might not have done much of what seemed outlandish to others: moved far and often, left jobs, traveled in search of spiritual teachers and communities, made unwise financial decisions, experimented with alternative lifestyles, diets, and healing modalities. But just because I may not have done these things without him, it wasn't that I disagreed with them. Rather, it was that on my own, I might not have had the courage to pursue ideals that ran so utterly and inexorably against familial and familiar habits and norms.

Through Philip, I came to know personally rather than theoretically that many of the blessings of our lives emerge from beyond the confines of comfort. He pushed against what was comfortable, encouraged doing and living toward what wasn't conventional, familiar, or practical in a worldly sense. His expanded perspectives and courage are what most attracted and challenged me from beginning to end.

Philip was always *other*, and thus, often misunderstood and threatening to people who did not share his longing to seek his own way, his own truth. He was principled and committed, intense and vehement. I agreed and chose to love him more than I can imagine ever loving again.

An early draft of this memoir was responded to with tactful expressions of anger.

"Why did you sacrifice your independence? What became of that young woman in her twenties who drove across the Rockies at midnight?" one friend asked.

"Where did that fearless adventurer go?" another asked. "The one who traveled the West Coast solo in search of herself and her soul."

"She joined forces with another even more fearless soul," I answered. "Have you not often expressed wonder and admiration for the adventures I've lived?"

"But Philip was domineering and you often gave way to him."

"What does that matter when the issues I gave way on were inessential and petty to me?" I replied with some heat. "How does eating chocolate compare to sharing a life with a remarkable human being? Have you known such love?"

I listened to the rare sensitivity of philosopher and geophysicist Xavier Le Pichon in conversation with Krista Tippett on her online show, *On Being*. The love and compassion we feel for another, he explained, cause us to want to do and be more of what that beloved person needs, particularly in his or her weakness, pain, or disability. He spoke of how honoring this fragility—this unavoidable frailty of our humanity—is what makes us more human and humane.

Our willingness to be generous with our time and affection allows our lives, our souls, and our egos to be worked upon—like kneading and softening stiff dough. We become both stronger and more flexible, move beyond our personal universes to see what is needed by others. Clearly, I often failed at this with Philip, felt resentful or burdened at times. And clearly, it is very difficult to walk the balance between living for oneself in a healthy and constructive way versus caring and compromising in order to maintain loving accord with someone else.

But surely these efforts at balance, and all the moments when we tip over into imbalance, are necessary parts of what we are here for, here to learn, here to become. Through loving Philip, I have gained greater esteem for interdependence right alongside independence. As much as I value and still often fiercely protect my newly regained independence, I know that our years of interdependence both softened and strengthened my heart.

Looking at myself today, after having spent thirty-seven years relying on and being relied upon by Philip, what am I now if not stronger, abler, more compassionate, and far less judgmental? Living beside his pain, vulnerability, and fragility, and now respecting my own as well as that of others, I inch toward my own more tender humanity.

48

His Siren Song

It's sadly ironic that in all Philip inspired, in all we tried and did together, in the end, it was I who was the more grateful for the outcomes. In our last long, quiet days at Highlands, we spoke of how we saw our many attempts and failures. He could not accept disappointed schemes, couldn't see the value in experiences that didn't go as he'd hoped. He couldn't see them as different but potentially worthwhile in their own right.

Challenging as many of our travels had been for me, each trip, person, and misadventure provided opportunity for inner expansion, adding a richness and a deeper texture to our relationship and to my individual unfolding. Through those final tropical afternoons, lying together on his bed, we recalled the many places where we'd tried or hoped to remake a life.

"I look back on each of these and feel how they have shaped and strengthened me, taught me resilience and pliability," I said to him. "They've contributed to the tapestry of my soul."

In sad contrast, even when facing the end of his life, Philip saw the failures only as disappointments. "No, I don't agree," he said. "I knew what I was seeking, and we never found it. All our mistakes were distractions and detours that interfered with finding what I felt such an insatiable longing for."

As we talked through those long afternoons with sometimes painful honesty, I cried quietly to hear him so unable to see meaning or value in pieces of a life that was so precious to me in its entirety.

I was learning, up to the very last days of his life, how utterly, impossibly committed Philip was to the vision of a life he had only ever glimpsed, as though spying but never reaching a distant, mist-shrouded shore. A jagged gemstone of longing forever cut into him like a splinter, even while glinting with ineffable beauty, a lodestone that reminded and foreshadowed, never allowing compromise.

"I still want to find a sanctuary with you," he'd said from his bed at Highlands just days before he died. "I want to find a simple, quiet, peaceful place in beauty to call home. I want to be at home with you. We still have so much to do and be. . . . We're not finished. I'm not finished."

Ceaselessly beckoned by the siren song of his soul, he could never silence or ignore its call. He wouldn't settle, but tragically could never clear his vision enough to manifest that elusive quality that so haunted him, never let him rest. Relentlessly driven, perhaps he was mistaken to seek outside himself for the beauty and safe haven he ultimately needed to find within.

Maybe finding one's true home requires recognizing that home is more a feeling than a place. Not wherever you go there you are, but wherever you are, and wherever you love, there you create a home.

Or maybe, just maybe, his place on the planet was just around the next corner. Who can say? If only he could have seen, as I did, the love that radiated from his laughter, that sang in his voice, that resonated in the musicality and poetry of his soul, he might have found the love that resided within. He might have discovered he was already and always at home.

I wonder if Philip—wherever his home is now—would agree.

Epilogue: Extending Hope

When I first read that a memoir of loss should end with some glimmers of hope, I felt anything but hope. Even three years after Philip's death, feeling defeated and deflated, I couldn't find a flicker. Much of the time I still don't know what I hope for. But I began to see that before I could grow into a new sense of hope, my understanding of death had to expand. Philip's death has shown me what medical doctor and author Rachel Naomi Remen calls "the view from the edge of life"—the view that encompasses even sickness and the messy, heart-rending collapse of the body.

The view from the edge of life includes dying and death. Death that puts everything into a totally, shatteringly different light. The view from the edge is nothing like what we see when we're in undisrupted, we-go-pleasantly-on-forever life. It's not the view seen in comfort or complacence. The view from the edge is what death—heartbreaking, right-in-front-of-me death—privileges me to see, to know, and to endeavor to live into: the deepening understanding of what matters and what doesn't, the essential aspects of being and living. It is the view that opens the way to living and dying well.

Remen says loss is "not the end of the story." For those who death leaves behind, it is a demanding, painstaking uphill climb that requires finding the inner resource and resilience—which can also be called hope—to sit with an appalling pain that was unimagined and unfathomed only minutes before life as we knew it was disrupted.

I've slowly come to realize that the pain of losing Philip is neither static nor deadly. Instead, with patience and trust, I feel it shift and soften me—hourly, daily, and, hopefully, always. And oddly, I do not want this sorrow to disappear entirely. Instead, I want to befriend it, because it too is love for Philip—not only the thorn, but also, the rose. I move gradually, creeping out from under crushing, shut-down, unable-to-move pain toward being able to carry it, much as I carried the weight of Philip's ashes in my backpack.

So, my understanding of pain extends. And I am creeping slowly, beginning to see that quietly waiting, joggling and bumping alongside the pain, sometimes bleeding into it, resides the love. The love for Philip that will never die, and the enormous comfort that accompanies both the love itself and the growing trust that love does not fade or diminish, even as it grows quieter. When something is good, it is forever good.

And in my backpack, safely cushioned in its own compartment, I carry the tiny shoots with their deepening roots to all the love for others and the world through which I move. I know now, living with grief and absence, that my understanding of hope is extending and expanding in different directions.

Hope isn't sunny, Pollyanna optimism.

It is strength—the strength to carry on, one foot in front of the other. One day after the next.

It is the honesty of vulnerability—the willingness to stay with every emotion, not to run, not to avoid, similar to the determination to stay with an impossible man so many years ago.

It is acceptance—the growing acquiescence to a lifetime ahead when Philip no longer wakes beside me.

It is courage—the courage to do and live on into the future without Philip, even to live in ways he wouldn't have chosen.

Hope embraces the capability to live with uncertainty, questioning, and doubt. The ability not to have certain faith in spirit, heaven, or God—but not to reject the possibilities, either.

Hope is also the trust in the constantly evolving understanding, the making real, the taking in and making part of me—in body, nerve, and heart, as well as in mind—the words and wisdom I have sought and read and begun to make sense of for myself. It is the slow and personal picking up off the pages the words of wisdom offered by others, the transforming of their meaning into my own evolving understanding. It is the digesting, absorbing, and assimilating for myself ideas that were at first merely ideas. It is an extending and expanding of apprehension and comprehension.

I am also beginning to find the strength and hope to stay with and move through the discomforting feelings of purposelessness and meaninglessness that descended like a heavy theater curtain with Philip's passing. Now, years down the road—without quite seeing how I got here—I find myself involved and engaged in writing, finding identity and purpose in a very different way through reflection and the crafting of words. While finding meaning in love for another was immediate, easy to identify, and by far the most exquisite experience of my life, discovering it in creative endeavor is quieter, solo, but ultimately fulfilling and rewarding. It leads me deeper into who I am becoming, brings meaning through reflection, and, oddly, connects me more fully to the world around me.

There are still hours and days when I cannot understand what or why I am when the source and recipient of love is no longer. I was recently asked what one emotion or quality I would choose to live for the rest of my life. I still choose love.

To find identity and meaning without Philip, who is and was love, remains an ongoing struggle. I am seeing, however, if ever so slowly, that Philip's death and his love ask me to extend my understanding of love rather than to close down. And even while I would still choose and wish to give and grow and live inside that one love in relation to that one person, a love I understood with little effort, I am now turning toward and acknowledging the value in all the other love I feel and receive.

As I begin to see and explore the affection that grows in family, in friendships, in the minute particulars of each day, and in all the multifarious beauty of the natural world through which I am privileged to walk, there is the quiet joy that comes from extending my capacity to give and receive in new ways. There is new life—enriched by a beautiful, painful past—and a growing sense of wonder in all of this.

So, for Philip, for love, for the sorrow of loss, and for the emerging sense of hope that glimmers in each new day, I am humbly grateful.

"They say it's a choice to be loving you.
If it was a choice then every day I would choose you."

—Danielle Anderson, of Danielle Ate the Sandwich